Hölderlin's
Major
Poetry

The Dialectics of Unity

Hölderlin's

Major

Poetry

The Dialectics of Unity

RICHARD UNGER

INDIANA UNIVERSITY PRESS
BLOOMINGTON · LONDON

Published in Canada by Fitzhenry & Whiteside
Limited, Don Mills, Ontario

Manufactured in the United States of America

Library of Congress Cataloging in Publication Data

Unger, Richard, 1939–
Hölderlin's major poetry.
Bibliography.
Includes index.
1. Hölderlin, Friedrich, 1770–1843—Criticism and
interpretation.   I.   Hölderlin, Friedrich, 1770–1843.
Gedichte.   English and German.   1975.   II.   Title.
PT2359.H2U45   1975   831'.6   75–28913
ISBN 0–253–32836–5   1 2 3 4 5 80 79 78 77 76

To My Mother

Contents

Preface

This book offers detailed readings of a number of Hölderlin's major poems. My readings are organized within the context of a problem central to his poetry. The problem, simply stated, is how the poet can best approach the phenomenon of "Eins und Alles"—unified totality or "All-Unity"—how he may experience the essential unity of all life or how he may best name that unity in a poem. This is the fundamental question of Hölderlin's ontology and of his art, and he confronted it in poem after poem, finding and testing new strategies for its resolution. In the pages that follow I shall try to show what some of Hölderlin's major poems mean in themselves and how they are related dialectically to each other in the development of his dominant poetic concern. The book therefore combines critical analysis of the individual poems with an historical account of the problem of All-Unity.

Because I seek to present a coherent (and somewhat original) view of the development of Hölderlin's poetry, my book is intended hopefully as a contribution to the specialized corpus of Hölderlin criticism, which is by now very extensive. But it is also written to serve as an introduction (and to that end translations have been provided) for American or English readers, especially readers interested in the phenomenon of European Romanticism, who may know Hölderlin mainly by reputation. I hope such readers may find their way to this book and come away understanding why Hölderlin is ranked, by those who know his poetry well, among the great poets of Western literature.

For readers who do not come to the book as specialists, an explanation of its organization and of my way of proceeding may be of use. The organization is primarily chronological; essentially the book is a study in poetic argument, partially emulative of such recent Romantic studies as Harold Bloom's *Blake's Apocalypse* (New York, 1963) and of such earlier standard works on Hölderlin as Paul Böckmann's *Hölderlin und seine Götter* (Munich, 1935). The basic argument, as I have mentioned, is the evolution of Hölderlin's concern with the problem of All-Unity; I intend to show that Hölderlin's preoccupation with this general problem gives rise progressively to the manifold particulars of his poetry. In tracing the development of the problem the reader must consider Hölderlin's major poems in exact detail; hence the individual chapters within the chronological order here are devoted primarily to detailed contextual interpretations of the individual poems.

Hölderlin's poetry is exceptionally difficult. Virtually every line of his more important poems has been subjected to intensive and often contentious exegesis by several generations of astute German critics. Poems like "Brot and Wein" and "Friedensfeier" have undergone explications as numerous and divergent as those devoted to "Lycidas" or "Ode on a Grecian Urn." It might thus be deemed unseemly (and impertinent) for anyone at this date to essay casual or cursory discussions of Hölderlin's major poems. But scholarly circumspection alone may not sufficiently justify voluminous and detailed explications in a study intended in part for nonspecialists. The best defense for such close reading must be the verbal complexity—and excellence—of the poems themselves. Like many of Shakespeare's sonnets, Hölderlin's major elegies and hymns are virtually inexhaustible as objects for interpretive reading and intellectual contemplation. They amply repay all the exegetical effort we can expend on them and seem always to require more. Successful interpretations of these poems can emerge only if the reader pays exact attention to the poetic details while carefully observing their thematic and esthetic coherence.

My own efforts to understand Hölderlin have, of course, been greatly assisted by my readings in the German secondary literature on his poetry. Foremost in general helpfulness have been studies by Friedrich Beissner, Wolfgang Binder, Bernard Böschenstein, Lawrence Ryan, and Jochen Schmidt; I have relied on Professor Beissner's definitive edition of the text of the poems. Equally important and stimulating for me were the Hölderlin seminars given by Paul de Man at Cornell, Professor de Man's forebearing direction of my dissertation (on "Patmos") in Zurich, and many long and animated conversations on Hölderlin with Jochen Schmidt at Bebenhausen. Frl. Maria Kohler, administrator of the Hölderlin-Archiv, has been unfailingly helpful during my many summer visits to the archives at Bebenhausen and in Stuttgart.

In my writing of this book, I was indispensably aided by the unflagging endeavors of Allan Bennett to assist me in adapting a Byzantine thought-style more closely to the conventions of standard English prose; wherever the book attains readability, it is owing chiefly to his help and advice. Professor de Man was good enough to read and comment on my finished manuscript. Also valuable has been the generous assistance of colleagues at Mississippi State University, particularly Price Caldwell, Richard Larry, Clyde V. Williams and Peyton W. Williams. Brenda Gail Bridges has been but the latest (and most excellent) of a long series of patient typists of various phases of my manuscripts. Finally, I would like to express my thanks to the College of Arts and Sciences and the English Department at Mississippi State University for their very timely profferings of direct and indirect financial assistance for the preparation of the book.

A Note on the Translations

Literal prose translations follow all excerpts of Hölderlin's verse quoted in this book. These translations are given solely to assist those readers whose knowledge of German is insufficient for full or ready comprehension of the original poems; they should not be appraised as if they were intended to be definitive or elegant recreations of the poems themselves. Readers in search of poetic excellence are hereby referred to Michael Hamburger's fine verse translations in Friedrich Hölderlin, *Poems and Fragments* (Ann Arbor, 1967).

My own translations are offered here only because they are consistent with, and based on, my own interpretations of the poems (other translators, of course, have their own implicit interpretations). It might be noted, however, that parts of these translations are not always verbally identical with the interpretive paraphrases that follow them. For whereas the paraphrases are designed primarily to elucidate (and hence to rationalize) the poems, the translations attempt to reproduce as nearly as possible the intellectual (though not the esthetic) experience of reading Hölderlin in the original; thus, while I have sought for clarity I have also, on occasion, respected the indisputable mysteriousness of some passages in the original German, and have presented them carefully but unsimplified to the reader for his contemplation. When a choice seemed unavoidable, I have tended (perhaps unwisely) to sacrifice the ease of the English version to a literal fidelity to the original poem. Thus, while the text aims at conceptual lucidity, these translations seek verbal exactitude. I have of course tried to avoid when possible the grotesqueness and gratuitous obscurantism that are constant dangers for anyone attempting literal translations of difficult German verse; but my failings here will, I fear, be sufficiently evident.

Hölderlin's

Major

Poetry

The Dialectics of Unity

1. Introduction

Hölderlin's major poetry develops through a dialectic of poetic responses to the metaphysical problem of "Eins und Alles" or "All-Unity." This topic was a principal concern for other German writers such as Goethe, Schelling, and Hegel, and was also of interest to major English poets of the nineteenth century. Shelley referred to the problem of All-Unity with respect to man in *Prometheus Unbound* ("Man, one harmonious soul of many a soul") and with respect to Being itself in *Adonais* ("The One remains, the many change and pass").[1] Much of Wordsworth's *Prelude* is concerned with the unity of experience as realized by "intellectual love" in its relationship to the Imagination. Wordsworth praises Coleridge as one to whom "the unity of all hath been revealed," enabling him to share his own awareness of "the mighty unity / In all which we behold, and feel, and are."[2] The topic is also present in Coleridge's own poetry ("the one Life within us and abroad, / Which meets all motion and becomes its soul") and in Coleridge's esthetics as the concept of "Unity and Multëity."[3] And in Blake's central myth, the Four Zoas with their emanations and fallen forms are fragmented aspects of one primal man, Albion; they tend toward apocalyptic reunion in man, who is to realize his own divinity and integral being.

In the twentieth century the problem of All-Unity—by whatever other term it may be called—has continued to be a major concern for many of our greatest poets and philosophers. Alfred North Whitehead's *Process and Reality* is to a large extent concerned with the resolution of the problem of the one and the many.[4] Paul Tillich defines God in all-unitive terms as the "ground of all Being." Yeats was notably obsessed with the question of "Unity of Being," as in his myths of Byzantium—where "religious, esthetic and practical life were one" —or, more ideally, of the Thirteenth Cone.[5] Wallace Stevens confronted the problems of unity and order in all his major poems. Both Eliot and Pound are preoccupied with the question of cultural cohesion, and Eliot's masterpiece *The Waste Land* takes the disintegration of Western culture as one of its central themes.

Eliot also serves to illustrate another aspect of the problem of All-Unity, for to the religious sensibility this problem inevitably raises the question of God's presence—or absence—in this world. The question has been one of the most intense of modern concerns. Divine absence may, however, be understood in two different senses. In one sense, as for Nietzsche, it may mean the ontological nonexistence of God; in its other sense, as for Eliot, it means the absence of God within human experience, a profound alienation from transcendent Being. It is this latter sense of divine absence which Eliot expresses in the following lines:

> Knowledge of speech, but not of silence;
> Knowledge of words, and ignorance of the Word.
> All our knowledge brings us nearer to our ignorance,
> All our ignorance brings us nearer to death,
> But nearness to death no nearer to God.
> Where is the Life we have lost in living?

Where is the wisdom we have lost in knowledge?
Where is the knowledge we have lost in information?
The cycles of Heaven in twenty centuries
Bring us farther from God and nearer to the Dust.[6]

Another of our greatest writers who is profoundly concerned with divine absence is Samuel Beckett. In *Endgame* Hamm attempts to lead his "family" in prayer: "Now let us pray to God." After several interruptions and false starts he abruptly abandons his pious attitude: "The bastard! He doesn't exist!"[7]

J. Hillis Miller's *The Disappearance of God* relates the problem of divine absence to the problem of unity in the case of certain Victorian writers.[8] Miller sees belief in the Incarnation, by which he means the benign immanence of God in the world, as a fundamental principle of coherence in the traditional world view. The symbolic interrelationships within man's experience were once sacramental in character and regarded as divinely ordained. However, with a loss of active belief in divine immanence the sense of coherence fostered by this belief disappears. Fragmentation occurs at all levels of experience—moral, intellectual, and religious, as well as esthetic:

> The history of modern literature is in part a history of the splitting apart of this communion. This splitting apart has been matched by a similar dispersal of the cultural unity of man, God, nature, and language.[9]

As a result of cultural disintegration, man experiences reality itself as fragmented, and his own deeper being as alienated from his empirical self, other selves, God, and from all the disconnected phenomena of his world:

> We are alienated from God; we have alienated ourselves from nature; we are alienated from our fellow men; and, finally, we are alienated from ourselves, the buried life we never seem able to reach.[10]

For Miller, this manifold alienation affects even the process of poetic composition itself. It is now the task of the poet to devise new unifying symbols to mediate among the discordant elements of experience. However, these symbols ideally should also function to "establish a new relationship, across the gap, between man and God."[11] For those nineteenth-century writers Miller terms "the romantics," God still exists but has withdrawn from the world. Until the poet imaginatively perceives a universal symbolism which mediates an authentic contact with the divine principle in Being, any order which we ourselves could impose on reality would be merely human, arbitrary in character, and hence ultimately devoid of meaning. The poet's business is "to bring God back to earth as a benign power inherent in the self, in nature, and in the human community."[12]

Miller refers to Hölderlin on the first page of his introduction as one of the poets most fully cognizant of the historical absence of God. He cites the elegy "Brot und Wein," in which Hölderlin devises a temporary solution to the problem of divine absence. The gods have deserted us and left the world without concrete participation in Deity. They may return some day, but until they do it is perhaps meaningless to write poetry, as the poet is now deprived of his most authentic subject matter. However, the gods have left us the gifts of bread and wine as tokens that they were once present on earth and will eventually return:

> Brod ist der Erde Frucht, doch ists vom Lichte gesegnet,
> Und vom donnernden Gott kommet die Freude des Weins.
> Darum denken wir auch dabei der Himmlischen, die sonst
> Da gewesen und die kehren in richtiger Zeit,
> Darum singen sie auch mit Ernst die Sänger den Weingott
> Und nicht eitel erdacht tönet dem Alten das Lob.[13]

Bread is the fruit of earth, but it is blessed by the light, and from the thundering god comes the joy of wine. Hence we also therewith think of the Heavenly who were once here and who will return at the right time, hence they also, the singers, sing in earnest the winegod, and praise not idly thought out resounds to the ancient one.

It may thus be the poet's task to celebrate those purely human joys and give comfort to men by fostering remembrance and anticipation of those gods who are now, for a time, absent.

Hölderlin here would identify Dionysus with Christ as spirits of earthly community, and equate dionysian rites with the Eucharist as communal ceremonies. But Hölderlin also implicitly subscribes to the Zwinglian concept of the Eucharist, in which, as Miller remarks, "the communion service becomes the expression of an absence."[14] Unlike Hopkins, Hölderlin felt it impossible to return to a belief in an abiding Incarnation, typified in the Real Presence of Christ in the Sacrament. And yet, for Hölderlin, the writing of poetry was a religious act, even the essence of religion itself. In this fundamental attitude he most resembles William Blake.

Like Blake, Hölderlin was not adequately valued or even partially understood until the twentieth century. And he has likewise remained permanently esoteric and "difficult" for us; critics are still grappling with the literal meaning of his major poems. But also, as in the case of Blake, it is perhaps the very quality of this difficulty which often intrigues us. For these poets sometimes appear to understand more than we do; they admittedly share our problems but we suspect they have seen these problems more clearly and in greater depth. And in our interpretations it may seem that (rather than explaining their "relevance") we are attempting to discover something which, in the silence of their texts, they already know.

As was indicated above, concern with the problem of All-Unity is not unique to Hölderlin. Hölderlin, however, is the poet who most exhaustively, in all his major works, concentrates on the problem of All-Unity: "Eins und Alles," the "One and All." Hölderlin was aware of the complex dialectic inherent in this problem. Any finite unity may become an element in a greater multiplicity, until this too is resolved in a higher unity. The All is simply the name for the greatest possible unity, the infinite form of the One, which is divine. The All-Unity designates God or (considered impersonally) Being or Life, which Hölderlin regards as divine. The name "Eins und Alles" designates the Hellenic pantheon in "Brot und Wein," and "die Natur" is equated with divine Being or Life in "Wie wenn am Feiertage," where it is termed "Allgegenwärtig," equivalent to the Greek *parousia* and one of the traditional attributes of the Christian Deity. All-Unity is thus Hölderlin's conceptual name for God. It is notably inadequate as a poetic name, for it appeals only to man's intellect, and the ultimate poetic naming of Deity must involve man's total being. Hölderlin's later poetry tries to find names which adequately express man's integral response to Deity. These names should articulate not only a subjective unity, speaking for all that man is, but also an objective unity comprehending Deity in all its various manifestations. Divine immanence would thus be reestablished through language.

Hölderlin's major hymns are primarily devoted to seeking an all-unitive divine name; as articulations of his most important poetic endeavor, they are generally (and properly) regarded as his greatest poetic achievements. They will thus be the principal focus of this book—which, as stated in the Preface, will offer interpretations of a number of Hölderlin's major works in terms of how they develop the problem of All-Unity.

As has already been noted, this problem, which was central for Hölderlin, has continued to be of concern for our own century, although our poets and philosophers may phrase the problem in other terms. Much has been said by critics on the topic of Hölderlin's modernity, and certainly this common concern with All-Unity accounts in part for our own responsiveness to him.[15] Yet the mere sharing of metaphysical concerns cannot account for the intense rapport that many readers now feel with this poet. Perhaps we may sense in Hölderlin—in the flawed total shape of his work—something profoundly like ourselves. For, despite isolated moments of hope in some of his later fragments, Hölderlin is a poet who failed ultimately to create (or discover) those principles of integration by which things could be made whole. Ultimately the structure crumbles; its self-destruction is inherent in its very nature—and this is the distinctly modern lesson. It may drive us to the reductiveness of logical positivism or the intense subjectivity of many of our postwar poets (for example, W. S. Merwin and James Wright); it may result in the acerbic self-mockery of consciousness we find in Beckett, or even the naive atavism of some countercultural phenomena. Hölderlin, like Pound, sought a poetry of cosmic dimensions and failed. Twentieth-century writers generally have been forced to confront the tragic realization that we can never create or discover a meaningful order within reality. After devoting the greater part of his creative life to the *Cantos*, Pound (in the 116th) makes the shattering admission: "I cannot make it cohere."[16] This is our condition; and this condition of radical incoherence—poetic, metaphysical, and finally existential—is what we confront in Hölderlin. That, perhaps, is the ultimate basis of his modernity.

2. The Topic of All-Unity in the Early Work

Although All-Unity is the dominant *topos* of Hölderlin's poetry, it had its origins as a philosophical "problem" in the works of the pre-Socratics, and has since been a sporadically recurrent theme in Western thought. A number of studies of Hölderlin have dealt with backgrounds, influences, and sources of Hölderlin's first interest in the topic.[1] However, Max Bäumer's 1967 article, "Hölderlin und das Hen Kai Pan," appears to be the most competent treatment to date of the backgrounds and details of Hölderlin's early preoccupation with the problem.[2] It might thus be helpful to refer to some of his findings here before going on to investigate how the topic is presented in Hölderlin's poetry.

Hölderlin probably first encountered the Greek phrase ἓν καὶ πᾶν

("One and All") in Friedrich H. Jacobi's *Briefe über die Lehre des Spinoza* (1785), which he read in 1791 while a seminarian at the Tübingen theological seminary.[3] The formula, which became a kind of metaphysical slogan for Hölderlin and his classmates Hegel and Schelling, had a rather complicated previous history. Although the Greek philosophers of the Eleatic school speculated at length upon the unity and totality of the cosmos, they presumably did not formulate the topic in that particular phrase.[4] Neither did their Hellenistic followers nor did the Neo-Platonists, who continued the tradition of speculation on the problem of the One and the All, and on the relationship of the Deity to this All-Unity. The topic was revived by the Renaissance Platonists and give a specifically "pantheistic" interpretation by Bruno and later by Spinoza, who formulated his concept of God as universal substance in the phrase *Deus sive Natura*. Spinoza himself, however, did not make use of the formula ἐν καὶ πᾶν, although the phrase was mistakenly attributed to him by Jacobi and Lessing in the late eighteenth century.[5]

It is not actually known when or by whom the Greek phrase was first given its definitive form. Perhaps its immediate progenitor was the German Pietist concept "Eins und Alles," referring to the experience of deific infinitude by the soul, rapt in ecstatic union with godhead.[6] The Greek equivalent might thus represent a secularization of the concept, moving it from a theological to a purely philosophical context and eliminating any reference to an orthodox Deity. Whatever its actual origin, the Greek formula appeared in current use among German writers of the "Sturm und Drang" period and soon attained the status of a cliché, seeming inexhaustible as an object of literary or philosophical elaboration.

Bäumer maintains that Jacobi's initial attribution of the phrase to Spinoza was not only factually inaccurate but also a distortion of the spirit of Spinoza's thought.[7] The latter was rationalistic and detached, whereas the various modes of "Sturm and Drang" pantheism were characterized by emotionalism and enthusiastic fervor. For such contemporaries as Herder, Hamann, and young Goethe, as well as for Hölderlin, All-Unity was more of a mystical than a rational notion, an experiential goal to be attained through intensity of feeling. Bäumer thus concludes that All-Unity has nothing to do with Spinoza's doctrine. It is rather

> a German invention, born of the German mania for Greece, very probably formulated by Lessing or Jacobi and used quite in accordance with the original, ancient meaning of "topos" as an expedient for the invention of proofs in rhetoric. Immediately afterwards, in the utilization of the phrase by contemporaries and participants of the "dispute over Pantheism," *"Hen Kai Pan"* became a "topos" in the sense formulated by Ernst Robert Curtius, a fixed cliché. As such it was also used by Hölderlin.[8]

In the German "Dispute over Pantheism," the Lutheran seminary at Tübingen was naturally a stronghold of orthodoxy, and any form of the heretical doctrine would have had the status of forbidden fruit for its inmates. Thus when Hölderlin's friend Hegel inscribed the notorious Greek phrase in his album beneath the Goethe quotation "Joy and love are the wings to great deeds," it could probably be regarded as a kind of anti-Establishment gesture.[9] However, it could also be taken as indicative of the special meaning these seminarians gave to the phrase. All-Unity is to be realized among persons as a bond of fellowship. It is to be attained and find its expression in the emotive forces of "delight and love" and thereby encourage its participants to "great deeds." Although one might explore the political implications of this syndrome,[10] it would be more to our purpose here to note its mode of expression in Hölderlin's poetry at the time.

Hölderlin's earliest verse had chiefly been imitations of Klopstock or such local Swabian poets as C. F. D. Schubart or Friedrich von Matthisson.[11] As Wilhelm Michel notes in his critical biography of Hölderlin, these early poems tend to be subjective meditations or analytical and occasionally tortured expressions of the poet's own feelings.[12] However, with his Tübingen series, the "Hymnen an die Ideale der Menschheit,"[13] Hölderlin turns to "philosophical" verse in imitation of Schiller's poetry, specifically such speculative poems as Schiller's "Die Götter Griechenlands" or celebrations of ideals like Beethoven's later favorite, "An die Freude."[14] The usual inner viewpoint of these poems is the generalized, impersonal ego of idealistic philosophy rather than the more confessional, "existential" poetic "I" of the earlier lyrics.[15] They therefore tend to exhibit a kind of false transcendence, an escape into pseudo-objectivity, which proclaims in serene confidence the aspirations of universal Man while ignoring the concrete problems of the author. This quality may account in part for the impression the poems often create of intellectual hysteria, a self-induced and unconvincing mood of rapt elation. And yet they are somewhat interesting both in themselves and as representing a formative stage in Hölderlin's poetic development.

One of the earliest poems of this series was the "Hymne an die Göttin der Harmonie," begun perhaps before Hölderlin's reading of Jacobi. As Bäumer notes, this poem was strongly influenced by the ecstatic variety of pantheism found in Wilhelm Heinse's novel *Ardinghello* (1787).[16] The poem takes as its motto a quotation from Heinse's work: "Urania, die glänzende Jungfrau, hält mit ihrem Zaubergürtel die Weltall in tobendem Entzücken zusammen" ("Urania, the gleaming virgin, holds the Cosmos together in wild delight with her magic girdle"). Several of the ideas and motifs in the poem are also to be found in Heinse, such as the cosmological myth of Urania's creation of a harmonious world out of chaos and the birth of Love from this goddess. Bäumer thus suggests that Heinse, rather than Jacobi or other philosophical writers involved in the "Dispute over Pantheism" had the most decisive influence on Hölderlin's concept of All-Unity. In Hölderlin's view, the cohesive force of Unity is universal Love; if we can participate in this Love, either through human affection or in the spiritual ardors of poetic inspiration, we can be subsumed into the divine All-Unity of the Cosmos itself.[17] There is of course nothing radically new in this doctrine; neither Heinse nor Hölderlin could be credited with having invented it. It can be traced back at least as far as Plato's *Symposium* and has survived in the Platonic tradition, finding articulate spokesmen in such writers as Jacob Böhme and Angelius Silesius and occasionally, as in the case of German Pietism, benefitting from ecclesiastical sanction.[18] But what interests us here is the specific form given these ideas in Hölderlin's poetry.

Hölderlin's early hymns are not (as they might at first appear) merely rhymed philosophical treatises. They are actually meant to be hynms in the religious sense, public songs addressed to a divine power.

They are deliberately enthusiastic and seek to convey this enthusiasm to a community of "brothers" or like-minded souls. Their willfull ecstasies thus have a quasi-liturgical function and are not meant to be expressions of private feeling. Such enthusiasm is a projective state which the writer or singer seeks to evoke in himself as well as his audience. And this enthusiasm is to be understood in the root sense of the term as a feeling of divinity within the self (or self in God: *en-theos*). If this divinity is not simply equated with the "true" self (as in some Idealists or in Blake), it is felt as the inner presence or nearness of a divine power.

In an orthodox Christian hymn this power would at once be acknowledge as the Christian God or Jesus, and the song would proceed to elaborate his praises. But in Hölderlin's poems, such as the "Hymne an die Göttin der Harmonie," the first task of the hymnist is to find an appropriate name for his deity. This divine power is near, its presence sensed in and through the poet's inspiration, although it is not necessarily easy to grasp or apprehend by the right name. The initial situation is thus already similar to that given in the opening lines of the later "Patmos": "Nah ist / Und schwer zu fassen der Gott" (Near is the god and difficult to grasp"). However, the poet does not yet see the problem in the profound and serious terms of his late work. The first strophe of the present poem manages to generate enough ebullience to bear the speaker over any initial difficulties:

Froh, als könnt' ich Schöpfungen beglüken,
Kün, als huldigten die Geister mir,
Nahet, in dein Heiligtum zu bliken,
Hocherhab'ne, meine Liebe dir;
Schon erglüht der wonnetrunkne Seher
Von den Ahndungen der Herrlichkeit
Ha, und deinem Götterschoose näher
Höhnt des Siegers Fahne Grab und Zeit.   [1:130]*

Happily, as if I could bless creations, boldly, as if the spirits revered me, my love approaches you to look into your sanctuary, Most Exalted One! The seer, drunk with bliss, is already aglow from the presentiments

---

* Textual references here and following are to volume and page number of Friedrich Hölderlin, *Sämtliche Werke*, Grosse Stuttgarter Ausgabe, Friedrich Beissner, ed., 7 vols. (Stuttgart, 1943–).

of splendor, and, ah, nearer to your divine womb the victor's flag
scorns grave and time.

The central image of this strophe is the poet as lover victoriously
approaching the bower of Transcendence. It does not seem to matter
that he has not yet determined his Beloved's name, and his confidence
is unshaken by her "sublimity." (The confidence is somewhat habitual,
as Hölderlin uses virtually the same opening speech on another Power
in his "Hymne an die Unsterblichkeit.") In the second strophe the
poet brings himself to the point of naming her:

> Tausendfältig, wie der Götter Wille,
> Weht Begeisterung den Sänger an,
> Unerschöpflich ist der Schönheit Fülle,
> Grenzenlos der Hoheit Ozean.
> Doch vor Allem hab ich dich erkoren,
> Bebend, als ich ferne dich ersah,
> Bebend hab ich Liebe dir geschworen,
> Königin der Welt! Urania.   [1:130]

> Thousandfold, like the will of the gods, inspiration blows upon the
> singer, the fullness of beauty is inexhaustible, the ocean of sublimity is
> boundless. But before all things have I chosen you out, trembling
> when I saw you from afar, trembling have I sworn love to you, Queen of
> the World, Urania!

The poet's inspiration is "thousandfold" as the fullness of intellectual
beauty is "inexhaustible" and the ocean of majestic sublimity ("Hoheit") is "without bounds." He is on the verge of being overwhelmed
by his own enthusiasm. And yet he has managed to "choose" at his
own discretion that configuration of divine power which seems to him
predominant, "Urania," the queen of the world.

In the following strophe the poet addresses his Urania as the Power
most responsible for his own experience of All-Unity. Her "face" is
thus the personal aspect of this experience for him: Urania personifies
All-Unity. But this is not the type of personification frequently employed in neoclassical poetry as an embellishment of what might better
be treated conceptually. The personal address to this Power entails
rather an admission that it cannot be apprehended in concept, since
it transcends the rational capacities of the poet's mind. Hegel, of

course, was later to project a cognitive grasp of All-Unity in his "Absolute," but Hölderlin was never to attain this degree of rational self-assurance. Whatever transcended his powers of comprehension ought to be treated as such; it was thus to be addressed as "Thou" rather than demoted to the experiential status of an "It" and objectified as a manageable concept.

The following section of the hymn (strophes 4–6) thus seeks to determine the mythical identity of this Thou-personage. Urania is the Heavenly Aphrodite who evokes and sustains harmony out of chaos through the power of cosmic Love. She herself thus personifies both Harmony and universal Love, which in Hölderlin's view constitute the cohesive principle of All-Unity. The seventh strophe depicts the emergence of the anthropomorphic Eros out of the more diffuse presence of the harmonizing Love manifest in nature. In the next three strophes Urania addresses Eros as her "son." Eros, or Human Love, is the concretized image ("mein Bild") of cosmic Love or Harmony, much as in orthodox theology man is the image and likeness of God. Humanized Eros·is thus the microcosmic image and representative of macrocosmic Harmony in the created world. In this capacity, Eros will serve to reharmonize and revivify earthly creatures by reviving their "Bund" of Love to mother Urania.

But in his most rarified form, Eros is the principle of the poet's own inspired enthusiasm. Urania speaks to her son in phrases the poet had used in the first strophe to describe his own experience: "Mir entströmt der Schönheit ewige Fülle, / Mir der Hoheit weiter Ozean" ("From me streams forth the eternal fullness of beauty, from me the wide ocean of sublimity"). The immanence of godlike love within the poet is thus to be maintained through dialectical relationship to its transcendent source. Yet the love felt by the poet must be shared by others and established as a concrete principle of human community. Situated within a community, Eros would thus provide a more stable image of the All-Unity than the inner enthusiasm of any one person. The poet therefore calls for the establishment of such a community, envisioned as an enthusiastically devoted group of friends.

In strophes 11–13 of the hymn the poet then addresses his fellows and exhorts them to a fitting worship and celebration of the goddess. This worship entails the service of Truth and the overcoming of obsolete delusion ("verjährtem Wahne"), which would distort or conceal the truth of cosmic harmony and thereby keep people from its full communal realization. The exhortation has revolutionary political implications.[19] Hölderlin and his friends at the seminary were devoted, if mostly inactive, adherents to the cause of the French Revolution. And there is a structural, if not a causal, relationship between Hölderlin's political and metaphysical views. However, it should be remarked that in this poem, as in most of his works at the time, the political sentiment appears as a function or consequence of poetic enthusiasm, rather than as its basis or actual cause. It is probably safe to assert that for Hölderlin, contrary to most Marxian literary doctrine, the poetic is always prior to the ideological or political, both logically and in value. The notable cooling of political fervor in Hölderlin's later works is probably a function of the growing difficulties in his poetic optimism, rather than an actual transference of hope from politics to poetical activity such as M. H. Abrams has observed in the case of several English Romantics.[20]

Whatever its political nature, the "priesthood" of Urania's devotees is to serve as privileged example or nucleus for a future world-brother-hood. Their communal liturgy is to be a celebration of Urania as the principle of cosmic Love. The deity summoned by them seems to approach them as the intensity of their fervor increases. The concluding strophes of the hymn thus anticipate the final moment of this approach. Strophe 15 celebrates the triumph of Harmony over discord, which had falsified the truth of cosmic order in the world. The next strophe foreseees the final consummation of human Eros in union with the goddess:

Stark und seelig in der Liebe Leben
Staunen wir des Herzens Himmel an,
Schnell wie Seraphin im Fluge, schweben
Wir zu hoher Harmonie hinan.
Das vermag die Saite nicht zu künden,
Was Urania den Sehern ist,
Wenn von hinnen Nacht und Wolke schwinden,
Und in ihr die Seele sich vergisst.   [1:134]

Strong and blissful in the life of love we stare amazed at the heart's heaven, quickly as seraphim in flight we soar forth to high harmony. The strings cannot proclaim what Urania is to the seer, when from hence night and cloud vanish and the soul forgets itself in her.

With this end in view, the concluding strophe functions as a last ex-hortation, now addressed to all mankind ("Millionen"), to join in ecstatic praise: "Heilig, heilig ist Urania!" ("Holy, holy is Urania!") It is important perhaps to note that the final union of the immanent human Eros with the transcendent principle of cosmic Love is here envisioned as a dissolution of the former into the latter. The soul can finally enjoy a beatific mergence with the All-Unity, but only at the price of "forgetting" its individual being.

The hymn thus consists of four main sections: an opening address, in which the transcendent principle is named; the mythical placement of this entity; an exhortation to worship; and the anticipation of an ultimate unity in which the poet's individual identity is somehow forfeited.

Other poems in the same group of Hymns to the Ideals of Mankind show a similarity in construction, as they also tend to alternate between ecstatic apostrophe and exhortation to greater and more communal ecstasies. Two other major poems in this series, likewise provided with opening quotations, are the second version of "Hymne an die Schön-heit" (1:152–156), which cites Kant, and "Hymne an die Mensch-heit" (1:146–148), which begins with a reference to Rousseau. These poems deal with different aspects of the subject treated in "Hymne an die Göttin der Harmonie." They are not actually addressed to distinct "ideals," but develop various implications of the central concept of Love or Harmony (here virtual synonyms) as the organizing principle of the cosmic All-Unity. The hymn to Beauty, which we shall exam-ine, is perhaps the more interesting of the two.

Hölderlin's "Hymne an die Schönheit," which is in some ways quite similar to Shelley's "Hymn to Intellectual Beauty," again calls upon Urania. This is not due to any confusion or mere uninventiveness on Hölderlin's part, but because his ideal Beauty is simply another aspect of his ideal Harmony, just as for Plato the Beautiful is ultimately to be identified with the One and the Good. The opening reference, adapted from Kant's *Critique of Judgment*, itself indicates how these ideas may be related: "Die Natur in ihren schönen Formen spricht figürlich zu uns, und die Auslegungsgabe ihrer Chiffernschrift ist uns im moralischen Gefühl verliehen" (1:152). ("Nature speaks figuratively to us in her beautiful forms, and the gifts of interpreting her ciphered writing is granted to our moral feelings.") The esthetic sensibility (by which we perceive beauty and significance in nature) is ultimately identical with the "moral feeling" of disinterestedness by which we acknowledge the validity of the moral law; both are aspects of our sense of harmonious order.

As this poem is ultimately addressed to the same personage as the hymn to the Goddess of Harmony, it might be expected that the two poems would be somewhat similar in construction. The hymn to Beauty likewise begins with an invocation of the Power (strophes 1–3). The opening address is again overtly erotic, and the personage is hailed first as the poet's "muse" or source of his enthusiasm, and next as the specific object of his enthusiasm, ideal Beauty. Once again the joyous nearness of deity has been felt and the poet has been incited to seek out the name of this giver of joy; the third strophe already anticipates the poet's union with his ideal.

The next section (strophes 4–7) recounts the growth of the poet's awareness of primal Beauty ("Schönheit in der Urgestalt"). He is led from an initial perception of beauty in the natural world and in the person of his earthly beloved, Antiphile, to an intuition of Beauty in its transcendental or ideal form. The poem thus retraces certain phases of discovery given in Plato's *Symposium* and parallels as well the general developmental structure of Shelley's hymn.[21] This particular section corresponds to the second part of the "Hymne an die Göttin der Harmonie," where Eros has been presented in mythical rather than experiential terms. Their respective third parts (here represented by strophes 8–11) are also parallel. In this hymn, the poet calls upon other poets (like himself, sons, lovers, and priests of ideal Beauty) to show more fervor in her service; in the other poem he exhorts his comrades to a more perfect celebration and earthly realization of cosmic love. And, as in the other poem, the spiritual commitment has its political implications:

> O! so lindert, ihr Geweihten!
> Der gedrükten Brüder Last!
> Seid der Tyrannei verhasst!   [1:154]

O you consecrated ones, thus ease the burden of our oppressed brothers!
Let tyranny be hated!

Just as political liberty is a prerequisite for equality and fraternity and
thus harmonious love among men, it is also necessary if poets are to
foster a cult of intellectual beauty. "Hymne an die Menschheit" and
"Hymne an die Freiheit," the two Tübingen hymns to Humanity and
Freedom, are in fact explicitly political. But, as we remarked earlier,
politics does not here become an activity divorced from poetry.

Urania's own address to her followers constitutes the concluding section of the hymn. In form it thus corresponds to strophes 10–12 of the
other hymn, where Urania speaks to Eros, but in "message" it resembles the other poem's conclusion, the promise of ultimate fulfillment
in reward for devotees' efforts. And, as before, this culmination is
envisioned as an unmediated union of the poet's soul with the divine
power. Whereas the poet in the other hymn enunciates his vision of
ecstatic self-forgetfullness, here it is Urania herself who holds forth
promises of celestial erotic delights:

Meiner Gottheit grossen Sohn
Lohnt der treuen Huldigungen
Lohnt der Liebe Wonne schon.   [1:156]

The bliss of loyal homages, of love, already rewards the great
son of my divinity.

The poet is to be identified again with Eros in his Oedipal union with
Mother Urania. As before, the emotional conventions of courtly love
are given an incestuous application in the poet's celebration of the
principle of universal Love-Harmony.

Most of the other poems in this group of Tübingen hymns ultimately have the same subject (in its various guises of Love, Friendship,
Genius of Youth, etc.) and the common structure previously noted.
Perhaps their single most characteristic feature, however, is their un-
derlying attitude towards time. All are directed to the future. Past and
present moments have significance only in reference to a future event:
the mergence of the poet and all mankind with the divine principle of
All-Unity. Past moments are either appraised as harbingers of this
event or consigned in memory to the darkness of "obsolete delusion."

The present itself, with all that differentiates it from future beatitude, is to be "destroyed," as proclaimed in the "Hymne an die Menschheit":

> Hinunter dann mit deinen Thaten,
> Mit deinen Hofnungen, o Gegenwart!   [1:147]
>
> Down then with your deeds, with your hopes, O Present!

Our anticipation of the ultimate mergence permits us to "scorn" time itself in its negative aspects of mutability and transiency:

> Ha, und deinem Götterschoose näher
> Höhnt des Siegers Fahne Grab und Zeit.
>
> Ah, nearer to your divine womb the victor's flag scorns grave and time.

These lines from the opening of the first hymn to Urania show a variety of optimism which Shelley, despite his alleged immaturity, specifically rejects in *Prometheus Unbound:* man will never be exempt, despite his inner mastery,

> From chance, and death, and mutability,
> The clogs of that which else might oversoar
> The loftiest star of unascended heaven,
> Pinnacled dim in the intense inane.[22]

Hölderlin's mind is generally free of such "clogs" in his early hymns, and sometimes shows a kinship to the "intense inane" that makes the achievement of his later poetry all the more astounding. Critics generally would blame the influence of Schiller for the stylistic deformities of these early poems. However, the tradition of the chosen genre itself may have had a more insidious effect. Hölderlin ultimately borrowed more than the generic name from the Christian hymn—he also appropriated its most characteristic attitudes towards the present and future life.

Hölderlin began work on his novel, *Hyperion,* in 1792, while he was still at Tübingen.[23] He worked on it intermittently, through a number of versions and revisions, until the second volume of the completed novel was published in 1799. In *Hyperion,* Hölderlin remains preoccupied with the question of All-Unity.[24] But the topic is not presented in the same way as in the Tübingen hymns. It is true that the novel's protagonist speaks of his longing for "Einigkeit mit allem, was lebt" (3:8). ("Unity with everything that lives.") And the novel might very well be treated, as Lawrence Ryan has shown, in terms of the hero's quest for this ideal. However, as Ryan has again pointed out, *Hyperion* is not to be regarded merely as an expressive "lyrical novel" but as a carefully designed, objective *Bildungsroman*.[25] Hölderlin as author is never simply to be identified with the protagonist; rather he describes with a certain detachment the very enthusiasms which were uncritically celebrated in the early hymns. And he presents not only the peaks of enthusiasm but also the fallings from these heights: "Auf dieser Höhe steh' ich oft, mein Bellarmin! Aber ein Moment des Besinnens wirft mich herab" (3:9). ("I often stand on this height, my Bellarmin! But a moment of recollection casts me down.") Hölderlin thus shows how these moments of imaginary subsumption into All-Unity (with their rapturous scorn for mutable existence and temporality) are themselves subject to the forces of mutability and time. This awareness perhaps constitutes the central irony of the novel.

The protagonist himself has come to a limited awareness of this situation by the novel's concluding epistle. He has finished telling his mute correspondent, Bellarmin, the story of his life, with its profound disappointments in friendship and political action and the recent catastrophe of his beloved's death. But a new mode of affirmation has been gained through his reflection on these events—one which seeks to resolve the dissonances of the violent alternations of depression and manic elation:

> Wie der Zwist der Liebenden, sind die Dissonanzen der Welt. Versöhnung ist mitten im Streit und alles Getrennte findet sich wieder. Es scheiden und kehren im Herzen die Adern und einiges, ewiges, glühendes Leben ist Alles. [3:160]

> Like lovers' quarrels are the dissonances of the world. Reconciliation is in the midst of strife and all things separated come together again. The veins separate and return in the heart and everything is one unified, eternal, glowing Life.

Although this might at first appear to be a restatement of the doctrine of the earlier hymns, there is a significant difference. In those poems All-Unity is a distinct reality, infused with a divine principle of Love, Harmony, or Beauty with which our soul could be ecstatically united. This cosmic totality is thus "ideal" in the Platonic sense. Here, however, the unity of life is regarded as a living organism which is itself subject to laws of development and change. It exists in a state of constant movement. And although the protagonist is united with this totality, he is joined to it as a part to a greater whole, to which he will never be equal. This mode of unity with the All is therefore not, as previously, a rapture of self-forgetfulness in a higher reality. It is rather a sobering, if somewhat comforting, reflection on one's own finitude as a mere part of this organism. And finite man is not free of time, but subject to all its vicissitudes. We might perhaps be justified in reading the novel's strange concluding statement as an expression of the awareness that even this final resolutive insight might be subject to mutability and revision: "So dacht' ich. Nächstens mehr" (3:160). ("Thus I thought. More very soon.")[26]

This modification of the concept of All-Unity can also be noted in the prefaces to two of the earlier versions of the novel. The introduction to the *Fragment von Hyperion* (3:163) speaks of the "eccentric course" ("exzentrische Bahn") from a condition of "simplicity" ("Einfalt"), in which we are naturally at one with ourselves and with the world, to a condition of complex "cultivation" ("Bildung"), in which we must organize and impose a kind of integrity upon our own natures.[27] The latter state, like the first, is an "ideal of our existence"; and the "eccentric course" of our development is to lead us to a condition which is specifically not perfection but a "more or less finished cultivation" ("mehr oder weniger vollendeten Bildung"). The projected goal here is obviously not ecstatic absorption into All-Unity as in the Tübingen hymns, but rather a self-attained condition of "more or less" complete cultural or psychic integrity.

The preface to the penultimate version (Die vorletzte Fassung) of the novel elaborates these ideas. One passage is especially important to our argument:

Die seelige Einigkeit, das Seyn, im einzigen Sinne des Worts, ist für uns verloren und wir mussten es verlieren, wenn wir es erstreben,

erringen sollten. Wir reissen uns los vom friedlichen ἐν και παν der
Welt, um es herzustellen, durch uns Selbst. Wir sind zerfallen mit
der Natur, und was einst, wie man glauben kann, Eins war, wi-
derstreitet sich jezt, und Herrschaft und Knechtschaft wechselt auf
beiden Seiten. Oft ist uns, als wäre die Welt alles und wir Nichts,
oft aber auch, als wären wir Alles und die Welt nichts. Auch Hyperion
theilte sich unter diese beiden Extreme.   [3:236]

Blissful unity, "Being" in the unique sense of the word, is lost for us
and we had to lose it if we are to strive after it and achieve it. We
tear ourselves loose from the peaceful One and All of the world in order
to establish it through our selves. We have fallen out with nature,
and what was once (as we believe) One is now in conflict with itself, and
mastery and servitude alternate on both sides. It often seems to us as
if the world were everything and we nothing, but often too as if we were
everything and the world nothing. Hyperion, too, shared in these
two extremes.

This is the first noted occurrence of the actual Greek phrase ἐν και παν
in Hölderlin's literary work.[28] Here it designates the original, uncon-
scious inclusion of ourselves in the world's All-Unity, and also that
unity with ourselves ("seelige Einigkeit") which constitutes our
"Being" as pure self-identity: "Seyn, im einzigen Sinne des Worts."
We no longer possess this simple being, for consciousness has transformed the world and our historical selves into objects and has thus
alienated us from them. (An "ob-ject"—in German, "Gegen-stand"—
is by root definition that which opposes.) As long as this division of
consciousness lasts, we will not be self-identical: we will not simply
"be" what we are.

And yet, although we have lost the condition of "Einfalt," we strive
to attain the self-integrity of "Bildung." We seek to restore not only
our unity and identity with ourselves but also our harmonious relationship with the external world. Still, as Hölderlin himself implies,
this undertaking is highly problematical. The opposition between self
and world has taken the form of a struggle for mastery. We do not
actually exist in harmony with the world but in a kind of reversible
master-slave relationship to it. At times (when depressed) we seem to
be at the world's mercy, we are "nothing" to it; and at other times (in
moments of elation) the world is as nothing to us. What may at first
seem a paragraph of pure metaphysical speculation can thus be under-

stood as a rather exact phenomenological description, not only of a manic-depressive cycle but also of the original and constantly renewed act of consciousness which estranges us from reality by converting reality into a congeries of dissociated objects. If the objects of our world are to be ordered, it is only through an act of our will. But since they often resist this ordering, the world seems to exert an opposing will, and our relationship to the world becomes something like a struggle for mastery.

We must recall that the problem of alienation was not an actual problem for the poet in the Tübingen hymns. In the earlier poems, the tyranny of the world was merely a contemptible illusion which could be overcome in the higher truth of enthusiasm. And this enthusiasm did not appear to disdain the world itself, but only its accidental delusions and falsifications. The truth of the world was of course the principle of cosmic harmony, and the poet approached this living principle not as a slave or master but as a confident lover. What has happened in the meantime is that Hölderlin managed to lose some measure of his philosophical innocence. Study of the critical philosophy of Kant and Fichte (whose influence is especially apparent in the previous passage) had convinced him of the naiveté of positing any such metaphysical entity as a principle of cosmic Love.[29] The All-Unity remains an important concept, perhaps necessary as a regulatory idea for our thought. But it is now perhaps to be regarded principally as an idea of and for our own consciousness, which has no existence apart from consciousness. This "critical" attitude can be seen even in the cautious wording of the preface: "wie man glauben kann . . . oft ist uns, als wäre . . . als wären. . . ."

Yet this harmonious unity remains for us as an ideal "goal of all our strivings":

Jenen ewigen Widerstreit zwischen unserem Selbst und der Welt zu endigen, den Frieden alles Friedens, der höher ist, denn alle Vernunft, den wiederzubringen, uns mit der Natur zu vereinigen zu Einem unendlichen Ganzen, das ist das Ziel all unseren Strebens, wir mögen uns darüber verstehen oder nicht.   [3:236]

To end that eternal conflict between our self and the world, to bring back the Peace of all peace, which is higher than all reason, to unite ourselves with nature to one infinite Whole, that is the goal of all our striving, whether we agree about it or not.

"The peace . . . which passeth all understanding" (Phil. 4:7) is of course an ideal of traditional religiosity, and for a while we may seem to be back in the optimistic world of the Tübingen hymns, with their implicit borrowings from Christianity and their promises of "peace" in ultimate union with the "one infinite totality." But the poet immediately qualifies his statement:

> Aber weder unser Wissen noch unser Handeln gelangt in irgend einer Periode des Daseins dahin, wo aller Widerstreit aufhört, wo Alles Eins ist; die bestimmte Linie vereiniget sich mit der unbestimmten nur in unendlicher Annäherung.   [3:236]

> But neither our knowledge nor our action can attain in any period of our existence to that point at which all conflict ceases, where All is One; the determinate line can be united with the indeterminate only through an infinite approximation.

Here the apparent promise is largely withdrawn. Neither in our knowledge nor in our actions (which might perhaps create social conditions to end alienation) can we ever wholly resolve the struggle between consciousness and its object, or between ourselves and the hostile forces of nature or society. It seems here that All-Unity can never be wholly achieved, either through concrete human love or through any participation in transcendent or world-immanent harmony. We can only hope to approximate this condition like lines that approach each other "infinitely" without ever actually becoming one. The total unity which was loudly proclaimed by the early hymns is here perceived as, ultimately, inaccessible to us.

Hölderlin's preface continues:

> Wir hätten auch keine Ahndung von jenem unendlichen Frieden, von jenem Seyn, im einzigen Sinne des Worts, wir strebten gar nicht, die Natur mit uns zu vereinigen, wir dächten und wir handelten nicht, es wäre überhaupt gar nichts (für uns), wir wären selbst nichts (für uns), wenn nicht dennoch jene unendliche Vereinigung, jenes Seyn, im einzigen Sinne des Worts vorhanden wäre. Es ist vorhanden—als Schönheit; es wartet, um mit Hyperion zu reden, ein neues Reich auf uns, wo die Schönheit Königin ist.   [3:237]

We would not have even an inkling of that infinite Peace, of that Being
in the unique sense of the word, we would not at all strive to unite
nature with us, we would not think and we would not act, there would
be nothing at all (for us), we ourselves would be nothing (for us),
if that infinite Unity, that Being in the unique sense of the word were not
nonetheless present. It is present—as Beauty. In Hyperion's words,
a new realm awaits us where Beauty will be queen.

Even if the attainment of All-Unity is finally impossible for us, Hölderlin implies, it is still desirable as the projected goal of our aspiration.
Even an approximate and imperfect unity with ourselves and the
world is of course better than total discord. We are therefore fortunate
that this harmony remains present to us in a phenomenal form, as
beauty. As an objective mode of harmony it serves as a model for the
subjective harmony which we seek. Hölderlin's ideas here are perhaps
derived in part from Kantian esthetics (as mediated by Schiller), in
which the beautiful object appears to us in a state of equilibrium or
peaceful repose, as "purposive" self-identity in which nothing can or
should be altered. Without such an example we would be unlikely to
strive for harmony within ourselves and with the world, and both the
world and our phenomenal selves would appear without promise and
without significant being for us. We would be left in a state of total
indifference, in which both ourselves and the world are as "nothing."

Beauty thus remains for Hölderlin what it was in the earlier hymn,
the revelation of a cosmic, primal harmony ("Schönheit in der Urgestalt") in which we can participate through our own beauty of spirit.
Now, however, the poet has realized that this participation can never
be consummated, that we can never really exhaust all possibilities for
ideal beauty in our own lives or be wholly united in ecstasy with
Beauty as a transcendent Idea. Yet the author joins his protagonist in
hoping for "ein neues Reich . . . wo die Schönheit Königin ist": not
a society in which transcendent Beauty is perfectly realized, but one
in which it is the dominant and controlling ideal.

But in the novel itself, Hyperion's efforts to establish such a society
through revolutionary action meet with total failure. And his attempts
to achieve a wholly integrated or harmonious life within himself meet
with only partial and temporary successes, as in moments of his friendship with Alabanda or, especially, his love for Diotima. Yet this does

not mean that he has given up the quest for such unity; the conclusion of the finished novel, as cited above, does not signify mere acquiescence. The "struggle" continues; "Versöhnung ist mitten im Streit" ("reconciliation is in the midst of strife") means that temporary reconciliations may be achieved even if they must be destroyed again through conflict. But "Alles getrennte findet sich wieder" ("All things separated come together again") : perhaps in the natural course of things, although our own efforts are required. Guided by the ideal example of objective beauty, man is somehow impelled to seek a progressively greater realization of unity within himself and with the external universe. Yet the awareness that each subsequent realization grows progressively more difficult will become obsessive in Hölderlin's later poetry.

3. The Frankfurt Poems

During the period of his work on *Hyperion*, Hölderlin continued to write verse. And during his years in Frankfurt, his poetry underwent an important change both in style and in content. This transformation corresponds to the poet's changing attitude toward the concept of All-Unity and the possibilities of its realization in experience. We have just noted briefly how the novel *Hyperion* indicates a change of attitude. If it is possible to speak of a turning point or "Wendung" in Hölderlin's poetry, it would have to be located in the verse of his Frankfurt years.[1] His later poems, up to the time of his madness, manifest a development and refinement of the problems and style which were given specific character at this time.

The poems of this period can be arranged for the most part in three main groups.[2] The first includes those addressed to "Diotima," a name borrowed from Plato's *Symposium* and given to the heroine of *Hyperion*. In these poems Diotima is the idealization of Frau Susette Gontard.[3] The second group comprises poems addressed to Nature and natural objects. The more important of these are written in hexameters or distichs, convey a generally elegiac tone, and show the influence of an older contemporary, Friedrich Leopold, Count of Stolberg. The third group consists of short and often epigrammatic odes. There are also a few tentative and experimental poems which are outside these categories and which we shall not consider here.

The chief poem addressed to "Diotima" exists in several versions.[4] The stanzas are rhymed and the tone and mode of writing are much as in the Tübingen hymns. Also characteristic of the earlier poems is the invocation of an ideal entity, a personification of some aspect of All-Unity. Here, however, the personage addressed is "Diotima"—a Urania-like cosmic principle of harmony, but also an actual human being, Frau Gontard. The middle version of the hymn (1:216–219) offers perhaps the clearest instance of the dialectic between Diotima as transcendent principle and Diotima as Susette.[5]

This poem may conveniently be divided into five sections of three strophes each. The first section (1–3) celebrates the revivification of the poet's "heart," which awakens to life again like trees or flowers in the spring. The ugly discords of life have been overcome in a new harmony reminiscent of childhood. The power responsible for this rebirth is hailed in the third strophe: "Diotima! Seelig Wesen!" ("Diotima! Blissful creature!") Since Diotima and the poet had long anticipated each other, they may now be sure that their heaven will endure.

The next three strophes (4–6) deal with the poet's life before their meeting. Her spirit first spoke to him as the voice of harmony in his childhood. Later, when the burden of time and everyday life had begun to alienate him from the world's beauty, Diotima appeared to him as the ideal Urania of the earlier hymns. This instilled in him the power and courage to seek the realization of his Ideal in life.

But now he has found her, and the next three strophes (7–9) are a celebration of her presence. She is even more beautiful and perfect than he had anticipated:

> Dieses Eine bildet nur
> Du, in ew'gen Harmonien
> Frohvollendete Natur!   [1:217]

> You alone, nature joyously fulfilled in eternal harmonies, are this One!

She is the perfection of Nature, and the happy realization of its eternal harmonies. Her joy and immutable beauty are as transcendent as the gods', and like Urania herself she stands inviolate amidst the ravages of time:

> Wie melodisch bei des alten
> Chaos Zwist Urania,
> Steht sie, göttlich rein erhalten,
> Im Ruin der Zeiten da.   [1:218]

> Like Urania, melodically amidst the contention of old Chaos, she
> stands, kept divinely pure, there in the ruin of the ages.

And, just as the poet had previously confronted the transcendent Ideal of All-Unity and had been alternately attracted and humbled by it, he now feels a similar ambivalence when confronted with its concrete realization: "Streit und Frieden wechselt hier" ("contention and peace alternate here") before the "angelic image."

The following three strophes (10–12) elaborate on this struggle between desire and feelings of unworthiness. All the "tones" of his own life have found accord within Diotima's harmony and he has prayed that she might "spare" him when her "heaven" appeared to him. He has lamented his own nothingness to her when "the god who inspired [him] dawned upon her brow" (1:218). Here we see the courtly love attitudes previously entailed in the poet's enthusiasm for transcendental ideals reapplied to a supernal human devotion. In the twelfth strophe the poet tells how the "heavenly being" now allays his anguish through an act of purely human grace. Because Diotima is both divine and human she can (as happens in Christian salvation) permit the poet to participate in divinity by condescending to the level of his humanity. But once Diotima has equalized herself in relation to the poet, she can no longer be regarded as transcending him. In bestowing her divine life she has forfeited her privileged claim to divinity, and what divinity they now share has become solely immanent.

The concluding three strophes of the poem (13–15) accordingly consider both Diotima and the poet as mortals, who yet share in the divine life:

Ha, wo keine Macht auf Erden,
Keines Gottes Wink uns trennt,
Wo wir Eins und Alles werden,
Da ist nun mein Element;
Wo wir Noth und Zeit vergessen,
Und den kärglichen Gewinn
Nimmer mit der Spanne messen,
Da, da sag ich, dass ich bin.   [2:1000]

Ah, there where no power on earth, no god's signal parts us, where we
become One and All, there now is my element! Where we forget
need and time, and never measure the paltry profit with the span, there,
there I say that I *am*.

In the unity of their love they fully participate in All-Unity, as their relationship is now its microcosmic image. They *become* "Eins und Alles"—Hölderlin's most exact conceptual term for Deity. Having become godlike, they are entitled to "forget" human need and temporality; they no longer need to "measure" by finite standards the "scant gains" or imperfect joys of mortal existence. The poet can now proclaim the deific certitude of his own existence: "Da, da sag ich, dass ich bin" ("There, there I say that I *am*"). It seems he has almost momentarily recovered "das Seyn, im einzigen Sinne des Worts" ("Being, in the unique sense of the word").

If such a height of being is achieved in the present moment, what can be thought of the future? The only appropriate aftermath for such bliss would be an ecstatic death. Just as the stars in their heavenly course are ordained to disappear beneath the waves on the horizon, so the lovers also are to find a "blessed grave" in the excess of their own divine "inspiration":

O Begeisterung! so finden
Wir in dir ein seelig Grab,
Tief in deine Wooge schwinden
Stillfrohlokkend wir hinab,
Bis der Hore Ruf wir hören,

Und mit neuem Stolz erwacht,
Wie die Sterne, wiederkehren
In des Lebens kurze Nacht.   [2:1001]

O Inspiration! Thus in you we find a blissful grave, quietly jubilant we
vanish deep down into your waves, until we hear the call of the
Horae and, awakened with new pride, return like the stars in the short
night of life.

The inspiration in which the lovers are to die (now as equals) is not
the overpowering transcendence the poet sought in the early hymns
as the all-subsuming Deity, but rather the simple excess of that feeling
which had already made them divine. They are already as gods, and
death would not essentially change their present being. Yet in addition
Hölderlin speaks here of a kind of rebirth, a return "into the brief
night of life." It is of course possible that these lines refer to a reawaken-
ing after sexual fulfillment, but this would be somewhat uncharacteris-
tic of Hölderlin, who generally tends to employ sexual metaphors for
spiritual experiences, rather than the reverse.[6]

In any event, the poet was apparently dissatisfied with the conclusion
to this version of the poem, for in the "Jüngere Fassung," the newer
version, he substitutes the following strophe:

Wie dein Vater und der meine,
Der in heitrer Majestät
Über seinem Eichenhaine
Dort in lichter Höhe geht,
Wie er in die Meereswoogen,
Wo die kühle Tiefe blaut,
Steigend von des Himmels Bogen,
Klar und still hinunterschaut:
So will ich aus Götterhöhen
Neu geweiht in schön'rem Glük,
Froh zu singen und zu sehen,
Nun zu Sterblichen zurük.   [1:222]

Like your Father and mine, who in serene majesty walks there in radiant
height above his oakgrove, as he, descending from the bow of
heaven, in clarity and silence looks down into the sea-waves where the
cool depths are blue: thus will I, newly consecrated in more
beautiful happiness, joyously to sing and to see, return now to mortals
from the gods' heights.

What we might first remark about these lines is a noticeable improvement in general poetic quality over the earlier version of the poem. Here natural objects are treated more sensitively than in any of the early poems; this will be characteristic of the group of Frankfurt poems we are to consider next. Along with this incipient change in style, however, there is also some change in attitude.

This strophe presents us with the first instance we have observed of the Deity as a paternal sky-god rather than a female principle of cosmic harmony. He is possibly to be identified already as "Vater Aether" who emerges as an important personage in the nature poems; whoever he is, he is certainly not to be equated simply with the God of orthodoxy, since the divine Father in Hölderlin's poetry henceforth bears only a generalized resemblance to the Biblical Jehovah or the First Person of the Trinity. Yet, this Deity is clearly transcendent, "personal," and maintains a paternal distance from mortals. The relationship of man to Deity is still that of love; however, this love does not lead to mergence or loss of individual being but maintains the essential distinction and radical otherness of God and man.

This doctrine of divine separateness is merely suggested at this point by the presence of a paternal God. The main burden of the strophe is a comparison which perhaps tends to blur these distinctions. Like the Father, who looks down from his heavens into the earthly seas, the poet will return to mortals from the divine heights of his love for Diotima. This highpoint of experience is deific because it is the moment of greatest emotive realization of All-Unity. But he must return to mortals because his sentiment of divinity cannot endure forever and he is himself a mortal. As was noted in *Hyperion*, moments of relative depression must alternate with those of elated joy. Here, however, the poet does not return from ecstasy simply to its absence; he brings with him what he considers an abiding happiness and a feeling of divine "consecration" to poetry, an endowment with the holy gifts of song and vision ("zu singen und zu sehen").

The change of attitude between the two versions of the poem's conclusion is fundamental. In the first version, both the poet and his beloved sink into oblivion through excess of their own holy raptures. If they are to be reborn, it is only to die again blissfully. In contrast to this spiritual *Liebestod*, the poet in the second version returns alone with renewed dedication to the human business of poetry. Only now (it is implied) he has a new purpose arising from his new consecration. The mission of poetry in the early hymns was, as we saw, to anticipate and work through self-exciting rhetoric to achieve a future mergence with All-Unity. But in "Diotima" the moment of divine unity has arrived, and the poem is written to celebrate its presence. Urania is finally realized in Diotima-Susette. This realization, however, means the exhaustion of the poems' previous subject matter; the poet may be left only with beatific silence. While such was implied by the poem's earlier conclusion, the later ending represents commitment to a new kind of poetry. Since the moment of ultimate participation in divine Life has already been achieved, the new poetry will have to regard this moment as something past. It will be a poetry of remembrance. And, in later poems to Diotima,[7] written after their enforced separation, she herself will appear almost in the form of a memory, a surviving presence of a more beautiful time: "Schönes Leben! du lebst, wie die zarten Blüthen im Winter, / In der gealterten Welt blühst du verschlossen, allein" (1.230). ("Beautiful Life! You live like the tender blossoms in winter; in the changed world you blossom locked up and alone.") As her real life is now in the past, she no longer has Urania's power to bring chaotic elements into harmony again: "Deine Sonne, die schönere Zeit, ist untergegangen / Und in frostiger Nacht zanken Orkane sich nun" ("Your sun, the more beautiful time, has set, and in frosty night the storms are quarreling now"). Urania was concretized in "Diotima" but this composite being, divinely-human, is now fading, like the poet's memory, into the simple, bothered humanity of Susette Gontard.

Past beatitude is thus for a while the chief concern of Hölderlin's poetry. This is generally the case in the nature poems and the later elegies which evolve stylistically from them. The odes, we shall observe, tend to focus on pure presence. And when futurity reappears as a basic poetic dimension in the later hymns, its form will be radically different from that of the Tübingen poems.

The Frankfurt nature poems in hexameters or distichs ("An den Aether," "Der Wanderer," "Die Eichbäume," and several fragments) are, as Adolf Beck notes, influenced in theme and style by the poetry

of Friedrich Leopold, Count of Stolberg.[8] Both Hölderlin's and Stolberg's poems have a common meter and a similar attitude of ecstatic
yet concretely detailed celebration of the natural world. Yet the poets
differ in their conception of the essential forces in nature. Stolberg
(rather like Dylan Thomas) proclaims an immanent, dionysiac life-
force which emanates from Mother Earth; for Hölderlin, on the other
hand, the source of Being is more ethereal.[9] But Stolberg's influence
was crucial for Hölderlin at this juncture. Beck speculates that Hölderlin came to a renewed belief in the divinity of nature through the
spiritual intensity of his love for Diotima, and that this new belief
demanded a new form of expression, which Hölderlin appropriated
from Stolberg's emulations of Greek hymns to divine powers.[10]

After Hölderlin's earliest, expressive poetry, the Tübingen hymns
used nature-imagery almost solely in the form of rhetorical decoration.
Natural objects were either associated with conventional myths or
used as stereotyped "examples" in argumentation. A relatively late
instance of such usage would be the constellations which dip beneath
the waves in the provisional conclusion to "Diotima." While even the
first versions of *Hyperion* had passages of sustained and detailed celebration of nature in prose, the scattered instances of natural imagery
in Hölderlin's poetry remained "artificial." Then the poet discovered
a stylistic precedent in Stolberg and adapted the form to his own ends.
Yet this was no mere stylistic experiment but rather an indication of
basic change in attitude. As noted, Hölderlin's exposure to critical
philosophy had almost convinced him of the impossibility of any
immediate comprehension of All-Unity such as that hypothesized in
"intellectual intuition." Hence, any attempt to discern the presence
of All-Unity in the natural world could only entail mediation through
a concept interposed between ourselves and nature. If only disjointed
phenomena can ever be discerned in Nature, we should perhaps abandon any search for unmediated vision of the noumenal essence of all
Being.

And yet, Hölderlin's love for Diotima-Susette seemed to give him
that immediate experience of mergence with All-Unity which before
had only been the object of his hopes. Through his supposed unmediated participation in cosmic harmony, he now seems able to view
its presence in the natural world; like Wordsworth, he is for a while

privileged "with an eye made quiet by the power / Of harmony, and the deep power of joy [to] see into the life of things."[11] For Hölderlin, though, this is no momentary trance-state as it is for the poet of "Tintern Abbey." It is rather a lingering metaphysical joy, a preternatural blessedness which seems to endure as long as the first intensity of being in love. And when this intensity passes away, the fading beatitude is yet recent enough that poetry can still be written in its light.

These poems thus seek to capture in concrete detail an intuition of the unitive Being or Life of nature.[12] In "Die Eichbäume" the poet achieves a certain degree of empathetic feeling for the trees. One passage might be regarded as an approximation of Keatsian empathy or an anticipation of Rilke's later attempts to pronounce the essence of things in his *Dinggedichte:*

> Und ihr drängt euch fröhlich und frei, aus der kräftigen Würzel,
> Unter einander herauf und ergreift, wie der Adler die Beute,
> Mit gewaltigem Arme den Raum, und gegen die Wolken
> Ist euch heiter und gross die sonnige Krone gerichtet.   [1:201]

> And joyfully and freely you press upwards out of the powerful roots among yourselves and, as the eagle his prey, you seize space with powerful arms, and your sunny crest is raised up serene and great towards the clouds.

Hölderlin's characterization of the oaks as "titans" a few lines earlier is no mere conceit; he effectively conveys in description of the trees a sense of powerful motion and growth. As one critic has remarked, this poem provides perhaps the first clear instance of those qualities of language which we associate with the mature Hölderlin; it might therefore be said to mark the turning point from his earlier work.[13] From this point, Hölderlin's poetry shows a continuous development in style and thought and a consistency in thematic structure that is maintained until the time of his madness.

The two most important achievements in this crucial group of poems are "An den Aether" (1:204–205) and "Der Wanderer" (1:206–208).[14] Both approach the general topic of All-Unity from the perspective of the poet's new, intuitive grasp of Nature. The first views all living things in terms of an hierarchical order in which things aspire to the transcendent source of their being, the blue air of heaven. Man feels this transcendental aspiration but often tends to displace his longing in horizontal quests, which still are ultimately for the "deeper ocean" of sky beyond the earthly sea's horizon. The poet, however, with his privileged intuition of universal Being in Nature, is content with the visitation of heaven's breezes at his own dwelling-place:

> Aber indess ich hinauf in die dämmernde Ferne mich sehne,
> Wo du fremde Gestad' umfängst mit der bläulichen Wooge,
> Kommst du säuselnd herab von des Fruchtbaums blühenden Wipfeln,
> Vater Aether! und sänftigest selbst das strebende Herz mir,
> Und ich lebe nun gern, wie zuvor, mit den Blumen der Erde. [1:205]

> But while I yearn upwards into the dusky distance, where you embrace
> foreign shores with the bluish wave, you, Father Aether, come
> rustling down from the blossoming tops of the fruit tree, and you yourself
> appease my striving heart, and now I live gladly, as before, with the
> flowers of the earth.

"Aether," the quintessence and transcendent principle of Being, is here invoked as "Father." In "Brot und Wein," "Vater Aether" is the name the Greeks give to their universal Deity. He is perhaps also the "Father" mentioned in the third conclusion to "Diotima." As was suggested above, Hölderlin's name for the Deity is here "personal" without being crudely anthropomorphic. It enables him to regard the transcendent source of Being as distinct from himself (a "thou") without reducing it to the status of an object (an "it"). Naming the Deity as Father has several advantages: it conveys the idea of source or sustained creation (the father begets and then provides for his children) and also the idea that this relationship is one of mutual love. However, as noted, it does not suggest the idea of immediacy or possible (incestuous) loss of autonomy, which could be aspects of any relationship with a maternal Deity. Hence the popularity of the Father-God for monotheistic religions. But Hölderlin's Father Aether has the added qualities of being literally above all entities (transcendent) and yet also an integral part of them (immanent): aether is all-pervasive. Again, he is a nonhuman god, not even conceived in man's image. This permits the poet to be wholly clear about the distinction between man and God. For God is divine Life itself, but he can be addressed only as that aspect of Life (or Being) which transcends our capacity for participation. God must appear as radically other than man, although man may partially share in God as Being. Also, as one critic remarks, the elusive quality of aether makes it an especially appropriate image for the divine essence, since the Deity not only transcends man's capacity for participation but also his ability to comprehend and describe.[15]

Thus "Vater Aether" remains for Hölderlin the most appropriate provisional poetic name for the Deity, just as "Eins und Alles" remains his preferred conceptual term for it. Yet, while Hölderlin's poetry continues to be preoccupied with the concept of All-Unity, "Father Aether" must eventually be considered inadequate as a definitive name. For this is only one of the modes in which divinity has manifested itself to us; man has discovered many other names for God, and though all are imperfect or partial, all have some validity. The poet in his later hymns will therefore attempt a poetic synthesis of the names of God.

In this poem, however, the poetic problem of naming has not yet become acute, and the poet expresses confidence in the title "Vater Aether." A similar contentment is evinced in "Der Wanderer," a poem of analogous structure. Divine Life appears here in another of its forms, the element of fire, which is to become Hölderlin's most characteristic designation of that mode of presence which, in its intensity, is potentially destructive of man's finite, individual being.[16] In this poem, the poet speaks merely of extremes of feeling: the unbearably intense presence or the desolating absence of deific Life as symbolized by the nearness or distance of the sun. In the African desert the fiery sun is so intense that little natural life can flourish; at the North Pole, however, the nearly complete absence of the sun is even more debilitating and no life at all can exist. The visit to the desert was valuable as an experience of intensity—"du erschienst mir feurig und herrlich" ("you appeared to me fiery and splendid")—and yet God's holy fire had once appeared to him in a "more divine and beautiful" form, presumably in his love for Diotima: "Aber ich hatte dich einst göttlicher, schöner gesehen." The arctic regions still anticipate the visitation of a warmer sun that will awaken in them the fires of immanent life. The poet, however, is pleased to return to his homeland where the sun's deific fire is present in moderation and a happy balance is maintained between transcendence and immanence:

Aber jezt kehr' ich zurük an den Rhein, in die glükliche Heimath,
    Und es wehen, wie einst, zärtliche Lüfte mich an.
Und das strebende Herz bensänftigen mir die vertrauten
    Friedlichen Bäume, die einst mich in den Armen gewiegt,
Und das heilige Grün, der Zeuge des ewigen, schönen
    Lebens der Welt, wandelt zum Jüngling mich um.   [1:297]

But now I return to the Rhine, to the happy homeland, and tender
breezes breathe upon me as before. And the familiar, peaceful trees, that
once rocked me in their arms, appease my striving heart, and the holy
greenery, the witness of the eternal, beautiful life of the world,
transforms me into a youth.

Here, as in "An den Aether," breezes ("Lüfte") are signs of divine
grace and, as in many of the later poems, trees and foliage are figures
of abiding immanence. Although the poet has been shaken by his experiences of religious extremes, he hopes that the idyllic beauty of his
fatherland, which is neither too hot nor too cold, will restore his soul's
youth:

Alt bin ich geworden indess, mich bleichte der Eispol,
    Und im Feuer des Süds fielen die Loken mir aus.
Doch, wie Aurora den Tithon, umfängst du in lächelnder Blüthe
    Warm und fröhlich, wie einst, Vaterlandserde, den Sohn.   [1:207]

In the meantime I have become old, the icy Pole made me pale, and my
locks fell out in the fire of the South. Yet, as Aurora does Tithonus,
you embrace your son amidst smiling blossoms, warmly and happily, as
before, Earth of the Fatherland.

The rest of the poem is an extended celebration of the naive, bucolic
joys of the poet's native Swabia.

What is notable about this poem is the poet's newly symbolical rep-
resentation of religious experience. As noted, the moment of complete
religious fulfillment is now seen as past: "I had *once* seen you more
divine, more beautiful."[17] This distance permits the poet to adopt a
new attitude of objectivity towards his experience. Since Hölderlin's
most intensely felt participation in All-Unity is now viewed as definitively past and can never again be experienced with the same original
intensity, any subsequent religious experience can only be judged with
respect to this standard as deficient, properly moderate, or excessive.

The notion of an excessive indulgence in divine presence might appear somewhat puzzling; however, it is a recurrent theme in Hölderlin's later work which becomes progressively more significant for him.

Briefly, the notion seems to be that once we have experienced our full "measure" of spiritual elation (whether or not we interpret this elation in conventionally religious terms) we can never experience it again. Until this moment of fulfillment has occurred, we do not know what it is. When it happens we recognize it; it is a moment of full clarity. And when it is past, we can only hope to keep it alive in memory. If we attempt simply to relive it, we destroy the memory, and if we attempt to exceed it we run the risk of destroying ourselves. For Hölderlin, happiness ("Glück") or joy ("Freude") is always a divine gift; if we seek to take it by force, we are unable to bear it.[18] In traditional terms, the gods would punish us much as they punished Icarus for coming too near the sun. The image of the offender chastened or destroyed by divine fire, Apollo's arrows, or Zeus's lightning, becomes an obsession for Hölderlin in his later poetry.

In the present poem, however, this threat is still muted. The poet sees the unhappy effects of prolonged and excessive exposure to the sun's fire, but this intensity is not yet considered lethal. It has simply caused his hair to fall out (an image probably without humorous intent), suggesting he will be less protected against such exposure in the future. And the dangers of excess are here neatly balanced against the miseries of deficient transcendence. One can here return to an idyll of contentment in moderate awareness of divine presence. "An den Aether" similarly recommends moderation: that we should let heaven's breezes come gently to us, rather than embark on a wild quest for the sky. And "Die Eichbäume" urges an analogous kind of moderation between the values of communal love or "geselliges Leben" and the more heroic values signified by the gigantic oak trees.[19]

Thus, the completed poems of this group, along with their other similarities, are alike in recommending the *via media*. The poet's supposed consummate religious experience has made possible a new empathetic participation in the Life of Nature and encouraged him to write a nature poetry of "negative capability." This experience has also satisfied all present desires, so that he may now content himself with the moderate joys of remembrance. For a while, he knows the certi-

tude of an untroubled faith in the reality of All-Unity. In "Der Wanderer," the totality of unified experience is figured geographically as
the poet visits the ends of the earth and then returns to what he considers its center. All-Unity is even more clearly present as a structural
principle in "An den Aether," which enumerates all living creatures
in their common aspiration to the blue air of heaven. As the poet is
able to comprehend them all in relation to what unifies them, he is
granted a conforting visitation from the divine principle of this unity,
Father Aether. The poem thus achieves a complex synthesis in theme
and structure of the poet's current attitude towards his principal topic.
However, such a synthesis was not to be permanently viable.

The attitude of momentary contentment expressed in the nature
poems, then, was not the only mood to prevail in Hölderlin's poetry;
he also wrote several odes in this period (1798). In his earlier years he
had written a number of lyrical odes in imitation of Klopstock, chiefly
of the loose pseudo-Horatian type. With the advent of the Tübingen
hymns Hölderlin abandoned the ode form temporarily, to take it up
again during his later Frankfurt years. These poems were written in an
attempt to achieve the structural precision of the ancient ode, without
being markedly pedantic in imitation of classical meter.[20] One of the
Frankfurt odes, characteristic both in formal exactness and in theme,
is entitled "Die Kürze":

"Warum bist du so kurz? liebst du, wie vormals, denn
Nun nicht mehr den Gesang? fandst du, als Jüngling, doch,
    In den Tagen der Hoffnung,
        Wenn du sangest, das Ende nie!"
Wie mein Glük, ist mein Lied. — Willst du im Abendrot
Froh dich baden? hinweg ists! und die Erd ist kalt.
    Und der Vogel der Nacht schwirrt
        Unbequem vor das Auge dir.   [1:248]

"Why are you so brief? Do you no longer love song, as before? Indeed, as
a youth, in the days of hope, you never found the end when you
sang!" Like my joy is my song. Do you want to bathe happily in the red
of evening? It's gone! And the earth is cold, and the bird of night
hums, uncomfortably, before your eyes.

The poem is itself an example of that "brevity" which it defends and
explains: "Wie mein Glük, ist mein Lied." The sun of the poet's

greatest joy is now seen disappearing beyond the horizon of his immediate consciousness. The restorative power of memory diminishes as its
object fades into the past; the joy derived from recollection lessens
each time it is consciously renewed.

Wordsworth, of course, was troubled by the same problem. Not only
does he lament the fading of his visionary gleam, but in *The Prelude*
he is unpleasantly aware of the occlusion of those "spots of time"
which were the sources of his later strength:

> The days gone by
> Come back upon me from the dawn almost
> Of life: the hiding-places of my power
> Seem open; I approach, and then they close;
> I see by glimpses now; when age comes on,
> May scarcely see at all . . .   [11.334–339: 1805 version]

And Wordsworth, like Hölderlin, seeks to capture the substance of
these memories poetically before they evanesced:

> . . . and I would give,
> While yet I may, as far as words can give,
> A substance and a life to what I feel:
> I would enshrine the spirit of the past
> For future restoration.   [11.339–343]

But *The Prelude* is a work of hard-bitten, grim optimism unlike anything in Hölderlin. The misgivings even in the 1805 version are often
quashed with a sometimes forced epic sublimity of style. Wordsworth
here refers only parenthetically ("as far as words may give") to the
capacity of poetic language to reconstitute experience. However, for
Hölderlin the problem of this capacity is to become a primary concern.

In this ode, written in the objective, even catechetical form of
question-and-answer, the brevity of poetry is explained by the brevity
of "happiness" or joyous inspiration. (Joy, like Yeats's "gaiety," is
always an essential element in poetic inspiration for Hölderlin.) With
the fading of his inspirational source, the poet is left only with the
"Vogel der Nacht," the conventional owl of an international Grave-
yard School. But the poet would be "uncomfortable" brooding upon
his own moroseness; he has no desire to write consciously uninspired
poetry.

This same laconic style is to be found in most of Hölderlin's odes of the period. They are highly objective in attitude despite the complexity of the poet's often tormented moods and feelings. Here for the first time Hölderlin consciously adopts a "mask" almost in the Yeatsian sense of a special personality expressed in the voice of the poems. This persona is notably more reserved and inclined to understatement than the highly excitable speaker of the early poems. The new voice inclines to terse formality, posing and then answering rhetorical questions, and shows a marked preference for indicative, simple statements as opposed to the exclamations and optatives of the Tübingen hymns. Through this mask (determined by the formal structures of the chosen genre) the odes do not appear spoken by the historical Friedrich Hölderlin, the now unhappy former lover of Susette Gontard, but as utterances of a dispassionate Poet aloof from any mere earthly event. Hölderlin's mask is thus ultimately of a different kind than Yeats's: the latter's persona not only speaks his poems but constitutes his ideal public personality; Hölderlin's is closer in general function here to Eliot's "escape from personality." It might thus be considered an anti-persona or mere voice by which the "medium" (to use Eliot's terms again) is "expressed."[21]

But the mask of Hölderlin's odes (with their severe objectivity and distance from the feelings and even ideas they present) is not apparent in most of his other poetry. The "I" of "Der Wanderer," for example, speaks of the events of the poem as personal experiences, and the poem's language is in immediate or reflective response to such experiences. That the events are figurative rather than historically literal does not affect the concrete relationship of the poetic "I" to the narrative happenings. Although the "experience" ("Erlebnis") is formally constituted, within this formal world the "I" responds authentically to whatever it encounters. Such is also generally the case with Hölderlin's later elegies and hymns. Although the poet's "I" may there assume prophetic character, the reader does not sense this character as an adopted mask (as in Shelley's prophecies, for example), but merely as a heightened dimension of the poetic "I's" own being as it encounters and freely responds to events of the poems. If we were to seek analogues in fiction, where point of view is more clearly defined, we might say that the "I" of the odes is like a near-omniscient observer who, even if he appears as a character, is always superior to the events. The "I" of the elegies and late hymns, however, is more like the first-person narrator who, as he is involved in the action, can only surmise the meaning of events as they occur.

Another way of noting this distinction would be in terms of the basic temporal structures of the respective genres. The early hymns, as noted, were chiefly directed towards the future. Futurity is also characteristic of the late hymns, although in a radically different form. In the elegies, as in the nature poems, the predominant reference is to the past, and the present is usually seen in some relationship to it. In the odes, however, an attempt is made to concentrate on the present moment as a kind of absolute. The earliest odes of the Frankfurt period evolve formally from the epigram, the succinct pronouncement of an isolated present idea; and most of the odes of 1798 remain essentially epigrammatic in character.[22] "Die Kürze," the eight-line poem discussed above, offers the rationale for this brevity. An isolated idea is stated only in terms of its own content; it is not elaborated upon or related to any other idea. The poet is interested neither in its (past) antecedents nor in its (future) possibilities. The idea is simply *presented* in its present form. Even when these poems have a narrative element, all events noted are referred to the present moment of insight, in which they are wholly comprehended and, often, definitively explained. There are no unintelligible memories; all past happenings are accounted for. Thus, in "Die Liebenden":

> Trennen wollten wir uns, wähnten es gut und klug;
> > Da wirs taten, warum schrökt' uns, wie Mord, die Tat?
> > > Ach! wir kennen uns wenig,
> > > > Denn es waltet ein Gott in uns.   [1:249]

> We wanted to part, fancied it to be good and clever; then when we did it, why did the deed frighten us like murder? Ah, we know ourselves little, for a god reigns in us.

This brief poem gives the impression that the poet has finally, definitively, come to terms with the experience of his parting from Susette. The past suffering is now wholly banished, the poet is calm and lucid, and he is able to give the final explanation for the horror caused by the break, as by a "murder." Although in general the lovers do not "know themselves" very well, the speaker of the poem is now implicitly dissociated from his identity as former lover through his mask of omniscient aloofness. He now knows perfectly: their relationship itself had the status of a god who was "murdered" when this relationship was destroyed by their parting. Although the poem is about a past event, the speaker's voice is isolated in the present moment of insight and thus the experience becomes—in the nonpejorative sense—depersonalized. The past event itself is presented only so that the definitive present "explanation" can be extracted from it. The past moment is virtually disposed of in the poet's use of it to consolidate the present.

In this poem, the question posed is thus immediately and finally answered. In most of the other odes as well, the only admissible questions are those with clear answers. The future simply does not exist except as a present hypothesis. There is no contingency beyond the present moment—it is almost as if the future has been emptied of significance. Thus, the four-line poems "Ehemals und Jetzt" (1:246) and, especially, "Lebenslauf" (1:247) speak of the poet's life as virtually over, and "An die Parzen" (1:241) proclaims his willingness to die in several months provided he has managed to express himself adequately in poetry by that time.

In the previous discussion I have indicated certain differences between the odes and the rest of Hölderlin's poetic work: their mask of aloofness and (occasionally) omniscience, the basic noninvolvement of the "I" in the feelings or events of the narrative, and the tendency to uphold the autonomy of the present moment. All of these qualities are also present in most of Hölderlin's later, more extensive odes written contemporaneously with the elegies and hymns. A number of the brief early odes, such as "Stimme des Volks," "Lebenslauf," "Die Heimat," and "An die Deutschen," are simply expanded later by adding more verses. In these, also, the present moment remains pivotal and the temporal structure is circular rather than progressive, so that the dominion of present insight is upheld rather than subjected to dialectical transformation. None of these qualities characteristic of the odes, however, are evident in that line of development in Hölderlin's poetry which clearly leads to the major hymns.

For these reasons I will not undertake any detailed analysis of Hölderlin's later odes in this book.[23] They comprise an important and highly interesting part of the poet's work, and are often close to formal poetic perfection. Yet they are not crucial to an understanding of his most important poems. While they are structurally unique, virtually all their themes and ideas are present (and more fully treated) in the elegies and major hymns. They may thus be regarded as constituting a kind of parallel path apart from the main course of Hölderlin's poetry.

4. Empedokles

One of Hölderlin's earlier odes was entitled "Empedokles." It commemorates the fifth century (B.C.) philosopher and poet who, according to legend, committed suicide by leaping into the crater of Mount Etna:

Das Leben suchst du, suchst, und es quillt und glänzt
    Ein göttlich Feuer tief aus der Erde dir,
        Und du in schauderndem Verlangen
            Wirfst dich hinab, in des Ätna Flammen.

So schmelzt' im Weine Perlen der Übermut
    Der Königin; und mochte sie doch! hättst du
        Nur deinen Reichtum nicht, o Dichter,
            Hin in den gärenden Kelch geopfert!

Doch heilig bist du mir, wie der Erde Macht,
　Die dich hinwegnahm, kühner Getödteter!
　　Und folgen möcht' ich in die Tiefe,
　　　Hielte die Liebe mich nicht, dem Helden.　　[1:240]

You seek life; you seek, and a divine fire wells up and gleams to you from
deep out of the earth, and, in shuddering desire, you throw yourself
down into Etna's flames. Thus did the arrogance of the queen dissolve
pearls in wine. And let her, if only *you*, O poet, had not sacrificed
your own wealth into the seething chalice! Yet you are holy to me like
the power of Earth, which took you away, you bold victim! And I
would like to follow the hero into the depths if love did not hold me
back.

We may notice here several formal characteristics common to Hölderlin's odes at the time: brevity, a certain restraint in treating an emotional topic, and (while the third strophe is more immediate in tone
than most of the odes) the self-certainty of the poetic "I" which, at
this moment, has attained a resolution that appears definitive. In
"Empedokles" the resolution is achieved by the following dialectic:
one may feel tempted to seek an unmediated, suicidal union with the
"divine fire" of all-unifying "Life,"[1] yet the poet is "held back" by the
community of love for others and thereby kept from sacrificing his
"wealth" of poetic powers as Empedokles had done.

Yet the Empedoklean temptation continued to fascinate Hölderlin
throughout the late 1790s. In these years he wrote the three unfinished
drafts of his play, *Der Tod des Empedokles,* and several related prose
sketches or meditations: an early "Frankfurter Plan," the somewhat
later "Grund zum Empedokles," and an outline of the third version
of the play with notes for its projected completion.[2] As the more fragmentary third version has immediate thematic relevance to the first of
Hölderlin's late hymns, it will be discussed in a later chapter. Since the
thematic contents of the first two versions are virtually identical and
several of the major scenes appear in both with only occasional differences in wording, no real distinction will be observed here between
them. This chapter will be concerned not with the tentative and fragmentary structures of the plays, but with their explorations of a radical
response to the problem of All-Unity.

The first two versions of the drama take up themes presented in the

Empedokles ode, but develop them in much greater complexity. The early "Frankfurter Plan" (although its outline is not followed) develops a characterization of the protagonist which appears to be consistently observed:

> Empedokles, durch sein Gemüth und seine Philosophie schon längst zu Kulturhass gestimmt, zu Verachtung alles sehr bestimmten Geschäffts, alles nach verschiedenen Gegenständen gerichteten Interesses, ein Todtfeind aller einseitigen Existenz, und deswegen auch in wirklich schönen Verhältnissen unbefriedigt, unstät, leidend, blos weil sie besondere Verhältnisse sind und, nur im grossen Akkord mit allem Lebendigen empfunden ganz ihn erfüllen, blos weil er nicht mit allgegenwärtigem Herzen innig, wie ein Gott . . . in ihnen leben und lieben kann, blos weil er, sobald sein Herz und sein Gedanke das Vorhandene umfasst, ans Gesez der Succession gebunden ist—
> [4:145]

> Empedokles, through his feelings and his philosophy long disposed to cultural hatred, to contempt for all very definite activity, all interest directed at diverse objects, a deadly enemy of all one-sided existence, and therefore dissatisfied, restless, miserable even in really beautiful conditions, merely because they are specific conditions and [because such conditions would] wholly fulfill him only when felt in the great accord with all living things, merely because he cannot live and love in [such conditions] with all-present heart, intensely like a god . . . , merely because, as soon as his heart and his thought embrace what is present, he is bound to the law of succession. . . .

This rather involved description of Empedokles' intellectual development shows sympathy without unqualified approbation. Empedokles is unhappy with specificity as such, for any specific thing is inevitably limited. He is unable to feel the infinite All-Unity of Life and thus cannot tolerate the fragmentary reality of everyday existence. Seeking total participation in divine Life, he aspires to attain absolute consciousness.

In the first two versions of the play, Empedokles, like Hyperion (or like the poet himself) is shown as one to whom the unity of all had been revealed. His present longing for participation thus has the character of nostalgia for a definite past moment.[3] A key passage in both versions shows how the revelation of the divinity of sunlight was an epiphany of All-Unity as the All-Vivifying: "die Allebendige."[4] Empedokles perceives sunlight to be the unifying principle of visible reality much as the informing "spirit" of a poem makes it a coherent whole:

> Doch als   [break in text]
>   der Geist mir blühte, wie du [Sonne] selber blühst,
> Da kannt' ich dich, da rief ich es: du lebst,
> Und wie du heiter wandelst um die Sterblichen,
> Und himmlischjugendlich den holden Schein
> Vor dir auf jedes eigen überstralst,
> Dass alle deines Geistes Farbe tragen,
> So ward auch mir das Leben zum Gedicht.
> Denn deine Seele war in mir, und offen gab
> Mein Herz wie du der ernsten Erde sich,
> Der Leidenden . . .   [4:17]

> Yet when . . . my spirit bloomed, as you yourself bloom, then I knew you, then I shouted, you live, and as you serenely move among the mortals, and in heavenly youthful fashion beam out the noble radiance before you upon each single thing, so that all things bear the color of your spirit, thus did my life also become a poem. For your soul was in me, and openly my heart, like you, gave itself to the somber earth, the suffering . . .

Through participation in this principle of integrating light, Empedokles' own mind achieves a sunlike, coherent lucidity that converts his life into a "poem." And Empedokles like the sunlight now devotes himself to the "Earth," the dark, suffering side of reality, helping to bring it into radiant clarity.[5]

The longer second version of this speech describes Empedokles' epiphany and dedication in more detail. His young disciple, Pausanias, has just suggested that the master ought to find maturity even more beautiful than youth had been. Empedokles begins his reply by positing a situation similar to that in "Die Kürze," where the poet is trying to revive a dying memory. Only now it is Empedokles himself who seems on the point of "vanishing away" from an abiding moment of the past. The passage merits quotation at some length:

> Und gerne sehen, wenn es nun
> Hinab sich neigen will, die Augen
> Der Schnellhinschwindenden noch Einmal
> Zurük, der Dankenden. O jene Zeit!
> Ihr Liebeswonnen, da die Seele mir

Von Göttern, wie Endymion, gewekt,
Die kindlich schlummernde, sich öffnete,
Lebendig sie, die Immerjugendlichen,
Des Lebens grosse Genien
Erkannte—schöne *Sonne!* Menschen hatten mich
Es nicht gelehrt, mich trieb mein eigen Herz
Unsterblich liebend zu Unsterblichen,
Zu dir, zu dir, ich könnte Göttlichers
Nicht finden, stilles Licht! und so wie du
Das Leben nicht an deinem Tage sparst
Und sorgenfrei der goldnen Fülle dich
Entledigest, so gönnt' auch ich, der Deine,
Den Sterblichen die beste Seele gern
Und furchtlosoffen gab
Mein Herz, wie du, der ernsten *Erde* sich,
Der schiksaalvollen; ihr in Jünglingsfreude
Das Leben so zu eignen bis zulezt,
Ich sagt' ihrs oft in trauter Stunde zu,
Band so den theuern Todesbund mit ihr.
Da rausch' es anders, denn zuvor, im Hain
Und zärtlich tönten ihrer Berge Quellen—
All deine Freuden, *Erde!* wahr, wie sie,
Und warm und voll, aus Müh' und Liebe reifen,
Sie alle gabst du mir.   [4:105–106; emphases in text]

And, when it is now about to decline, the eyes of the rapidly disappearing
one, the thanking one, gladly look back one more time. O that time!
You raptures of love, when my soul, waked like Endymion by gods, my
childlike slumbering soul opened up, vitally recognized the ever-
youthful ones, the great genii of life—beautiful *Sun!* Men had not taught
it to me, my own heart drove me immortally loving to the immortals,
to you, to you, I could find nothing more divine, quiet light! And just as
you are not sparing with life in your day, and carelessly release your
golden plenitude, so also did I, your own man, gladly give the best of my
soul to mortals and, fearlessly open, my heart, like you, gave itself
to the somber *Earth*, full of destiny, in youthful joy to adapt my life to
her until the last, I said it to her so often in an intimate hour, thus
I confirmed the dear bond of death with her. Then it murmured differently than before in the grove, and the springs of her mountains
sounded tenderly. All of your joys, *Earth*, truly, as, warm and full, they
ripen from effort and love, you gave them all to me.

Empedokles' spiritual birth is first described in the conventional mythic
terms of the awakening of Endymion. Since his heart was responsive

to the immortal presences of the natural world, he soon, untaught, recognized the sunlight as the first principle of divine presence in nature: "ich könnte Göttlichers / Nicht finden, stilles Licht!" Thus, unlike Wordsworth in the "Immortality Ode," Empedokles consciously achieves an intuition of divine essence in the light of common day. His act of recognition evokes a response from the heavenly power and permits a sharing in its divine essence and functions. His own soul, as a divine agent, now illuminates men and "the grave Earth, full of destiny," the mother of the mortal part of man.[6] And as soon as Empedokles fully realizes his sunlike divinity he immediately commits himself to this unhappy earth and swears "a dear bond of death with her." In this, of course, he somewhat resembles the Christ of orthodoxy, who freely humbled himself to earthly existence at the Incarnation.[7] The parallel between Christ and Empedokles becomes even more significant in the third version of the play with Empedokles' sacrificial death. Yet, Empedokles is never explicitly compared to Christ in the first two versions, and even in the third the comparison is problematical.

The first result of Empedokles' dedication to earth is a sense of joyous sharing in the All-Unity manifest in earthly life. In the first version he declares: "In mir, ihr Quellen des Lebens, Strömtet ihr einst / Aus Tiefen der Welt zusammen, und es kamen / Die dürstenden zu mir . . ." (4:14)—all of the "sources" of Life were joined in his own soul, and other men, thirsting for this unitive Life, came to him as to its fountainhead. In return, he was able to sympathize with the tribulations of mortals while sharing in their earthly joys. At times his empathy with suffering earth became painful to him; but at these moments, the paternal "Aether . . . breathed healingly upon his love-wounded breast," just as it comforted the earth. Then his cares left him like Shelleyan "clouds of flame" and dissolved in the high azure of heaven, which again became his native element. The young Empedokles was thus involved in a beneficent dialectic of Earth and Heaven, mortal and divine, and truly deserved to be called a "Son of Heaven." Yet, although he had lived as "comrade" ("Genosse") of the divine powers in nature and was able to hear her primal harmony ("deinen alten Einklang, Natur!"), he has now been "cast out" from heavenly fellowship and therefore has no further blessings to offer.

One of the chief problems of the drama is Empedokles' loss of his

sense of divine unity. This loss is presented most generally as the result of "hubris."[8] In the soliloquy preceding the conversation with
Pausanias (4:103–104), Empedokles speaks of his sin as drunken in-
gratitude towards his divine benefactors resulting from overindulgence
in heavenly "nectar." But such drunkenness is of course a metaphor
which cannot lucidly account for Empedokles' fall.

An analytical account is provided by Mekades (Kritias in the first
version) and Hermokrates, conservative priests who view Empedokles'
various revelations of All-Unity as posing a gnostic threat both to positive faith and to established society. Men should be kept from such
doctrines for their own good. Hermokrates explains his priestly strategy:

> Drum binden wir den Menschen auch
> Das Band ums Auge, dass sie nicht
> Zu kräftig sich am Lichte nähren.
> Nicht gegenwärtig werden
> Darf Göttliches vor ihnen,
> Es darf ihr Herz
> Lebendiges nicht finden.   [4:91]

> Therefore also do we tie the band about the eyes of men, so that they may
> not too powerfully nourish themselves on the light. The divine must
> not become present before them, their heart must not find the Living.

This deliberate mystification helps prevent the disaster that arises
when men forget the radical distinction between themselves as mortals (subject to an established order) and the gods (who have supposedly imposed this order). One of the most grievous consequences
of such blasphemous pride would be revolution. Empedokles is himself guilty of inciting crowds to sacrilegious frenzy. Mekades cites an
example of his subversive teaching, according to which All-Unity
would be the basis of an unmediated, unstructured communion of
mortals and divine forces (thereby obviating the need for priests as
mediators):

> Mir tauschen
> Die Kraft und Seele zu Einem
> Die Sterblichen und die Götter.   [4:95]

> For me, the mortals and the gods exchange and unify power and soul.

Empedokles also claimed to unite men with one another, since he himself possessed the absolute fulfillment of human wisdom; he could therefore remedy the various deficiencies of others' partial minds, reconciling them in the unified totality of the One Mind or *Logos:*

                                    denn ich
       Geselle das Fremde,
       Das Unbekannte nennt mein Wort
       Und die Liebe der Lebenden trag'
       Ich auf und nieder; was Einem gebricht,
       Ich bring es vom andern, und binde
       Beseelend, und wandle
       Verjüngend die zornige Welt,
       Und gleiche keinem und Allen.   [4:95–96]

For I associate what is foreign, my word names the unknown, and the love of the living I bear up and down; what is lacking to one I bring from the other, and bind together, vivifying, and transform, rejuvenating, the angry world, and I resemble none and all.

"So sprach der Übermutige," concludes Mekades.

"Übermut" is the priests' term for Empedokles' hubris, whereby he "forgot the difference" between men and gods: "Weil er des Unterschieds zu sehr vergass" (4:11). On this basis, Hermokrates provides a rather elaborate analysis of how Empedokles fell from grace. Because Empedokles felt too much love for the common people he betrayed the gods' secrets to them, thereby inciting the people to frenzy. But then even his own words sounded unreal and inadequate to himself. His growing, painful awareness of the insufficiency of his words began to make him self-conscious and faltering in his delivery, and his lack of confidence made the people realize his mortality. Empedokles had failed them as a god, and they turned against him. Perhaps Empedokles was forced to proclaim his own divinity in order to regain his self-confidence and the devotion of the crowd. In encouraging their adulation he became as blasphemously "superstitious" as they. As a result of Empedokles' attempted self-deification, the gods withdrew their grace and power from him.

In the soliloquy of the play's first version Empedokles himself offers a clearer and more existential account of his fall:

als die Genien der Welt
Voll Liebe sich in dir vergassen, dachtst du
An dich und wähntest karger Thor, an dich
Die Gütigen verkauft, dass sie dir,
Die Himmlischen, wie blöde Knechte dienten!   [4:15]

When the genii of the world, full of love, forgot themselves in you, you
thought of yourself and fancied, pitiable fool, that the benevolent
ones were sold to you, that they, the Heavenly, served you like timid
slaves!

Although his own explanation does not account for the dialectical
relationship between himself and his followers, it is perhaps more co-
gent than Hermokrates' theory. In Empedokles' view, the dialectic was
essentially between himself and the divine powers or "genii" of nature,
his "gods." They abandoned themselves in love to him, expecting him
to reciprocate in a loving abandonment of his own selfhood to them:
anyone who wishes to partake in All-Unity must share in its cohesive
spirit of love.[9] Empedokles, however, "thought of himself" and regarded the powers of nature as agents of his will, almost his "slaves."
We saw a similar master-slave dialectic in the preface to *Hyperion*.
Here, however, Empedokles tries to enslave the gods themselves; he is
a kind of pre-Socratic Faust.[10] But from the beginning of the play he
is a repentent Faust, chiefly interested in proclaiming his guilt and
finding some way to be reconciled with the deities he has offended.

His chosen way to effect this reconciliation is suicide. In the first,
most complete version of the play he actually leaps into the volcano,
and Pausanias commemorates his death with fine sentiment: "Der
sterben muss, weil er zu schön gelebt, / Weil ihn zu sehr die Götter
alle liebten" (4:85). ("Who must die because he lived too beautifully,
because the gods all loved him too much.") In the more fragmentary
second version of the play, there is every indication he will jump. (The
third version is somewhat more problematical; yet the notes for its
completion suggest that here, too, he will kill himself, although with
slightly different motives.) The motives in the early versions are fairly
clear, and can be separated into subjective and objective reasons.[11]
The more objective or public reasons are eloquently given in a scene
where the leaders of the people urge him to reconsider his suicidal

decision and return to them. Empedokles replies that he has already told them all he could, and that he cannot now continue to live:

> Ihr dürft leben
> So lang ihr Othem habt; ich nicht. Es muss
> Bei Zeiten weg, durch wen der Geist geredet.
> Es offenbart die göttliche Natur
> Sich göttlich oft durch Menschen, so erkennt
> Das vielversuchende Geschlecht sie wieder,
> Doch hat der Sterbliche, dem sie das Herz
> Mit ihrer Wonne füllte, sie verkündet,
> O lasst sie denn zerbrechen das Gefäss,
> Damit es nicht zu andrem Brauche dien'
> Und Göttliches zum Menschenwerke werde.   [4:73]

You may live as long as you have breath, not I. He must betimes depart, through whom the spirit spoke. Divine Nature often reveals herself divinely through men, so that the much-attempting race may recognize her again. Yet once the mortal, whose heart she filled with her bliss, has proclaimed her, O let her then break the vessel, so that it might not serve for another use, and what is divine become a human work.

Empedokles presents here a variant of what might be termed an "instrumental" theory of divine revelation. The misuse of the "vessel" might be the exploitation of sacred knowledge for profane ends, a temptation Empedokles had already experienced. To preclude such possible sacrilege, the divine spokesman must be permitted to die. Those who are "happy" in divine insight should die before they "perish in arbitrariness, frivolity and shame." This is Empedokles' fate.

It might seem that it is already too late for Empedokles to move to retain his happiness or prevent his degradation. However, once he resolves to die, some measure of his former serenity and harmony with the gods is restored. In anticipation, he already enjoys a union with divine powers of Nature that will be consummated in the volcano's fires. This desire for rapturous reconciliation with the gods is the more subjective motive for his suicide.

The gods seem to favor his resolve. Thus, when he begins to climb Mount Etna and takes a drink of springwater, he hails the deities as his restored friends; his sense of harmony with them "blossoms" in euphoric anticipation before it "ripens" in actual return to unmediated divine Life. He is eager to attain the top of the mountain, for the gods of nature are "more present on the heights," and from this perspective one achieves a more comprehensive, all-unifying view of the world. There the sunlight appears "splendidly youthful," just as when its divinity was first manifest. Above him are the more remote presences, the "eternal constellations," and of course the "Aether," here seen as the paternal "Spirit" that is "Mover of all things":

> Dann glänzt um uns und schweigt
Das ewige Gestirn, indess herauf
Der Erde Gluth aus Bergestiefen quillt
Und zärtlich rührt der Allbewegende,
Der Geist, der Aether uns an, o dann!   [4:52–53]

Then the eternal constellation gleams in silence around us, while the glow of Earth gushes up out of mountain depths, and, tenderly, the all-moving, the Spirit, the Aether touches us—O then!

These lines also note the presence of a third form of divine fire: besides sunlight (heavenly fire mediated in warmth and light) and the stars (fire in its purely transcendent mode) there is the unmediated, wholly destructive fire of the volcano, "the glow of the earth." Although this form is nearest and most accessible to us, it is also the most dangerous. It is the deific fire of earthly Life, the immanent principle of All-Unity in nature that focuses reality into a living whole. In its mediated form it constitutes the life force of earthly things; unmediated, however, it can only destroy those finite beings it would otherwise foster. Empedokles' final leap into the fires of Etna is thus not merely a symbolic death: it is the actual destructive merging of his mortal being in the infinite divine Being of Nature. This lethal fusion is a grim mutation of the mergence with All-Unity (as heavenly Urania) desired in the early hymns. For, once the limit of one's participation in divine Life has been attained, any attempt to reattain or exceed it can only mean death. When the poet of the early hymns speaks of oblivion, the meaning is essentially figurative; but when Empedokles now hails "O, Vergessenheit! Versöhnerin!" (4:74) ("O Oblivion! Reconciling One!") he can only mean oblivion in its literal—and permanent—sense.

But Empedokles' sacrifice will reconcile him not only with the gods but with other mortals. In his final soliloquy, he again expresses a joyous determination to fulfill his destiny:

> Aber freudig quillt
> Aus mutger Brust die Flamme. Schauderndes
> Verlangen! Was? am Tod entzündet mir
> Das Leben sich zulezt? und reichest du
> Den Schreckensbecher, mir, den gärenden,
> Natur! damit dein Sänger noch aus ihm
> Die lezte der Begeisterung trinke!
> Zufrieden bin ichs, suche nichts, mehr
> Denn meine Opferstätte. Wohl ist mir.   [4:80–81]

But joyously gushes the flame from a courageous breast. Shuddering desire! What, is my life at last ignited by death? And you, Nature, extend to me the cup of terror, the seething, so that your singer may still drink from it the last of inspiration! I am satisfied, seek nothing more than my place of sacrifice. It is well with me.

He is not only "satisfied" as he moves toward his place of sacrifice but feels divine "inspiration" flare up within him again at the thought of death. But soon he will be a sacrificial victim rather than a priest of divine All-Unity when his selfhood is consumed in the raging volcanic fire.

Some possible misgivings about Empedokles' suicide are raised in the speech of Manes, Empedokles' former teacher, who comes to challenge his decision in the brief third version of the play. As mentioned above, the Manes scene will be considered in a later chapter; however, we might note here that this scene and the projected outline for the third version signify an important alteration of Hölderlin's views, a development leading directly to the attitudes formulated in the late hymns. Nonetheless, the idea that Hölderlin expressed in his ode to Empedokles appears to remain constant throughout the several versions of the play. The poet considers Empedokles "holy" because of his heroically uncompromising devotion to the divine powers. But the poet feels no compelling desire to imitate him. "Love" holds him to this life and forbids his squandering poetic gifts even in the most heroic sacrifice.

5. Toward The Elegies: "Menons Klagen um Diotima"

We have observed that the general direction of Hölderlin's earlier work is towards a greater objectivity in the poet's apprehension of All-Unity and an increasing awareness of its problematical nature. There is a clear dialectical progression from the naively subjective celebrations of the Tübingen hymns to the complexities of the objective problems in Empedokles.

The elegies, Hölderlin's next major group of poems, are both formally and thematically continuous with the earlier Frankfurt nature poems.[1] In the elegies the movement toward problematical objectification of All-Unity continues. As noted previously, the Frankfurt poem "Der Wanderer" ends with the poet, after experiences of climatic extremes, returning to the temperately diffused divine presences of his native Swabia where memories of past joy still comfort him. In the poem's later, elegiac version, however, the poet encounters problems not present before:

> Vater und Mutter? und wenn noch Freunde leben, sie haben
> Anders gewonnen, sie sind nimmer die Meinigen mehr.
> Kommen werd' ich, wie sonst, und die alten, die Nahmen der Liebe
> Nennen, beschwören das Herz, ob es noch schlage, wie sonst,
> Aber stille werden sie seyn. So bindet und scheidet
> Manches die Zeit. Ich dünk' ihnen gestorben, sie mir.
> Und so bin ich allein.   [2:82–83]

> Father and Mother? And if friends still live, they have won others, they are no longer mine. I will come as before, and name the old, the names of love, conjure the heart if it yet might beat as before, but they will be still. Thus many things are bound and severed by time. I seem dead to them, they to me. And so I am alone.

Here the poet experiences a radical sense of estrangement from the people who were once closest to him, an alienation brought about by the passage of time and his own unsettling religious experiences. He now can find consolation and communion *only* with Nature, whose divine elements seem to constitute a naturalistic trinity: "Ihr einigen drei." This later version of "Der Wanderer" thus reveals a theme that becomes dominant in the elegies—the alienation of the poet who once experienced all-unitive vision, and who now must ask how authentic community can be reconstituted. An early elegy where this question arises is "Menons Klagen um Diotima,"[2] Hölderlin's last poetic treatment of the Diotima experience.

Like other elegies, "Menons Klagen um Diotima" speaks from an unredeemed present, looks back upon a past moment of happiness, and anticipates a future analogous to the past. The poet's dialectical attitude towards this past and its mode of relationship to present or future moments constitutes the matter of the poem.

Most of the poem is concerned with working out a series of contrasts between current dejection and past bliss. The opening section (the sections vary in number of distichs) likens the speaker to a wounded deer; his spirit, like the animal, can no longer find solace in nature.[3] The solution proposed in the conclusion to "Der Wanderer" is untenable here: nature has apparently betrayed a loving heart and no longer responds sympathetically to an estranged mind. Appropriately, then, the elegy abandons the animal analogy to detail the problem in somewhat more conceptual terms. Sections two through six develop imagistically related contrasts between present and past states. The principal opposition is between darkness and light, the absence or presence of joyous participation in the all-unitive force of Love. Mythically, the present world of the dead is opposed to the land of the living where the speaker had experienced divine presence in nature through the deific quality of his love for Diotima.

The second section, then, expresses both the futility of struggle against present captors, the "gods of the dead," and the stubborn persistence of euphoric hope. As in the Tübingen hymns, the spirit of joy can find its fullest expression only in community; the isolated individual must sustain himself in hope for such communal happiness. The ideal occasion of such joy is the "feast" which the poet can merely anticipate.[4] He awaits some return of the "light of Love," the illuminating divine presence of former blessedness. The third section begins with a recall of this light:

Licht der Liebe! scheinest denn auch Todten, du goldnes!
   Bilder aus hellerer Zeit leuchtet ihr mir in die Nacht?   [2:76]

Light of love! Then you also shine on the dead, you golden light?
Pictures from brighter times, do you gleam for me even in night?

His mind's eye recalls natural forms associated with love, chiefly images of springtime. Yet, as with Wordsworth, flowers in May now remind him of loss, and his awareness of the current lack of any visionary gleam leads to a meditation on transiency and human time:

Wohl gehn Frühlinge fort, ein Jahr verdränget das andre,
   Wechselnd und streitend, so tost droben vorüber die Zeit
Über sterblichem Haupt, doch nicht vor seeligen Augen,
   Und den Liebenden ist anderes Leben geschenkt.
Denn sie alle die Tag' und Jahre der Sterne, sie waren
   Diotima! um uns innig und ewig vereint;   [2:76]

Indeed the springs go by, one year crowds out the other, changing and quarreling, thus time rages past above mortal heads, yet not for

blessed eyes, and to lovers a different life is allotted. For, all of them, the
days and years of the stars, they were, Diotima, fervently and eternally at one with us then;

The Tübingen hymns made an absolute contrast between the chaotic
mutability of temporal existence and the beatific eternity of divine
life. Hyperion, as noted, came to regard temporality as an alternation
of varying degrees of participation in all-unitive Being. Here, however,
the vicissitudes of temporal existence are regarded as a zone of being
inaccessible to the poet, who is dead even to the experience of time.
The poet is even farther beneath the attention of gods and of lovers,
who by their love participate in eternal divine Life. For such lovers as
he and Diotima, reality was a fixed paradigm of eternally recurring
forms; as in a Platonic cosmos, they were beyond mutability and their
only divisions of time were the "days and years of the stars."

But the poet has now fallen from this vision of eternity and can
evoke it only through metaphor. In the fourth section he declares that
he and Diotima had been like two swans, Platonic symbols for the soul.
In the divine life of their love, the world had not been the dark earth
of mortality and suffering, but a beatific reflection of heavenly transcendence. Even when occasionally subjected to external annoyances
and the cold north winds of life, they had their deific love (the "Gott
in uns" of the earlier ode) to keep them warm. And even the hostile
forces of reality could not disrupt their blessed transquility:

> Ruhig lächelten wir, fühlten den eigenen Gott
> Unter trautem Gespräch; in Einem Seelengesange,
>   Ganz in Frieden mit uns kindlich und freudig allein.   [2:76]

... we calmly smiled, sensed our own god amidst intimate conversation,
in one song of our souls, quite at peace with ourselves, like children
joyfully alone.

Their close awareness of the indwelling god of love found expression in
a "song of [their] souls," kept to themselves in childlike, joyous peace.[5]
But such divine contentment has now deserted the poet, leaving him
disconsolate:

> Aber das Haus ist öde mir nun, und die haben mein Auge
>   Mir genommen, auch mich hab' ich verloren mit ihr.

Darum irr' ich umher, und wohl, wie die Schatten, so muss ich
   Leben, und sinnlos dünkt lange das Übrige mir.   [2:76]

But now my house is desolate, and they have taken away my eye, even
my self I have lost with her. Therefore I wander around, and indeed
I must live like the shades, and for a long time everything else has
seemed senseless to me.

The gods of spiritual death have taken away his "eye," Diotima as
mediator of his former vision.[6] And along with his visionary power
he has lost authentic selfhood. His existence is now that of a "shade,"
insubstantial as his world.

The fifth section describes his present desolation. Though he would
like to celebrate, he cannot, for he now lacks everything divine:

Feiern möcht' ich, aber wofür? und singen mit Andern,
   Aber so einsam fehlt jegliches Göttliche mir.   [2:77]

I would like to celebrate, but for what? And sing with others, but in such
loneliness everything divine is lacking to me.

In his present situation, the poet cannot even hope for a more joyous
state. Like Coleridge in "Dejection," a grief without a pang separates
him from the beauties of nature, the inaccessibility of which only intensifies his gloom:

Und die Pflanze des Felds, und der Vögel Singen mich trüb macht,
   Weil mit Freuden auch sie Boten des Himmlischen sind,   [2:77]

... and the plants of the field, and the singing of birds makes me gloomy,
because with joy they also are messengers of the Heavenly,

He sees, yet cannot feel how beautiful they are. He cannot respond to
such messengers of divine joy, nor be receptive to the natural grace of
sunlight. Even the heavens themselves no longer reveal transcendence
but are felt as a "load" above his head.

The sixth section seeks to articulate this predicament in terms of
historical myth. The joys of the poet's own youth resembled those of
mankind, the Greeks who like Empedokles were guilty of blasphemous
overindulgence in the feast of divine graces. But all of man's divine
guests have since departed, and mankind in general has been living in
a desolate underworld such as the poet is now experiencing personally.

All mankind, however, may some day reawaken to communal feasting and divine presence in nature:

> bis dereinst sie
> Eines Wunders Gewalt sie, die Versunkenen, zwingt,
> Wiederzukehren, und neu auf grünendem Boden zu wandeln.—
>   Heiliger Othem durchströmt göttlich die lichte Gestalt,
> Wenn das Fest sich beseelt, und Fluthen der Liebe sich regen,
>   Und vom Himmel getränkt, rauscht der lebendige Strom,
> Wenn es drunten ertönt, und ihre Schäze die Nacht zollt,
>   Und aus Bächen herauf glänzt das begrabene Gold.—   [2:77]

... until once again the force of a miracle will compel them, the lost ones, to return and anew to walk on the greening ground.—Holy breath divinely streams through the luminous form when the feast comes to life, and floods of love are in motion, and, watered by heaven, the living stream roars when it resounds beneath, and the night renders her treasures, and up out of brooks the buried gold gleams.—

The renewed manifestation of divinity in nature is depicted as a return of Spring after the desolation of Winter; the "flood of Love" is again flowing in the world. The speaker has tentatively identified his own present desolation with that of the race, and hopes to share some day in the general rejuvenation.

While "Brot und Wein" will elaborate this historical view, the present elegy now returns to the poet's special case. The seventh section recalls the moment of his parting from Diotima. The poet's ecstatic love for her had given him a new understanding of his vocation: to proclaim the divine presences revealed in his all-unitive vision. Diotima had then "inspiringly taught" him to "see the Great and more happily to sing the gods"; but he was unequal to these sublime instructions. She now appears to him again in memory:

> Götterkind! erscheinest du mir, und grüssest, wie einst, mich,
>   Redest wieder, wie einst, höhere Dinge mir zu?   [2:78]

... You child of gods, do you appear to me and greet me as before, speak again, as before, of higher things to me?

Yet still she cannot effectively inspire him to "higher things," and he is left ashamed of his inability to respond with anything but tears.

But in the eighth section (preparing for the poem's hopeful conclusion) the remembered image of Diotima is hailed as an enduring image of all the attributes of the lost world of light and joyous divine Life. Her godlike radiance keeps her before him as a "heroine" of beatitude, a persevering figure of holy benevolence. Her own spirit is constantly in flower and repose among her "playmates," the roses of the year. Father Aether himself sends her gently-breathing muses with songs to lull her. In her beatitude Diotima appears as a miraculous survivor of the Hellenic world, an "Athenian" ("die Athenerinn"). She remains a source of divine luminosity for fallen mortals;[7] and by her enduring example of bliss she can now finally inspire the poet to his task:

> Und wie, freundlicher Geist! von heitersinnender Stirne
>   Seegnend und sicher dein Stral unter die Sterblichen fällt;
> So bezeugest du mir's, und sagst mir's, dass ich es andern
>   Wiedersage, denn auch Andere glauben es nicht,
> Dass unsterblicher doch, denn Sorg' und Zürnen, die Freude
>   Und ein goldener Tag täglich am Ende noch ist.   [2:78]

> And, friendly spirit, just as from your serenely contemplative brow your
> ray descends, securely blessing, among mortals, so you witness to
> me, and tell me, that I might repeat it to others, for others too do not
> believe it, that indeed joy is more immortal than care and annoy-
> ance, and a golden day is daily still at the end.

As a shaft of light flashes from her brow, she testifies that a golden day of divine presence and inspirational joy will endure beyond man's present destitution. The poet can now convey this message in poetry to fallen mankind.

The concluding ninth section proclaims a poetic recommitment to joyous hope. The speaker can now pray in grateful anticipation:

> So will ich, ihr Himmlischen! denn auch danken, und endlich
>   Athmet aus leichter Brust wieder des Sängers Gebet.   [2:78]

> Thus then, you Heavenly ones, I will also give thanks, and finally the
> singer's prayer breathes again from a free breast.

Such expectant gratitude will become an increasingly important aspect of the poetic function.[8] Presaged (and prefigured) by Diotima, the return of divine presence can now be joyfully sung by the poet. His new consummation in divine joy will be through poetry itself, unlike his previous inarticulate fulfillment in personal love. The poet now wills to live and to return to the temporal realm of seasonal change where the new Spring begins with an awakening of poetic energies. He calls on Diotima to rejoin him within this "time-world" of modulating joy, and in his new poetic quest:

> Komm! es war wie ein Traum! Die blütende Fittige sind ja
>   Schon genesen, verjüngt leben die Hoffnungen all.
> Grosses zu finden, ist viel, ist viel noch übrig, und wer so
>   Liebte, gehet, er muss, gehet zu Göttern die Bahn.   [2:78–79]

> Come, it was like a dream! Indeed the bleeding wings have already
> healed; rejuvenated, all the hopes live! To find the great means much,
> much still remains, and whoever so loved, his path *must* proceed to
> the gods!

His nightmare of desolation is past and the "wings" of song are healed, permitting new poetic flights.[9] His "great" fulfillment in love with Diotima still means "much," but no longer exhausts all spiritual possibilities. Past consummation now serves to guarantee a greater future beatitude: whoever loved with such intensity "must" proceed on a path to the gods. The poet's goal resembles the mythical Isles of the Blessed:

> Bleibt so lange mit uns, bis wir auf gemeinsamen Boden
>   Dort, wo die Seeligen all niederzukehren bereit,
> Dort, wo die Adler sind, die Gestirne, die Boten des Vaters,
>   Dort, wo die Musen, woher Helden und Liebende sind. . . .   [2:79]

> . . . remain so long with us, until we on communal ground, there where
> the blessed ones are all ready to descend, there where the eagles are,
> the constellations, the Father's messengers, there where the muses are,
> whence heroes and lovers are. . . .

This will be a communal ground for the gods who are "ready to descend again" and a place of reconciliation for men and deities where "all" aspects of unitive divine Life will again be present.[10] We will then participate in deific All-Unity—not subjectively, as in the Tübingen hymns, nor in the mode of fire, as in *Empedokles*, but in objective terms. All forms of deity ("die Seeligen all") must now be objectified, since the poet has already exceeded his capacity for subjective intensity in his love for Diotima. The divinity they knew in love will be restored to the lovers, though now in the mode of otherness.

But these lovers dwell now in a state of anticipation, an "island" of merely human happiness in which human time is experienced only in its most idyllic form:

> Dort uns, oder auch hier, auf thauender Insel begegnen,
>   Wo die Unsrigen erst, blühend in Gärten gesellt,
> Wo die Gesänge wahr, und länger die Frühlinge schön sind,
>   Und von neuem ein Jahr unserer Seele beginnt.   [2:79]

> There, or even here, on a dewy island we meet, where for the first time
> our own are blossoming conjointly in gardens, where our songs are
> true, the springs are beautiful longer, and where, anew, a year of our souls
> begins.

This "dewy island," like other islands in Hölderlin, is a place of asylum from the stormy aspects of time.[11] The lovers experience time organically as a "year of our souls" presumably reaching fruition at the moment of the gods' return. But in the meantime "true songs" of anticipation will bloom with flowerlike inevitability.

Like other principal elegies, "Menons Klagen" is structured in terms of a reconciliation with the past and a turning to hope made possible only through confrontation with this past. It overcomes nostalgia through a recommitment to poetry itself. For the all-unitive vision can be restored only through poetry; the remembered moment of happiness, no longer merely an object of futile longing, has been transformed into a model of poetic imitation. The poet's ultimate experience of divine Unity, now past, must somehow be *reachieved* through poetry and not merely recollected by it. The elegies thus point the way for the later hymns. Moreover, the sixth strophe's tentative optimism (which refers briefly to the possibility of restoring the harmony known to the Greeks) will be accorded extensive development in Hölderlin's greatest elegy, "Brot und Wein."

6. "Brot und Wein"

In "Brot und Wein" the entirety of Greek civilization serves the poetic function attributed to the idealized figure of Diotima in the previous elegy. The Hellenic world is now the locus of a total divine presence such as the poet might hope to reattain through poetry. This transference of symbolic function is partially anticipated in "Menons Klagen," where Diotima is "die Athenerinn"; and henceforth Greece itself will fill Diotima's previous role as hierophant of deific All-Unity. The most comprehensively helpful study of the present poem, Jochen Schmidt's *Hölderlin's Elegie "Brod und Wein,"* has provided an exhaustive reading.[1] My own discussion, though not attempting to duplicate such work, seeks to indicate in detail how the poem develops Hölderlin's concern with the problems of divine All-Unity and of divine absence.

We might first consider the overall structure of the poem. Schmidt observes that the nine strophes are divisible into three parts of three strophes each.[2] The first triad treats of "night" in general: the arrival of night, its nature and effects, and nocturnal inspiration. The middle section deals with the "Grecian day" and "Hölderlin's idea of culture": the beginning of culture, its development, and its culmination. The final triad of strophes concerns "Hesperian night," night as figure of the present condition of Western man. Thus, in Schmidt's account, the seventh strophe treats of "Hesperian night as interim," the eighth deals with "bread and wine, luminous traces of gods in the night," and the ninth strophe considers the eschaton: "Orcus, Elysium."

While agreeing in principle with this outline of the poem, we might note another significant aspect of the poem's structure. The poem is centered, with the focal point at the actual center of the elegy, the fifth distich of the fifth strophe.[3] These lines relate the precise moment at which the gods reveal themselves to the Greek world: "dann aber in Warheit / Kommen sie selbst" ("but then they themselves come in truth"). This is the crucial instant in the development of Greek "culture"; and the balanced equal sections of the central triad of strophes, before and after this distich, tell of events among the Greeks before and after this moment. As Schmidt notes, there is overall symmetry in the poem's general structure, with the first triad balanced by the third. But the individual strophes themselves also appear to have symmetrical arrangement. Thus the seventh, arguing that it is "too late" for a certain kind of poetic enthusiasm, appears to answer the third, an exhortation to precisely such inspired vehemence. The second, asking what night means for us, is answered by the eighth, which sketches the poet's nocturnal duties of celebrating bread and wine. And night itself, which the first strophe pictures in empirical (if mysterious) detail, is given a definitive mythical interpretation in the ninth strophe. The entire poem thus appears symmetrically focused on the central distich which tells of the gods' arrival "in truth" to the Greeks. Centered about this moment of truth, the three major sections may be considered parts of a dialectical process of discovery: an inquiry about the present, a turning to the past as a possible model for the future, and a subsequent authentic understanding of the present moment in terms of this past and (projected) future. Finally, the poem is a process by which the poet comes to discover his own function in terms of an achieved understanding of history. The history of the world is essentially a history of the religious consciousness which, basically for Hölderlin, is history of what it means to be a poet.

The poem's first section thus presents the situation of night, inquires into its meaning for us, and tentatively exhorts us to a course of action. The first three distichs of the evocative first strophe depict the ending of day as a time of cheerful busyness and mundane concern with the practical details of living:

Satt gehn heim von Freuden des Tags zu ruhen die Menschen,
    Und Gewinn und Verlust wäget ein sinniges Haupt
Wohlzufrieden zu Haus;   [2:90]

Men go home to rest full of the pleasures of the day, and a judicious
head weighs profit and loss well-satisfied at home;

However, the quietude of evening may also be an occasion for desire or nostalgic longing, as when a "lover" or "lonely man," making music, attempts to express and assuage a certain pang of absence. For such men the pleasant inactivity of nightfall is not especially restful, but fosters consciousness of deprivation. They find the incessant flowing of nocturnal fountains analogous to the persistence of time, while bells and the cries of watchmen enforce their awareness of time's divisions and its transiency. These sounds thus induce authentic consciousnes of temporality. The coming of night itself is announced by a breeze, natural figure of poetic inspiration,[4] and by the mysterious arrival of the moon, "shadow-image of our earth." The sudden presence of night is confronted as a troubling mystery. It (or "she") is a "stranger among men" who is "little concerned with us"; she appears inscrutable and alien. The radical otherness of Night may move us to mute wonderment or to rhapsodic fantasy. Yet, because she first appears as an obscure and unknowable power, the poet does not know how to respond to her here.[5]

The second strophe meditates upon these problems. Though seemingly unconcerned, Night affects our world:

Wunderbar ist die Gunst der Hocherhabnen und niemand
Weiss von wannen und was einem geschiehet von ihr.

So bewegt sie die Welt und die hoffende Seele der Menschen,
   Selbst kein Weiser versteht, was sie bereitet, denn so
Will es der oberste Gott, der sehr dich liebet, und darum
   Ist noch lieber, wie sie, dir der besonnene Tag.   [2:90]

   Wonderful is the favor of the most sublime one, and no one knows
from whence or what happens to someone from her. She so moves
the world and the hoping souls of men that not even a wise man understands what she makes ready, for this is the will of the highest god,
who loves you greatly, and therefore the rational day is dearer to you than
she.

Greatly exalted, her favor is as wonderful (and mysterious) as a supernal providence whose effects are not known; she is a self-conscious
power obscurely at work in our lives and in history. Our ignorance of
her designs is benevolently ordained by the "Highest God" himself,
who provides for our customary distraction by practical concerns. The
poet would here discourage us from questioning her transcendent will.
Yet, authenticity requires a certain concern with Night:

Aber zuweilen liebt auch klares Auge den Schatten
   Und versuchet zu Lust, eh' es die Noth ist, den Schlaf,
Oder es blikt auch gern ein treuer Mann in die Nacht hin,
   Ja, es ziemet sich ihr Kränze zu weihn und Gesang,
Weil den Irrenden sie geheiliget ist und den Todten,
   Selber aber besteht, ewig, in freiestem Geist.   [2:90–91]

But at times even a clear eye loves the shade, and tries sleep for pleasure
before there is need, or even a true man likes to look into the night;
yes, it is fitting to dedicate wreaths to her, and song, because she is sacred
to those gone astray and the dead, but she herself subsists eternally
in freest mind.

These lines discern two possible responses: night may be a time of
sleep, when ever a "clear eye" may seek respite from lucidity before
actual "need" of weariness compels it to rest, or it may be an occasion
for devout celebration. As the realm of those "straying" and the
"dead," Night is the domain of alienation and death, associated with
the amorphous outer mystery and everything beyond the structures
of daily existence.[6] And yet, Night subsists eternally knowable only to
herself, existing in absolute mind ("in freiestem Geist").

But Night herself must also grant us means to endure what she represents. She must offer us her gifts of "forgetfulness," "holy drunkenness," and "holy remembrance," enabling us to remain watchful by night. The "holy remembrance" is consistent with "forgetfulness" of trivia and with holy intoxication which serves actually to heighten consciousness.[7] Remembrance is here an intense awareness of what must be recalled: the lost "day" of divine presence. Night herself gives inspiration essentially through this remembrance; the enthusiasm manifest in poetic rapture is best realized in a lucidity which, holding the past in memory, remains wakeful in present night towards a desired future.

The third strophe, then, elaborates on a possible response to night: the free acceptance of her apparent gifts, the benefits of a lucid (and "holy") intoxication. Such enthusiasm is again depicted as "divine fire," here striving to break out in the intensity of inspired joy: "Göttliches Feuer auch treibet, bei Tag und bei Nacht / Aufzubrechen" ("Divine fire also urges, by day or by night, to break out") (2:91). Knowing the divinity of the joy within us, we are exhorted to give full vent to our enthusiasm:

> So komm! dass wir das Offene schauen,
>   Dass ein Eigenes wir suchen, so weit es auch ist.
> Fest bleibt Eins; es sei um Mittag oder es gehe
>   Bis in die Mitternacht, immer bestehet ein Maas,
> Allen gemein, doch jeglichem auch ist eignes beschieden,
>   Dahin gehet und kommt jeder, wohin er es kann.   [2:91]

So come, that we may behold the Open, that we may seek what is our
own, however far it may be. One thing remains certain: whether it
be at midday or whether it goes into midnight, a measure always exists,
common to all, and yet everyone is also allotted his own, and each
man goes and comes there, wherever he can.

We must seek what is our "own" ("Eigenes"), the limit or measure ("Maas") of how much enthusiasm or intensity of divine joy we can bear.[8] Man's limit of intensity can be discovered and tested only through repeated experiences. At this point Hölderlin appears to agree with Blake's infernal dictum: "You never know what is enough unless you know what is more than enough."[9] Our holy drunkenness may be intensified to "jubilant madness," and defy all repressive forces by a daemonic will to self-utterance:

Drum! und spotten des Spotts mag gern frohlokkender Wahnsinn,
Wenn er in heiliger Nacht plözlich die Sänger ergreift.   [2:91]

Therefore! And jubilant madness may gladly mock mockery when in holy night it suddenly seizes upon the singers.

This poetic frenzy is an ecstatic participation in Deity which intensifies as the god approaches, somewhat as in the Tübingen hymns. But the "coming god" here seems to approach us from the past, from ancient Greece where all men supposedly experienced their limit of deific feeling in divine presence. The concluding lines of the strophe thus exhort a return to the site of this limit-situation: "Dorther kommt und zurük deutet der kommende Gott" ("Thence comes and there points back the approaching god") (2:91). The god points backwards to the Greek holy land, indicating the fountainhead of our nocturnal enthusiasm in a past when divine forces were visibly manifest in the world.

In the fourth strophe the poet, so exhorted, returns in spirit to Greece and hails the land as a place of universal epiphany. The Greek landscape itself is regarded as a setting for gigantic festivities of the gods;[10] the floor of this "hall" is the sea and its tables are mountains "especially" designed for this purpose. However, the poet realizes that his imagined pilgrimage to Greece is not equivalent to an actual return to the moment of divine celebration. That moment is irrevocably past; all concomitants of the sacred feasts now appear missing. The poet wonders what has become of the Greek destiny, the fulfillment of an oracular "word" with the character and efficacy of lightning. This portentous "word" (or phrase) was the most appropriate name of divine transcendence:

Vater Aether! so riefs und flog von Zunge zu Zunge
Tausendfach, es ertrug keiner das Leben allein;
Ausgetheilet erfreut solch Gut und getauschet, mit Fremden,
Wirds ein Jubel, es wächst schlafend des Wortes Gewalt
Vater! heiter! and hallt, so weit es gehet, das uralt
Zeichen, von Eltern geerbt, treffend und schaffend hinab.   [2:92]

Father Aether! So it called and flew from tongue to tongue, thousandfold, no one endured Life alone; when distributed, such a blessing
gives pleasure, and exchanged with strangers it becomes a jubilation, the
power of the word grows in sleep: Father! Serene! and there
resounds, as far as it goes, the ancient sign inherited from parents, striking and creating downward.

The act of naming divine transcendence as Father Aether is itself, for
Hölderlin, the constitutive act of Greek religious awareness and of the
entire Greek experience.[11] This lucid naming effectively convokes the
community of divine joy that unified the Hellenic world. The name,
inherited from ancestors, increased in significance as it became more
widely recognized among the Greeks; its effectiveness spread like
lightning's fire, as no one sought to keep the good news to himself or
bear the "Life" of such divine joy alone.[12] "Distributed" among neigh-
bors the word gave joy, and when "exchanged" with strangers it became a "jubilation."

The fundamental pattern here is the development of a sense of All-
Unity; the word itself is principle, germ and agent of this development.
The word's significance as a name of God is constituted in and by our
recognition. But each individual's capacity for recognition (and joyous
response) is necessarily finite. The significance or "power" of the word
thus increases phenomenally for each individual when increasingly
recognized by more men, and the unity of religious awareness is intensified in its unitive force as it grows more inclusive. But authentic
participation in all-unitive power always entails participation in divine
Life. The consequent interaction of immanence and transcendence,
realizing Deity both within and beyond our own mode of being, constitutes the radiance of manifest divine presence, the light of man's
"day":

Denn so kehren die Himmlischen ein, tiefschütternd gelangt so
    Aus den Schatten herab unter die Menschen ihr Tag.   [2:92]

For thus do the Heavenly enter, thus, deeply shuddering, does their day,
down from the shadows, arrive among men.

The central fifth strophe of the poem relates how this unaccustomed brilliance of divine presence is eventually perceived by men as the clearly differentiated forms of Hellenic gods. The "Heavenly Ones" are at first "unperceived": their presence is sensed only as joy and unbearable radiance, a source of happiness too "bright" and "blinding" to confront.[13] Although the children "strive toward" these gods, the adult prudently shies from them and even a "demigod" could hardly know them by name. But the gods' magnanimity soon overcomes human reluctance to accept their gifts; man's heart is then filled with joys the gods have urged upon him. And yet, still uncertain of their source, he remains confused about the gifts' meaning and function. Like a poor person coming unexpectedly into an inheritance, he is inclined to squander his benefice. He tends to lavish it about, sometimes blessing undeserving things, so that "what is unholy almost becomes holy to him."

The gods "tolerate" such indiscretion as long as possible, and then, as if exasperated, they finally show themselves in the full clarity of their being:

Möglichst dulden die Himmlischen diss; dann aber in Wahrheit
Kommen sie selbst . . .   [2:92]

The Heavenly tolerate this as long as possible, but then they
themselves come in truth,

As previously noted, these lines, constituting the focal point of the poem, are also at its exact center. Because the deities are now present "in truth" in the visible forms depicted by poets and sculptors, men have clear objects for their gratitude and are grown accustomed to gazing upon them; that is, upon All-Unity:[14]

und gewohnt werden die Menschen des Glüks
Und des Tags und zu schaun die Offenbaren, das Antliz
Derer, welche, schon längst Eins und Alles gennant,
Tief die verschwiegene Brust mit freier Genüge gefüllet,
Und zuerst und allein alles Verlangen beglükt;   [2:92]

and men grow accustomed to the happiness and the day and to look upon
the manifest ones, the faces of those who, for a long time named
One and All, deeply filled the silenced breast with free satisfaction and
were the first and only ones to satisfy all desire.

The divine All-Unity is experienced as harmony and beatitude, total achievement of Being; and participation in all-unitive Life is the only way man can ever fulfill his own being, satisfying all desires. This all-unitive harmony, long anticipated by the Greeks, is now visibly manifested in the distinct forms of their gods.

The final distichs of the strophe moralize on the above events and state the Greeks' necessary response to them:

> So ist der Mensch; wenn da ist das Gut, und es sorget mit Gaaben
>   Selber ein Gott für ihn, kennet und sieht er es nicht.
> Tragen muss er, zuvor; nun aber nennt er sein Liebstes,
>   Nun, nun, müssen dafür Worte, wie Blumen, entstehn.   [2:92–93]

> Such is man: when the blessing is there, and a god himself provides him
> with gifts, he knows and sees it not. First he must endure; now,
> however, he names his dearest possession; now, now the words for it must
> come into being like flowers.

The Greek experience is generalized as appropriate to all men. When a god proffers gifts of divine joy, man does not immediately recognize the benefiee; he is unable, in the subjectivity of euphoria, to objectify the gifts or their source. At first he must "bear," even suffer from, the intensity of confused happiness.[15] "Now," however, at the moment of epiphany, when gods come in truth, he succeeds in naming the divine presence. And for this act of naming, "words must now originate like flowers."[16] We are perhaps reminded of Keats's dictum "that if Poetry comes not as naturally as the Leaves to a tree it had better not come at all."[17] Hölderlin, like Keats, is here insisting on spontaneity or naturalness in the origin of poetic language: poetry must be unforced and seem as beautifully inevitable as organic growth. But the poet is specifying how poetry had to originate for the Greeks at this historical moment; he is not actually proclaiming his own view of poetry. Further, it might be noted that the present strophe implies a fairly complicated attitude toward poetry. The gods' epiphany is simultaneous with their formal recognition; they arrive "in truth" at the precise moment when they are fittingly named by words of flower-like origin. In the summary distichs the crucial event of the gods' apparition is not explicitly mentioned as such. What is conveyed is the intensity of joy that must be borne and the extreme urgency of the thrice-repeated

"now": "nun aber nennt er sein Liebstes, / Nun, nun. . . ."[18] The
moment is urgent because it is the very instant of the gods' arrival,
and "words" are needed to effect this epiphany in the act of naming.
There is of course no simple causality involved, as if the Greeks could
somehow conjure the gods, forcing them to appear. In the phenome-
nology of religious perception, the gods appear only when (and as)
recognized; and for Hölderlin sufficient poetic naming is essential to
any recognition.

The sixth strophe tells what follows upon the gods' arrival. Man now
"thinks to honor the blessed gods in earnest," and not merely in a
restricted "religious" sphere of activity. Rather, "everything must actually and truly proclaim their praise." "All" of Greek life and civilization is unified by this one purpose, and therefore everything must be
perfect. "Nothing may see the light, that does not please the high"
gods, and nothing idly attempted deserves to stand before "Vater
Aether." This need for perfection accounts for the varied splendors of
Greek civilization. The "peoples" of the Hellenic world arise in the
"splendid orders" of their diversity before the gods and build beautiful
temples and cities as articulations of divine praise. Like the words for
the original naming of gods, this concrete language of worship itself
comes into being "like flowers." The peoples "arise" ("sich auf-
richten") in order to "stand" ("stehen") in the presence of the heavenly ones. Their temples and cities also "rise" ("emporgehen") above
the waters. The particular structures of Greek life themselves constitute a poem of holy praise.

The remaining distichs of the sixth strophe are a series of questions
about the fate of these structures. Their flowerlike character is here
more explicit:

> Aber wo sind sie? wo blühn die Bekannten, die Kronen des Festes?
> Thebe welkt und Athen;   [2:93]
>
> . . . but where are they? Where do the known ones blossom, the crowns
> of the feast? Thebes withers, and Athens;

The "known . . . crowns of the feast" are the cities of Thebes and
Athens, envisioned here as "crowns" or blooms of flowers; but now
both cities are "wilting."[19] While the questions in the fourth strophe

inquired generally about religious functions in Greece, the questions here specifically ask what has happened to the religious festivals. The concluding distichs wonder why a god will now no longer mark a man's forehead with the sign of divine genius. This god, who personally arrived at the conclusion of the "heavenly feast," assumed human form and "comfortingly" brought the celebration to completion. The identity of this personage will be clarified later in the poem.

In the previous three strophes Hölderlin has viewed Greek history from a perspective that regards poetic naming as the highest expression of religious consciousness. Thus, the subjective (though shared) experience of divine joy is realized through the power of a poetic name, "Father Aether." The appearance of the gods in objective, distinctly visible form occurs when they are named through words that originate like flowers, and the ensuing celebration of praise is articulated through all structures of civilization which partake in the character of flower-like poetic language. These strophes have also given a history of various modes of all-unitive divine presence. The community of divine joy fostered by the name of Father Aether is all-unitive in force and character. The Greek gods who appear in a pantheon of visible forms are those who "had long been called One and All." And the festivities of Greek civilization are simply a concrete objectification of the earlier subjective community of all-unitive joy.

As noted, the seventh strophe is an effective answer to the problems raised in the third. The third strophe exhorts a return to Greece to find a formal object for inspired emulation and to meet the approaching deity. The intervening strophes, however, have traced the history of sacred inspiration in the Greek world. This history is now seen as finished; all its forms are irrevocably past. Adequate "imitation" of the ancients is thus viewed as ultimately impossible; like Hegel, Hölderlin here regards the achievements of Greek art as stages in a dialectic of religious awareness completed long ago.[20] The immediate function of this strophe, then, is to correct the unconsidered excitement of the third. The third strophe had urged poets to "come" to Greece ("Drum an den Isthmos komm! dorthin . . ." ["Therefore come to the Isthmus! There . . ."]); but in his own imaginary visitation the speaker found only absence. The seventh strophe thus begins with a lament that the poet and his "friend" (Wilhelm Heinse, to whom the poem is dedicated)[21] had arrived too late:

Aber Freund! wir kommen zu spät. Zwar leben die Götter,
   Aber über dem Haupt droben in anderer Welt.   [2:93]

But friend, we come too late. Indeed the gods live, but over our heads there in the other world.

They are too late because the "Heavenly Ones" have departed and now dwell solely in heaven. In this transcendent realm the gods function only as Ideas for us; they no longer affect our lives or even seem to notice whether we live. Yet their seeming disregard is really a willingness to "spare" us. The "weak vessel" of the human soul is not always capable of "holding" the gods; we can endure divine fullness only at specific "times," not simply at the bidding of enthusiastic will, as assumed in the third strophe. In the earlier passage, the possibility of fulfillment "subsists always . . . at midday or all the way to midnight," and "everyone" can "go and come" to this limit "whenever he can"; "jubilant madness" ("frohlokkender Wahnsinn") need only have the bravery of conviction to deride cautionary misgivings. In the later passage, however, such possible "fullness" is determined by history. The Greeks experienced their own fulfillment of divine intensity, but we at this moment cannot. Yet our inability to do so is ordained by gods who wish to "spare" us.

Whenever divine fullness might safely recur, of course, man would again know complete happiness: his own life would become a dream of gods, an occasion for free realization of deities in this world. However, man must first prepare himself for such intensity:

Traum von ihnen ist drauf das Leben. Aber das Irrsaal
   Hilft, wie Schlummer, und stark machet die Noth und die Nacht,
Bis dass Helden genug in der ehernen Wiege gewachsen,
   Herzen an Kraft, wie sonst, ähnlich den Himmlischen sind.
Donnernd kommen sie drauf.   [2:93–94]

Thereupon life is a dream about them. But wandering helps, like slumber, and deprivation and night make us strong until heroes enough have grown in the brazen cradle, hearts which, as before, are equal to the Heavenly in strength. Thundering then they will come.

Night is traditionally a time of "slumber," and, as in the second strophe, is sacred to those wandering astray. Here these activities are mentioned again as ways of enduring privation; for night is now clearly understood as a time of dearth and divine absence. A toughening process, steeling men to live without gods, will continue until (paradoxically) men's hearts become so strong that divine presence can in fact be endured. The cradle of spiritual deprivation may ultimately nurture enough "heroes" whose hearts are capable of again bearing the rigors of divine epiphany. When the gods see that men can withstand them again they will return to the world "thundering" in power and glory—much as they had first come down among the Greeks.

In the meantime, however, all gods and all authentic earthly communities are absent and the speaker is without true "companions," human or divine. There are no immanent deities to praise, and no godly community to provide the intersubjective basis for private enthusiasm. It is perhaps better to sleep, to relent from poetic efforts completely, than to attempt to be a poet in time of deprivation ("in dürftiger Zeit"). The night of divine absence is thus experienced by poets as a time when the manifest (and proper) source or object of poetry is lacking.[22] Therefore the question arises, why be a poet? Since poetry can be justified principally as celebration of divinity (as with the Greeks) a negative answer is suggested. The concluding distich of the strophe, however, implies that Heinse ("du") has shown a way out of the dilemma:[23]

> Aber sie sind, sagst du, wie des Weingotts heilige Priester,
> Welche von Lande zu Land zogen in heiliger Nacht.   [2:94]

> But they are, you say, like the holy priests of the winegod, who went from land to land in holy night.

That is, in this historical night the poets are to be like the "holy priests" of the winegod Dionysus, who in ancient times proceeded "from land to land in holy night." Their priestly activities provide a model for poets in times of divine absence. Hölderlin is here reviving an old tradition which regards poets as dionysian votaries.[24] His special interpretation of their priesthood is clarified in the following strophe, which also answers the second strophe's questionings of the meaning of night.

The eighth strophe begins with a reinterpretation of the end of the Greek world. The time since the Greeks "seems long" to poets, since this has been an era of poetic incapacity. At the demise of the Greek world the gods "all" ascended, the "Father" turned his countenance from men, and "mourning" rightfully began on earth. Finally, a "quiet genius" appeared who offered heavenly comfort, announced the end of the gods' day, and departed. This comforting "genius" is a living spirit of consolation. While he might suggest both Christ and Dionysus, he is perhaps not specifically identical with either, but is rather their simple concurrence in mythic-historical function.[25] He presumably is the god in human form who concluded the "heavenly feast" at the end of the sixth strophe.

This Comforter is representative of the gods' will to console man in their absence:

Liess zum Zeichen, dass einst er da gewesen und wieder
    Käme, der himmlische Chor einige Gaaben zurük,
Derer menschlich, wie sonst, wir uns zu freuen vermöchten,
    Denn zur Freude, mit Geist, wurde das Grössere zu gross
Unter den Menschen und noch, noch fehlen die Starken zu höchsten
    Freuden, aber es lebt stille noch einiger Dank.   [2:94]

. . . the heavenly chorus left behind them, as a sign that they had once
been here and would return, some gifts in which humanly, as before, we
might take pleasure—because for spiritual joy anything greater
became too great among men, and even now there are none yet strong
enough for the highest joys, but a little gratitude quietly lives on.

The "heavenly chorus," gods considered in unitive harmony, left behind some gifts as "signs" that they were once on earth and would return. The gifts function both as a reminder and as a promise. But they are also a source of present, merely "human" joy such as men knew even before the gods' epiphany. As explained above, divine joys are now impossible for us since the divinely transcendent became "too great among men" for "spiritual joy"—that bliss which involves all man's being and all he knows in comprehensive divine lucidity. Yet, although those strong enough to endure the highest joys are still absent, some residual gratitude survives. Such quiet gratitude is our most authentic way of relating to absent gods; when immediate participation is lacking, gratitude is always possible. By reminding us of the necessary reality of donors, such gratitude helps foster hope in their return. Also, communal thanksgiving for shared gifts itself constitutes a vestigial structure of true community, at best reminiscent of the communion of divine praise that founded Greek civilization. With rediscovered hope, the poet also views this quiet community of thanks as foreshadowing the ultimate communion, to be reestablished when the gods return.

The divine gifts are specifically bread and wine, the focus of the traditional "communion" service:

> Brod ist der Erde Frucht, doch ists vom Lichte geseegnet,
>   Und vom donnernden Gott kommet die Freude des Weins.
> Darum denken wir auch dabei der Himmlischen, die sonst
>   Da gewesen und die kehren in richtiger Zeit,
> Darum singen sie auch mit Ernst die Sänger den Weingott
>   Und nicht eitel erdacht tönet dem Alten das Lob.   [2:94]

> Bread is the fruit of earth, but it is blessed by the light, and from the
> thundering god comes the joy of wine. Hence we also therewith think of
> the Heavenly who had once been here and who will return at the
> right time, hence they also, the singers, sing in earnest the winegod, and
> praise not idly thought out resounds to the ancient one.

The gifts are, as noted, emblems of remembrance and hope that the gods will return at the "right" time. Bread is the product of Earth and Light, the dark and luminous aspects of our mortal existence, themselves revered as elemental deities. The "joy of wine" comes from the "thundering god," Zeus himself. Hölderlin here utilizes the myth in which Dionysus is the son of Zeus and Semele;[26] the joy of wine is thus ultimately identical with Dionysus, who is always present in the grateful communal spirit of vinous euphoria. Dionysus is also the spirit of hopeful remembrance of other gods, and he abides with us (in and through his gifts) as a divine Comforter. In this function he is identical with the "stiller Genius" mentioned above and is yet undifferentiated from Christ himself, who is traditionally considered present through remembrance at the communion ceremony.[27]

And "therefore," Hölderlin concludes, the poets have discovered their authentic task in the era of night. They are to hymn the Comforter and themselves give comfort. In "holy night" they are effectively to serve as priests of Dionysus (an abiding presence) and foster awareness of the abiding absence of the other gods. This is the poem's major statement.

The final strophe of the elegy returns to something like the first strophe's mood of wonderment; the wonder is now, however, at the solutions to the original problem. "Brot und Wein" is a poem not of exposition but of discovery. The speaker has returned to his initial mood, but in the course of his meditation he has gained a new understanding of history and of his historical situation as a poet. This understanding is not, however, closed or dogmatic; the tone of the conclusion is still one of openness and expectation. The initial lines of the strophe celebrate Dionysus, the new patron and focus of song. As mediator between night and day, Dionysus also mediates historical eras of light and darkness, divine presence and absence; for even in night he is the spirit of abiding joy, "joyous at all times." He remains and himself brings the trace of departed gods down amidst the darkness to godless ones. Not merely nocturnal, the "darkness" is the obsecurity of an underworld bereft of divine presence. The Hades where the poet found himself alone in "Menons Klagen um Diotima" is now the allotment of the entire human race in our post-Hellenic era.

And yet the hope discovered in the eighth strophe presages a speedy return of blessedness. The ancient poets and prophets had foretold the return of the Golden Age when all men should become "children of God." We may note that Hölderlin here syncretizes Hellenic predictions of a renewed Saturnian Age with Biblical prophecies of the return of Christ.[28] In the chiliastic view of this poem, these prophecies are to be fulfilled perhaps even in our generation.[29] The process of fulfillment is here as inevitable as the ripening of fruit (the golden apple of the Hesperides), an organic consummation of time. The poet has foreseen this fruition and now proclaims his belief to others. Yet he is forcibly reminded of our present situation. "So much is happening" in our world and still "nothing takes effect." Our very actions and the events of our era are fundamentally unreal without the direction or significance of divine participation. We remain powerless to evoke still distant gods whose will cannot be conjured; our being is still that of insubstantial "shades" in this underworld and we remain "heartless,"

incapable of feeling participation in divine Life. We are condemned
to this shadowy existence "until our Father Aether, recognized, belongs
to each and all of us." The recognition of Father Aether as the transcendent principle of immanent All-Unity was, we recall, a precondition for visible manifestation of the Greek gods. And this same recognition, achieved by "each and all" ("jeden und allen"), must constitute the basis of the new universal participation in divine Life.

The situation is implicitly problematical, though any problems are
concealed in the hopeful tone of the concluding strophe. Although the
general return of the gods will occur with seeming inevitability, it is
stipulated that the paternal Deity, Father Aether, must first be recognized and "belong" to one and all. Such recognition demands an act
of our wills; and yet, we recall, our wills are debilitated and powerless
("nothing takes effect") until such recognition is already achieved.
These lines thus pose an agonizing dilemma, the problem of poetic
freedom versus historical necessity. This problem will dominate the
later hymns, where the poet's hopes for divine epiphany are paradoxically heightened even as his struggle with the dilemma itself becomes more intense.

In the conclusion of this elegy, however, even the hope is somewhat
muted. The final strophe ends with a vision not of the future but of
the present, and with the poet functioning not as prophet *in extremis*
but as priest of the Comforter. In the strophe's allusion to the harrow-
ing of hell, the "Syrian," the "Son of the Highest" who comes as
torchbearer, is of course Christ.[30] He still performs essentially the same
function as Dionysus, bringing consolation to the nocturnal underworld. In this respect, then, the mythic identities of Christ and Dionysus still remain undifferentiated, subsumed in the role of the eighth
strophe's unspecified "stiller Genius."[31] The coming of Christ here is
not yet to redeem mankind but simply to offer comfort; the torch he
carries is a light of hope to make the night more bearable. The "blessed
wise ones" able to understand the decrees of providence see this; a
smile radiates from their still captive souls and their benighted eyes
"thaw out" somewhat to the light. At least a minimal capacity for joy
and vision is thus fostered by this comforting spirit. Moreover, just as
the poet's vocation is now to be "priest" or ministering agent of this
spirit, so the spirit himself has a somewhat poetic character: his effect

is comparable to that of Orpheus on his visit to the underworld. Cerberus, representing forces of violence and aggressive evil, is lulled and rendered harmless by the same wine which gives renewed hope and comfort to mortals.[32]

While the elegy thus ends with a restatement of the more humble functions of poetry, it has also achieved a vision of history, and of the present, which Hölderlin will now generally maintain. It situates the ultimate, definitive experience of All-Unity in the definite past moment of the ancient Greek world. Henceforth, much of Hölderlin's poetry will consider our mode of relating to this moment. As the concluding strophe declares, Father Aether as transcendent principle must again be recognized by each and all, constituting a universality of awareness akin to that achieved by the Greeks. And yet this elegy implicitly raises a number of problems. The gods will not return with their day until "night and privation" have made us "strong" enough to endure new fullness of ecstasy. But how might we abet this toughening process in our own souls? The poetry proclaimed here can only help us to endure suffering by mitigating our hardships. We are further told that any human activities must remain ineffectual until Father Aether is again universally recognized. Yet we hear nothing about how this recognition might once more be achieved, or about the poet's specific role in any proclamation of an epiphanic divine name.

These are precisely the problems which must be confronted in the major hymns, where they constitute principal themes. First, however, Hölderlin will write a final elegy, "Heimkunft," seeking to resolve poetic problems on a personal rather than historical basis.

7. "Heimkunft"

The elegy "Heimkunft" attempts, and apparently fails, to establish an authentic community (based on religious gratitude) apart from historical process. This apparent failure indicates that ahistorical religiosity itself is ultimately impossible—all the hymns that follow must deal necessarily with history. In "Heimkunft" Hölderlin also reaches an impasse in elegiac form, which (as noted) evocatively recalls some blissful experience of the past and reconciles us to that experience through a present moment of achieved serenity.[1] Such consolation is earnestly sought here but the poem ends in irresolution and a sense of uncertainty about the future; the present itself is no longer harmoniously self-contained. (The hymns will look *through* the present to some future reattainment of all-unitive vision.) I will not here seek to interpret "Heimkunft" in detail, as was necessary with "Brot und Wein," a crucial work introducing the basic structure of Hölderlin's historical vision.[2] In discussing this poem I will instead concentrate on those sections which have most direct bearing on Hölderlin's major religious and poetic concerns.

The opening strophe, aside from its thematic importance, is also distinguished by complexity and gnarled, paradoxical compression. It begins:

Drinn in den Alpen ists noch helle Nacht und die Wolke,
   Freudiges dichtend, sie dekt drinnen das gähnende Thal.
Dahin, dorthin toset und stürzt die scherzende Bergluft,
   Schroff durch Tannen herab glänzet und schwindet ein Stral.

                                           [2:96]

   Inside in the Alps it is still bright night and the cloud, composing the joyous, covers the gaping valley within. Hither and yon roars and plunges the sportive mountain breeze, abruptly down through fir trees a beam of light glitters and is lost.

This describes an Alpine landscape at sunrise. The mountain valley is still in "bright night," an oxymoric expression possibly designating light before dawn;[3] the valley, "gaping" like an abyss between mountains, is covered by a cloud which is put into turbulent motion by a "sportive mountain breeze." The resultant breaks in the cloud permit an occasional beam of light ("Stral") to intrude, shining abruptly and momentarily through the pines on the slopes. As is evident from the character of the diction, this description is not merely objective. Nor is the landscape allegorized as in an eighteenth-century "loco-descriptive" poem like Pope's *Windsor Forest*. Rather, as in Shelley's "Mont Blanc," a poet is here transforming the described landscape into poetic myth through interpretive language.[4] Antithetical constructions, compound verbs, and especially oxymora signify the tension in language between description and interpretation. Thus, the cloud is said to be "composing the joyous" ("Freudiges dichtend")—a phrase that would have no meaning in naturalistic description. Here it serves to indicate that the poet, like Shelley, is interested in problems of poetic composition and that the scene is interpreted in terms of poetic process.[5] To speak of the cloud as "composing" the "joyous" is to suggest the function attributed to poetry in "Brot und Wein." The following lines depict the cloud's appearance and movements in dionysian terms:

> Langsam eilt und kämpft das freudigschauernde Chaos,
>   Jung an Gestalt, doch stark, feiert es liebenden Streit
> Unter den Felsen, es gährt und wankt in den ewigen Schranken,
>   Denn bacchantischer zieht drinnen der Morgen herauf.   [2:96]

Slowly hastens and struggles the joyously shuddering chaos, young in form yet strong it celebrates loving strife among the rocks, it seethes and wavers in the eternal confines, for more bacchantically does the morning arise within.

The oxymoron ("slowly hastens and struggles") indicates once again the paradox of an interpretive description which seeks to express the subjective workings of the poetic process in naturalistic terms. Insofar as these words depict any objective thing, it is a trembling mass of cloud which, though amorphous, appears to be struggling for form and whose parts, while moving rapidly in relation to each other, move slowly as a whole in relation to other things.[6] The mass of cloud is "young in form," just emerged out of formless darkness into the light that permits form itself to be visible. And, though young, the cloud is "strong" in its movements and celebrates "loving struggle" among the rocks where it "seethes and wavers in eternal confines." Virtually all aspects of this description may refer to the process of composition. For Hölderlin, as for Coleridge, one begins with a "chaos," the amorphous preconception of what is to be said. This chaos is "joyously shudder- ing" in the vibrant eagerness that precedes and accompanies poetic creation. The poetic idea "struggles" for articulation in deliberate haste, restrained avidity, much as Coleridge observes in the *Biographia*.[7] The nascent poem is "young in form," just coming into shape and yet strong in the energy of its inspiration. It festively celebrates its "loving strife" toward appropriate form "among the cliffs" where it seethes and wavers in "eternal confines."

The following line refers more explicitly to the visual scene, though retaining a figurative dimension: "For more bacchantically does the morning arise within." This statement clearly suggests the dionysian commitments of "Brot und Wein": since the poet is a priest of Diony- sus, the activity of composition will have a somewhat "bacchantic" character. Moreover the entire scene itself might be referred to the last strophe of the previous elegy, where the present historical era of divine absence is depicted as a nocturnal underworld anticipating a new dawn. Here, the scene is of an abyss-like mountain valley immediately before sunrise, darkened into a kind of temporary underworld by a dense, covering cloud. The situation of the valley is thus closely analogous to that of our present world.

This opening passage may thus be read on three related "levels" of meaning: as an objective depiction of a scene, in terms of consistent visual imagery; as a reflection on poetic process, in terms of its conceptual diction; and as an emblem of an historical situation, in reference to symbolic values already established. The remaining lines of this strophe may likewise be read in cognizance of its pictorial, poetic, and historical references:

Denn es wächst unendlicher dort das Jahr und die heilgen
    Stunden, die Tage, sie sind kühner geordnet, gemischt.
Dennoch merket die Zeit der Gewittervogel und zwischen
    Bergen, hoch in der Luft weilt er und rufet den Tag.
Jezt auch wachet und schaut in der Tiefe drinnen das Dörflein
    Furchtlos, Hohem vertraut, unter den Gipfeln hinauf.
Wachstum ahnend, denn schon, wie Blize, fallen die alten
    Wasserquellen, der Grund unter den Stürzenden dämpft,
Echo tönet umher, und die unermessliche Werkstatt
    Reget bei Tag und Nacht, Gaaben versendend, den Arm.   [2:96]

For the year grows more infinitely there and the holy hours, the days, are
more boldly ordered and mixed. Nevertheless the storm bird notices
the time and between mountains, high in the air, hovers and calls out the
day. Now also the little village awakens and within in the depths,
fearless, intimate with the high, looks up from beneath the peaks. Anticipating growth, for already, like lightning-bolts, fall the old
sources of water, the ground steams beneath the cascades, echo
reverberates around, and the immeasurable workplace, distributing gifts,
wields its arm night and day.

Again, as in "Brot und Wein," time is viewed as organic growth. The "holy" hours of the year, the days, are here "more boldly ordered" and "mixed." The pattern of growth formed by these days is complex, and yet this temporal growth towards fruition constitutes an order decreed by a transcendent God. For God's messenger, the eagle or "storm bird," is aware of this order and hovers between mountains "high in the air" above the tumult to announce the advent of day.[8] The inhabitants of the village are also aware that the hour of day has come and look up among the peaks fearlessly, since what is "high" is familiar to them: they have trust in the powers above and faith in transcendent will. Moreover, the entire scene now appears an "immeasurable workplace" that, dispensing gifts, wields its arm day and night like Blake's Los at his forge. This workshop or site of growth is literally the ensemble of storms, waterfalls and melting glaciers; its "gifts" are the streams that originate at this source and convey various blessings, natural and human, to surrounding countrysides.

Historically, then, the beginning of each day here serves as an emblem for the return of a universal day of divine presence to the world. But the entire strophe may also be explicated in terms of its poetic significance. The priesthood of Dionysus is comforting or even pacifying in its effects (the "gifts" to surrounding areas), but as a vocation for the poet it involves intense, tumultuous activity (the seething clouds and vital energies of waterfalls). The cloud in its joyous self-conflict is the figure of nascent poetry. It is the source of present gifts, but also heralds the "more bacchantic" arrival of morning in the "more infinite" growth of the year. Poetic composition is thus figuratively regarded as having a dual function: to supply present comforts and consolations (the elegiac mode) and, in the process, to encourage chiliastic expectations.[9] Each authentic poetic act may be considered a prefiguration of the redemption of history in its achievement of order and clarity out of tumult and darkness.

As noted, the first strophe accomplishes a perfect fusion of form and content by expressing stylistically in oxymora the conflict and tension it describes. Such yokings of opposites might be regarded as a striving for harmony in discord, that *concordia discors* which (as Earl Wasserman has observed) was a standard item of faith for the classicistic *Weltanschauung*.[10] Yet, as Wasserman notes, with the breakup of traditional "cosmic syntax" such order could no longer be regarded as given; it must somehow be achieved through the poet's own efforts. Thus for Hölderlin now, any vision of All-Unity, whether universal or microcosmic, must come as an actual accomplishment of poetry, not as its mere presupposition. Discord may be given; concord must be achieved. The antithetical structures in this strophe are thus expressions of a limited totality (cloud or poetic process) which has not yet found its harmony in definitive form. And yet when harmonious serenity is actually realized (in the beginning of the next strophe) it is attained only through a transcendence of conflict, an actual rising above the clouds into pure, untroubled light and the presence of the transcendent God dwelling above light itself.[11] The second strophe thus begins:

> Ruhig glänzen indess die silbernen Höhen darüber,
>   Voll mit Rosen ist schon droben der leuchtende Schnee.
> Und noch höher hinauf wohnt über dem Lichte der reine
>   Seelige Gott vom Spiel heiliger Stralen erfreut.   [2:96]

> Meanwhile the silver heights gleam calmly above this, the luminous snow is already full of roses up there. And still higher above there dwells over the light the pure, blessed God delighted with the play of his holy beams.

This Deity is identified as Father Aether, "Der ätherische":

> Stille wohnt er allein und hell erscheinet sein Antliz,
>   Der ätherische scheint Leben zu geben geneigt,
> Freude zu schaffen, mit uns,   [2:96]

> Quietly he dwells alone and his face appears bright, the Ethereal seems inclined to give life, to create joy with us,

The God dwells "silently, alone." Like the "Power" Shelley perceives enthroned above Mont Blanc, this Deity is described essentially in terms of radical transcendence. Unlike Shelley's inaccessible horror, however, he is seen as benevolent and generous to men. The remainder of the strophe describes the various workings of his benevolence. Conscious of the "measure" of human capacity noted in "Brot und Wein," the Deity is always "hesitant and sparing" in dispensing "well-considered happiness" to us in our communal "cities and houses." His gifts to our natural surroundings are also benign, in the forms of "mild rains" to "open the lands," "brooding clouds," "most tender breezes," and "gentle springs." And, for our suffering, the Deity "gives joy again to the sad" with a restrained "slow hand." This "creative" (and re-creative) God "renews the times," revivifying the human experiences of time itself and perhaps preparing for a rejuvenation in historical process.[12] He refreshes and seizes upon the "quiet hearts of aging men," giving them again youthfully joyous awareness of his presence. Fi-nally (in terms applying both to nature and human life) the Deity "works down into the depths, and opens and illuminates, as he loves to," so that "now a life begins again, graciousness blooms as before and present spirit comes, and a joyous courage [Muth] swells the wings again" into new activity. As in the elegy "Stuttgart"—"alle gebund-nen / Fittige wagen sich wieder ins Reich des Gesangs" (2:86)— the "wings" are those of poetry. The grace that penetrates into the depths of life and the soul also provides a renewed impetus to poetic flights.

Thus, after the first strophe's discord, the poet is granted a vision of God, Father Aether, who in pure transcendence embodies the serenity and unitive harmony no longer immanent either in the world or in poetic thought. The divine *principle* of All-Unity is thus seen as radi-cally divorced from its disjointed components in objective actuality and in the finite mind. Hölderlin will later complain that if we strive for totality we achieve only a multiplicity, the disharmony of which becomes evident when we seek to grasp its unity. As discovered in "Brot und Wein," all-unitive experience is no longer (or not yet) his-torically possible. When we now seek to experience totality we find discord, as in the first strophe where the poet attempts to comprehend the various aspects of nature (height and depth, peace and tumult, darkness and light) visually present in the Alpine landscape. Har-mony can exist only *above* discord; it can no longer be realized in the midst of it ("mitten im Streit") as at the conclusion of *Hyperion*. Likewise, unity can no longer be a property of actuality, but only of the abstract, "pure" vanishing-point that transcends the extended, vis-ible universe, a moment detached from earthly experience. In "Heim-kunft" the poet is granted a private vision of this transcendent princi-ple and names it God.

He thus claims a lucid perception of God, and even communication with him. The third strophe begins:

Vieles sprach ich zu ihm, denn, was auch Dichtende sinnen
  Oder singen, es gilt meistens den Engeln und ihm;   [2:97]

Much did I speak to him, for whatever poets think about or sing, it is
meant mostly for the angels and him;

In this ingenuous, offhand remark Hölderlin admits to a very radical
conception of the poet's role. The major concern of poetry is not
mimesis, effect, self-expression, or even the contrivance of artifacts for
their own sakes: the principal task of poetry is attention to Deity and
his mediators.[13] The poet had "much" to say to God because he had
already thought and written much about him. He also made petition-
ary prayers for his fatherland, Swabia, to which he is now (in the third
strophe) coming home after a brief stay in Switzerland. A returning
traveller would naturally think of his homeland and countrymen, but
the poet's prayers here have a particular urgency resulting from the intensity of his religious vision, and are complicated by his awareness of
the need for moderation in religious joy. His first prayer is that the
ecstatic "spirit" of joy should not too "suddenly" come upon his fellow
Swabians, lest they be overwhelmed with rapture.[14] He also prays for
those preoccupied with the cares of everyday life, ordinary "countrymen" to whom "fugitives" like himself return in "holy gratitude,"
grateful not merely that they are returning, but that they will have
opportunity to share in communal thanksgiving. (Religious gratitude
is always so compounded for Hölderlin; ultimately, such gratitude is
grateful for itself.) The poet thus sees his homeward journey, after his
vision of God, as a quest for the communal basis of thanks that may
adequately respond to divine benevolence.

The remainder of the elegy is concerned with the poet's quest and
its problematical conclusion. What first greets him on coming home
is an intimation of communal joy. In flowerlike naturalness this communality is even reminiscent of Greece in "Brot und Wein." Thus
Lindau, the first town he encounters, appears to rise up above its shores
like a Greek city: "und jezt blühet und hellet die Stadt   /   Dort in
der Frühe sich auf" (2:97). Everything appears fresh, nascent, wel-
coming; the people he meets all seem familiar to him, friends or even
relatives: "es scheint jegliche Miene verwandt" (2:97).[15] Encouraged,

the speaker opens the fourth strophe with an oblique but optimistic statement of his quest:

> Freilich wohl! das Geburtsland ists, der Boden der Heimath,
>   Was du suchest, es ist nahe, begegnet dir schon.   [2:97]

> Yes indeed, it is your birthland, the soil of your homeland, what you
> seek, it is near, coming to meet you already.

The joyous community he desires is already "near," even coming to "meet" him. Lindau seems to greet him as a "son" while he "seeks loving names" to praise it in song. The rest of the strophe elaborates the present mood of blessedness—how, though vistas all beckon to joyous wanderings, he chooses to continue homeward where "blooming paths are known."

The fifth strophe anticipates the poet's return to his native town whose voice, like his mother's, will evoke in him old remembrances and feelings: "du triffest, du regst Langegelerntes mir auf!" ("You strike and stir up in me what was learned long ago!") And the present reality still corresponds to his memories—nothing and no one has changed in its serenity:

> Dennoch sind sie es noch! noch blühet die Sonn' und die Freud' euch,
>   O ihr Liebsten! und fast heller im Auge, wie sonst.
> Ja! das Alte noch ists! Es gedeihet und reifet, doch keines
>   Was da lebet und liebt, lässet die Treue zurük.   [2:98]

> Yet they are still the same! The sun and joy still blossom for you,
> O you most loved ones, and almost brighter in your eyes than before. Yes,
> it's still the way it was! Everything thrives and ripens, yet no one
> who lives or loves there has abandoned loyalty.

In "Der Wanderer," we recall, the poet made a similar discovery that no one at home had changed. There, however, such awareness estranged him, for the poet thought himself spiritually altered by his suffering and his deific experience of All-Unity; his alienation drove him to seek communion with the divine presences in Nature. Here the seeming changelessness of people at home fills him with delight. In "Brot und Wein" the poet had reappraised his own situation regarding Deity and the question of All-Unity, and had discerned his own participation in man's common destiny. He now discovers a new relationship to his own family as mortals sharing this destiny and seeks from them an intersubjective confirmation for his own religious awareness.

He realizes that in life the greatest intensity and purity of joyous peace are reserved for innate and achieved simplicity, the young and the very old.[16] And yet he intends to speak of his holy "joy" with his family as they partake in the "holidays of spring" and go out to look on blossoming fields and trees which may suggest models for their lives. He will tell them of his recent vision of God:

> Vieles hab' ich gehört vom grossen Vater und habe
>   Lange geschwiegen von ihm, welcher die wandernde Zeit
> Droben in Höhen erfrischt, und waltet über Gebirgen.   [2:98]

> Much have I heard of the great Father and have long kept silent about
> him, who refreshes wandering time up there on the heights and
> reigns over mountains.

He had "heard" of the "Great Father" as giver of heavenly gifts, inspirer of hymnic song and dispatcher of angelic "good spirits"—all of which may correspond to the traditional theology he had learned from his family. Until now he had "long kept silent" about God, having no real experiential basis for speaking. Now, however, since he is personally acquainted with this Deity, he has a private gospel to tell his conventionally religious family, as he enthusiastically awaits God's general epiphany. He calls on God's "angels" to come and impart heavenly joy to all aspects of common life, hailing them as "preservers" of existence. This again coincides with orthodox theology, which considers direct or mediated divine attention essential to maintaining all things in being. Hölderlin, however (owing perhaps to his Pietistic background) attributes an ecstatic character to this preserving action.[17] Angels who bless aspects of human time (like the year) or human spatiality (like a house) are called upon to flood all "veins of life" with rapturous joy. These joyous blessings may "ennoble" and "rejuvenate" experience so that "nothing which is humanly good, . . . not one hour of the day" might be without angelic presences, and that even "such joy as now when loving people encounter each other again" should be "fittingly consecrated as is appropriate" for such happiness.

And yet even in prayer the poet has misgivings. *All* such joys must be

fittingly consecrated; each blessing received must be properly recipro-
cated with words of gratitude. But the finding of such words constitutes a problem. The poet thus continues in a different tone:

> Wenn wir seegnen das Mahl, wen darf ich nennen und wenn wir
>   Ruhn vom Leben des Tags, saget, wie bring' ich den Dank?
> Nenn' ich den Hohen dabei? Unschikliches liebet ein Gott nicht,
>   Ihn zu fassen, ist fast unsere Freude zu klein.
> Schweigen müssen wir oft; es fehlen heilige Nahmen,
>   Herzen schlagen und doch bleibet die Rede zurük?   [2:99]

> When we bless the meal whom may I name, and when we rest from the
> life of the day, tell me, how shall I offer thanks? Do I name the
> High One thereby? A god does not like what is unfitting, and our joy is
> almost too small to grasp him. We must often remain silent; holy
> names are lacking, hearts beat and does speech yet hold back?

Whom is the poet to name when the members of his family bless the
meal, and how shall he offer thanks when they rest from the life of the
day? True joy must be gratefully articulated, and real gratitude must
be addressed to someone who is named. Otherwise thanks is impossible and joy itself, unarticulated, becomes unreal. Authentic happiness
and community founded upon gratitude are thus dependent on the
availability of divine names. It is implied that the name of the Christian God has lost its evocative power, sacred words being subject to
radical mutability.[18] Furthermore, the conventional Christian prayers
of thanksgiving are no longer viable expressions for a poet who has
experienced God's radical transcendence. Dwelling "above the light,"
the Deity surpasses not only the world but our present resources of
language. This is not due to technical deficiencies in semantics; rather
(as explained historically in "Brot und Wein") our capacity for holy
joy seems no longer great enough to make possible an articulation of
an adequately holy name. The result is enforced silence, necessary
frustration of any expressions of gratitude confirming our joy.

  This question is not really answered in the remaining lines of the
poem, which offer a kind of consolation—yet weaker and more tentative than that of previous elegies:

> Aber ein Saitenspiel leiht jeder Stunde die Töne,
>   Und erfreuet vieleicht Himmlische, welche sich nahn.

Das bereitet und so ist auch beinahe die Sorge
  Schon befriediget, die unter das Freudige kam.
Sorgen, wie diese, muss, gern oder nicht, in der Seele
  Tragen ein Sänger und oft, aber die anderen nicht.   [2:99]

But a lyre gives to each hour its tones and perhaps gives joy to Heavenly
ones who approach. Let that be made ready, and thus the care that
came amidst our joyousness is almost already stilled. Cares like
these, gladly or not, a singer must bear in his heart, and often—
but not the others.

A limited harmonizing of life can be achieved by the naive, unproblematical music of a lyre. Such euphony may "perhaps" give pleasure
to angels possibly coming to fill our lives with deeper, more ecstatic
joy. This lesser music is merely to serve as possible invitation to the
greater bliss—which is now put into question by the poet's "care"
about our limited capacities for response. The lesser harmony might
also serve to distract us somewhat, so that our care is almost (but not
completely) placated. The poem thus ends on a note of resignation.

  This poem of "homecoming" is addressed "to the relatives" ("An
die Verwandten"). But, as Martin Heidegger notes, it ends paradoxically in an abrupt exclusion of the relatives, the "others" at home:
"aber die anderen nicht."[19] Despite his anticipation of a joyous community, the poet is still left unhappily with a sense of alienation. Obsessed with cares which others cannot share or even comprehend, the
poet (*as* poet) has unique concerns which unavoidably set him apart
from the others. A closer reading of the strophe's central lines will
reveal grounds for such isolation:

Wenn *wir* seegnen das Mahl, wen darf *ich* nennen, und wenn *wir*
  Ruhn vom Leben des Tags, saget, wie bring' *ich* den Dank?
Nenn' *ich* den Hohen dabei? Unschikliches liebet ein Gott nicht,
  Ihn zu fassen, ist fast *unsere* Freude zu klein.
Schweigen müssen *wir* oft; . . .

While expressions of religious gratitude must be communal articulations, they require proper words; and the poet *alone* must find and give
appropriate expression to these words. It is precisely his "care" for
words and proper forms of invocation that sets the poet apart from
that very community whose common gratitude he must express.

Hence the unhappy dialectic of the above lines: "When *we* bless the meal, whom may *I* name . . . when *we* rest from the life of the day . . . how shall *I* offer thanks? Do *I* name the High One thereby?" It is only the result of the poet's lonely failure that is shared: "*Our* joy is almost too small to grasp him, *we* must often remain silent." The poet's present inability to discover adequate names for God effectively precludes an authentic community which, like the Greeks', can only be founded in communal awareness of a divine name ("Vater Aether"). "Heimkunft" is thus finally about the radical impossibility of the "homecoming" announced in its title. We cannot return home for we can have no home on earth until we reconstitute an authentic community celebrating a name of God.

Thus "Heimkunft" confirms in private experiential awareness the conclusion attained through historical reflection in "Brot und Wein": "Denn wir sind herzlos, Schatten, bis unser / Vater Aether erkannt jeden und allen gehört." Such all-unitive recognition can be achieved only through poetry. Only the poet can redeem us from our "heartless," shadowlike existence. Not even a return to the seemingly unproblematical joys of home life can relieve a poet of this burden, for no joy (even the simplest) can be real until this poetic task has been accomplished. The conclusion of "Heimkunft" introduces us directly into the problematical world of the major hymns—impassioned meditations on the necessity (and possibility) of achieving an all-unitive divine name.

8. Toward the Major Hymns: The "Manes Scene"

We have observed the process by which Hölderlin virtually exhausted the possibilities of the elegiac form. His major elegies, as noted, originate in the tension between the present moment and a past instance of divine visitation. The remembered epiphany assumes various forms: The poet's deific love for Diotima in "Menons Klagen," the Greeks' "day" of divine presence in "Brot und Wein," and the personal vision of a transcendent Father-God in "Heimkunft." In each case a remedy for the present moment's unhappiness is sought through reconciliation with the deific past. Yet the elegies treat futurity, if at all, merely as an extension of a line that joins the past to the present moment. In "Menons Klagen" the future is envisioned simply as a vague repetition of past beatitude. In "Brot und Wein" hope is evoked for the gods' return, but their return is only vaguely foreseen. In "Heimkunft," of course, the poet finally encounters poetic frustration, so that "cares" rather than hopes come to dominate his vision of the future. This impasse in the poet's confrontation with futurity necessitates his recourse to the hymnic form.

As previously noted, the major hymns resemble the earlier Tübingen poems only in generic label and in their preoccupation with relating the present to a projected future moment. In the Tübingen hymns, the projected moment is a completed subjective rapture, an ecstatic personal experience of All-Unity. The structure of these poems is autorhetorical, designed to evoke an emotive state in the poet himself or in his immediate audience. The meditative structure of the later hymns, however, is designed to help the poet envision and clarify the ultimate goal of poetry. As indicated, this goal is usually seen as the articulation of an apposite divine name that might effectively designate the all-unitive character of deific Life and unite all men in communal recognition. The major hymns are perhaps best understood as a series of intricate questionings and responses on the meaning of this poetic task.

The formal aspects of Hölderlin's hymns have been treated in a number of perceptive studies;[1] here, we have examined how the elegiac form is superceded by the hymnic form, with its emphasis on futurity. Thus, as Peter Szondi indicates in his *Hölderlin-Studien*,[2] the hymns might be said to "follow" the elegies in the "inner chronology" of Hölderlin's work. And yet, as Szondi acknowledges, this internal chronology does not correspond with the actual sequence of poetic composition. Hölderlin's first attempts in the later hymnic style were begun before he had completed the last elegies; "Heimkunft" was written considerably later than the fragmentary hymn "Wie wenn am Feiertage," whose themes and attitudes are already those of the major hymns. To examine the hymnic structures in their incipience, it will be necessary to explicate the "Feiertag" hymn in some detail. Since, however, this is a most cryptic and difficult poem, we will first consider briefly a nearly contemporaneous work where identical themes and images occur in less complex form—the "Manes Scene" from the sketchy third version of *Empedokles*.

As noted in the discussion of the earlier versions of *Empedokles*, the crucial scene of the third version is of immediate thematic relevance to the hymns.[3] The first two scenes of this version rework familiar matter: Empedokles expresses desire for spiritual release and oblivion in the fires of Etna but discourages Pausanias from following him in sacrificial death. The third scene, however, presents a new episode: Empedokles' old teacher, Manes, arrives from Egypt and seeks to dissuade the protagonist from his suicide, reminding him of the divine wrath that awaits mortals who tempt the gods.[4] He then describes to Empedokles the only case where sacrificial suicide might be justified. It could be "right" solely for one:

Nur Einem ist es Recht, in dieser Zeit,
Nur Einen adelt deine schwarze Sünde.
Ein grössrer ists, denn ich! denn wie die Rebe
Von Erd' und Himmel zeugt, wenn sie getränkt
Von hoher Sonn' aus dunklem Boden steigt,
So wächst er auf, aus Licht und Nacht geboren.
Es gärt um ihn die Welt, was irgend nur
Beweglich und verderbend ist im Busen
Der Sterblichen, ist aufregt von Grund aus.
Der Herr der Zeit, um seine Herrschaft bang,
Thront finster blikend über der Empörung.
Sein Tag erlischt, und seine Blize leuchten,
Doch was von oben flammt, entzündet nur,
Und was von unten strebt, die wilde Zwietracht.   [4:135–136]

In this time it is right only for one, your black sin can ennoble only one man. He is a greater man than I! For as the vine bears witness to Earth and Heaven when, imbued by the high Sun, it emerges from the dark ground, so does he grow up, born of Light and Night. The world about him is in ferment, whatever is at all moveable and perishable in the bosom of mortals is stirred up from its foundation. The Lord of Time, anxious about his sovereignty, sits enthroned looking darkly over the insurrection. His day is extinguished, and his lightnings illuminate, yet what flames from above and what strives from below only inflames the wild dissension.

This demigod would be born of "light and night," like the grapevine; his parentage would be both earthly ("dunklem Boden") and divine ("hoher Sonn'"). He must be true to both parents at an historical moment of crisis when the world is in "ferment." The transcendent God, "Lord of Time" and of cosmic order, is then "anxious about his sovereignty" and sits enthroned in heaven "looking darkly over the insurrection"; on earth, the "day" of God's benevolent presence is extinguished and only the lightning of his rage illumines the darkness. Yet mortals respond with even greater defiance so that the conflict is exacerbated. In this moment of imminent catastrophe the demigod, loyal both to God and man, steps forward as mediator and "Savior":

> Der Eine doch, der neue Retter fasst
> Des Himmels Stralen ruhig auf, und liebend
> Nimmt er, was sterblich ist, an seinen Busen,
> Und milde wird in ihm der Streit der Welt.
> Die Menschen und die Götter söhnt er aus
> Und nahe wieder leben sie, wie vormals.   [4:136]

> Yet the one man, the new Savior, calmly seizes upon the beams of
> Heaven, and lovingly he takes whatever is mortal to his bosom, and the
> conflict of the world becomes mild in him. He reconciles men and
> gods, and they live near to one another as before.

The new Savior subdues God's rage at mortals by taking it upon himself. The "conflict of the world" becomes "mild" in him, for he settles it completely within himself and in such a way that this microcosmic solution is universally valid. The all-unitive harmony attained in his own soul is thereby—first vicariously, then actually—established as the renewal of harmony in the cosmos. However, he must die as an individual if such universal concord is to be perfectly effected:

> Und dass, wenn er erschienen ist, der Sohn
> Nicht grösser, denn die Eltern sei, und nicht
> Der heilige Lebensgeist gefesselt bleibe
> Vergessen über ihm, dem Einzigen,
> So lenkt er aus, der Abgott seiner Zeit,
> Zerbricht, er selbst, damit durch reine Hand
> Dem Reinen das Nothwendige geschehe,
> Sein eigen Glük, das ihm zu glüklich ist,
> Und gibt, was er besass, dem Element,
> Das ihn verherrlichte, geläutert wieder.   [4:136]

And so that, when he has appeared, the son be not greater than the
parents, and that the holy Spirit of Life not remain forgotten, enchained
above him, the only one, therefore, he, the idol of his time, turns
away, he himself, so that what is necessary might be done to the pure with
a pure hand, shatters his own happiness, that is too happy for him, and
gives what he possesses, again purified, back to the element that glorified
him.

The mediator between men and God must not, even unwittingly,
become an object of blasphemous adulation; it would be better for
him to die. Moreover, the "Holy Spirit of Life" can be released and
made universal only after the Savior's death, just as (in an analogue
later explicit in "Patmos") the Pentecostal manifestation of the Holy
Spirit was possible only after the death of Christ. Yet, Manes' hypothetical Savior is not a typological Christ-figure but represents an archetype of pure possibility, of which Christ is a particular example. Hölderlin's interest here is not in the specific identification of this Savior,
but in his ideal function and in the seeming necessity of his death.

As might be gathered from Hölderlin's own discursive treatment of
the question in "Grund zum Empedokles," there is an inherent con-
tradiction whenever a universally valid achievement of All-Unity is
realized in one man; only by destruction of this particular individual
can the universality of the solution be recognized among all.[5] One
man's realization of All-Unity in himself tends to fixate others' attention; only his death can free the others from his intimidating personality and permit his "spirit," the living force of his accomplishment,
to be reconstituted among all men. It is thus to prevent adulation and
to make possible the promulgation of the all-unitive "Life-Spirit" that
the death of Manes' "new Savior" is deemed necessary. In his case
suicide is commendable, because he, the potentially dangerous "idol
of his time," should "himself, in order that the necessary might hap-
pen to the pure by a pure hand, shatter his own happiness which is too
happy for him, and give back what he possessed purified to the element
that glorified him." That is: his "pure" life with its dangerous excess
of happiness can be fittingly destroyed only by his own "pure hand,"
returning the divine fire, "purified" through his life, to its primal form.
As such suicide is appropriate only to the "Savior," Manes concludes

by asking Empedokles: "Bist du der Mann? derselbe? bist du diss?" (4:136). ("Are you that man? The very same? Are you this?")

In his lengthy response, Empedokles clearly implies that he is. He recounts his spiritual autobiography, effectively reinterpreting his own life in terms of Manes' ideal Savior. He relates how he was startled from his initial serenity by the people's turbulence, and how he recognized the presence of divine wrath:

> Da fasste mich die Deutung schaudernd an:
> Es war der scheidende Gott meines Volks!
> Den hört' ich, und zum schweigenden Gestirn
> Sah' ich hinauf, wo er herabgekommen.
> Und ihn zu sühnen, gieng ich hin.   [4:137]

> Then the meaning seized me, shuddering: it was the departing god of my
> nation. Him I heard, and looked up to the silent stars from whence
> he had come, and to atone him I went forth.

He managed to reconcile the angry God with mortals and, like Manes' Savior, brought about a momentary rejuvenation of life: "Noch wurden uns / Der schönen Tage viel. Noch schien es sich / Am Ende zu verjüngern" (4:137). ("Still many beautiful days were given to us. Things seemed still to be rejuvenated at the end.") He now realizes that he was merely the instrument of divine "Spirit," chosen to articulate the "swan song" of the dying civilization:

> Denn wo ein Land ersterben soll, da wählt
> Der Geist noch Einen sich zulezt, durch den
> Sein Schwanensang, das lezte Leben tönet.
> Wohl ahndet ichs, doch dient' ich willig ihm.
> Es ist geschehen.   [4:138]

> For when a country is to die, the Spirit then chooses one more man
> for himself at last, through whom his swan song, the last life, resounds.
> Indeed I suspected this, yet I served him willingly. It has
> happened.

He has now fulfilled his function and is resigned to quit this world: "Den Sterblichen gehör' ich / Nun nimmer an" (4:138). ("Nevermore now do I belong to mortals.") In keeping with Manes' terms, he claims that he is summoned to death by his immortal "parents," the Earth and the God of Heaven, since the divine elements now actively seek consummation in return to "primal unity" ("Der alten Einigkeit"). The Earth in volcanic eruption is extending "Feuerarme" heavenward; the "Ruler" of Heaven is about to descend through his fiery lightning bolt. Heaven and Earth thus seem on the verge of fiery reunion. Empedokles proposes to join them, and follow "into the holy flames as a sign that we are related" to the Ruler of Heaven. Manes of course declines, and is unconvinced by Empedokles' implicit claim to be the Savior. The dialogue soon breaks off, with Empedokles still resolved to die.

In Hölderlin's tentative outline for completion of this version, the bulk of the action seems devoted to attempts to reconcile Empedokles and his royal brother, Strato, now representative of the established order. Manes, however, seems assigned to deliver the final speech after Empedokles' death. Hölderlin's note reads:

> Manes, der Allerfahrne, der Seher erstaunt über den Reden des Empedokles, und seinem Geiste, sagt, er sei der Berufene, der tödte und belebe, in dem und durch den eine Welt sich zugleich auflöse und erneue. Auch der Mensch, der seines Landes Untergang so tödtlich fühlte, könnte so sein neues Leben ahnen. Des Tags darauf, am Saturnusfeste, will er ihnen verkünden, was der lezte Wille des Empedokles war.   [4:168]

> Manes, the all-experienced, the Seer, astonished at the speeches of Empedokles and at his spirit, says that he [Empedokles] is the chosen one who kills and gives life, in and through whom a world is at once dissolved and renewed. Even that man who so mortally felt his land's perishing could thus anticipate its new life. On the following day, at the Feast of Saturn, he intends to proclaim to them what the last will of Empedokles was.

Hölderlin thus appears inclined to vindicate Empedokles; in the "Grund zum Empedokles" he seems to view his case as historically inevitable, a necessary moment in the destiny of a civilization—although he considers Empedokles' accomplishment problematical rather than definitive.[6] At any rate, Hölderlin has come to regard Empedokles' life as beyond good and evil, shaped by divine compulsion and no longer subject to moral judgment. Empedokles' destiny itself is no longer of special interest to the poet in his later works. Yet, as noted, the themes and images of the Manes Scene were taken over (slightly altered) into the fragmentary "Wie wenn am Feiertage," and thence were generally assimilated into the thematic structures of the later hymns.

9. "Wie wenn am Feiertage"

The first two strophes of the "Feiertag" hymn constitute an extended epic simile.[1] The rhetorical structure and even the syntax of this simile are highly complex; its major parts, however, are clearly defined. The first strophe is an elaborate "as when" clause; the whole is governed by "Wie wenn" and ends with emphases indicating a conclusion. The second term ("So stehn . . .") comprises the opening four lines of the second strophe:

Wie wenn am Feiertage, das Feld zu sehn
Ein Landmann geht, des Morgens, wenn
Aus heisser Nacht die kühlenden Blize fielen
Die ganze Zeit und fern noch tönet der Donner,
In sein Gestade wieder tritt der Strom,

Und frisch der Boden grünt
Und von des Himmels erfreuendem Reegen
Der Weinstok träuft und glänzend
In stiller Sonne stehn die Bäume des Haines:

So stehn sie unter günstiger Witterung,
Sie die kein Meister allein, die wunderbar
Allgegenwärtig erzieht in leichtem Umfangen
Die mächtige, die göttlichschöne Natur.   [2:118]

> As when on a holiday, to see the field, a countryman goes in the
> morning, when from hot night the cooling lightning bolts fell the entire
> time and the thunder still sounds from afar, the stream steps back
> into its banks, and the ground greens freshly, and from the joy-giving rain
> of heaven the grapevine drips, and gleaming in the quiet sun stand
> the trees of the grove:
> Thus do they stand under favorable weather, they, whom no master
> alone, whom the mighty, the divinely beautiful Nature educates,
> wondrously all-present, in gentle embrace.

"Nature" is here not inert physical reality (*natura naturata*) but the divine, unitive Life Force (*natura naturans*); she is both powerful and "divinely beautiful," for beauty is an attribute of manifest divine power or Life.[2] Since Nature is objective all-unitive Life, she is "wonderfully all-present" in the education of poets. The "embrace" of her wondrous all-presence educates them in gentle, sensuous immediacy. The poets' understanding of Nature will therefore be spontaneous and intuitive, like that of young Empedokles. Such intuitive immediacy with Nature will be (presumably) more important for them than the rules of poetic craft taught by a human "master."

In the controlling simile, these naturally educated poets stand in favorable weather as the trees of a grove stand when glistening in quiet sunlight.[3] Other clauses of the strophe develop the details of this comparison. The trees shine in the peaceful sun of a holiday morning, having just survived the night's violent storm. As Martin Heidegger cannily surmises, the "countryman" ("Landmann") of the opening clause goes out to see whether the storm has damaged his "field."[4] But, though the storm (the controlling image of the entire poem) has raged "the whole time," it has been beneficial. The poets stand radiant against a refreshed and rejuvenated landscape; and the "grapevine," associated both with Dionysus and with Manes' ideal savior, is also revivified and refreshed.

The relationship between the poet and "all-present" Nature is developed in the remaining lines of the second strophe:

Drum wenn zu schlafen sie scheint zu Zeiten des Jahrs
Am Himmel oder unter den Pflanzen oder den Völkern,
So trauert der Dichter Angesicht auch,
Sie scheinen allein zu seyn, doch ahnen sie immer.
Denn ahnend ruhet sie selbst auch.   [2:118]

Thus when at times of the year she seems to sleep in the heaven or among
the plants or the nations, the poets' faces mourn too, they seem to
be alone, yet they are always surmising. For she too surmises as she rests.

As the force of All-Unity, Nature is of course not conceptually limited to physical reality, but is present in transcendence ("Heaven") and in the historical being of "nations." Her vitalizing force seems dormant during winter months for the plant world, and in analogous wintry periods of divine absence or national torpor. At such times of dearth the "faces" of the poets are in mourning, as Nature, their loving teacher, is no longer manifest. The poets seem alone, cut off from unitive Life. Yet, in innermost awareness, they have intimations of this Life and foreknowledge of its return. For they sense a corresponding awareness in Nature herself, who "rests" always in the confidence that she will return. The time of deprivation which "Brot und Wein" envisages as a night of nearly two thousand years is viewed here as a brief season of seemingly untroubled hope.

Nature's return is proclaimed in the third strophe:

Jezt aber tagts! Ich harrt' und sah es kommen,
Und was ich sah, das Heilige sei mein Wort.
Denn sie, sie selbst, die älter denn die Zeiten
Und über die Götter des Abends und Orients ist,
Die Natur ist jezt mit Waffenklang erwacht,
Und hoch vom Aether bis zum Abgrund nieder
Nach vestem Geseze, wie einst, aus heiligem Chaos gezeugt,
Fühlt neu die Begeisterung sich,
Die Allerschaffende wieder.   [2:118]

But now it dawns! I waited and saw it coming, and what I saw, may the

Holy be my word. For she, she herself, who is older than the times
and is above the gods of the evening and orient, Nature is now awakened
with the clash of weapons, and from high in the Aether to down in
the abyss, according to fixed law, as once before, engendered from holy
Chaos, inspiration, the all-creating one, feels renewed.

"Now however it dawns!" Nature is manifesting herself, and will illuminate the world again. Foreknowing, the poet says, "I waited and saw
it coming." And he wishes to tell us of her arrival. But first he prays:
"and what I saw, may the Holy be my word." He wishes not merely to
tell of something holy, but prays that his naming of it, his own "word,"
may itself be holy. What he is about to name is no mere personal
experience—it is the advent of divine presence, manifest all-unitive
Life.[5] And what is divine may not be named by any word that is not
itself "holy." This insistence, we recall, is the basis of the problem encountered in "Heimkunft"; "es fehlen heilige Nahmen." ("Holy names
are lacking.")[6] The finding of this holy word, a principal concern in
all the major hymns, is the central problem of this poem. Here, however, in his initial enthusiasm, the poet does not yet *realize* the problematical nature of the desire. He merely prays, and hopes that the
prayer will answer itself: "may the Holy be my word."

Though thoroughly ambiguous in intent, the following sentence
might possibly be construed as an actual, impassioned attempt to name
divine All-Unity. The whole rhetoric of the sentence works to identify
the "all-creating inspiration" with "Nature." For, as we have seen,
divine All-Unity may be considered either objectively as Nature or
subjectively as supernal inspiration; these are merely two aspects of the
one metaphysical reality.[7] Nature is thus termed "older than the
times"; divine Being is ontologically prior to human temporality or
history. She is above the gods of occident and orient because divine
Nature herself is the unified totality of which the individual deities are
partial manifestations (for example, the early pagan gods of the East
or the Christian God of the "Abend-land"). Nature is now aroused by
the clash of arms, the cataclysmic events of the French Revolution and
the ensuing wars which many of Hölderlin's generation considered
portents of apocalypse.[8] These events here "awaken" Nature to a new
epiphany as divine all-presence in the form of "all-creating . . . inspiration." Inspiration is no longer the amorphous, ecstatic, dissolving

power of the Tübingen hymns; it is now the force which creates order out of chaos, an order implemented according to unchangeable "laws." While creation is revitalized, its basic structure remains fixed. Inspiration does not create its own laws, but is recreated as the energizing force of a fixed structure. The permanent order of reality is manifestly revivified from the transcendent realm of Aether down to the abyss. In Nature's awakening as all-unitive Being, all things are again aware of the one Life permeating all.

Nature is thus tentatively named as universal Inspiration ("Begeisterung,") the self-sentient force of divine All-Unity. Unlike the Urania of the Tübingen hymns, Nature is not personified here or viewed in anthropomorphic terms, though attributed with consciousness and sentiment of being.[9] It is remarkable that no image is evoked in this strophe's attempt to name Nature[10]; there is no figurative language because, clearly, if the poet's word is to be "the Holy," it must be unevasive. It should not seek to interpose the figure of some particular entity between itself and universal Being. Whatever the poet may achieve in this strophe is, however, necessarily subject to the inherent dialectic of the problem. Any particular designation of All-Unity immediately negates some facets of the universal and suggests the possibility of amplification, thereby revealing its exclusiveness and ultimate inadequacy.

The very continuance of this poem beyond the third strophe indicates that no definitive, "holy" naming of divine Life or Nature has been attained. The remaining strophes are actually concerned with determining a possible mode in which such naming might be achieved. The fourth strophe tells of promising preconditions for such an accomplishment:

Und wie im Aug' ein Feuer dem Manne glänzt,
Wenn hohes er entwarf; so ist
Von neuem an den Zeichen, den Thaten der Welt jezt
Ein Feuer angezündet in Seelen der Dichter.
Und was zuvor geschah, doch kaum gefühlt,
Ist offenbar erst jezt,
Und die uns lächelnd den Aker gebauet,
In Knechtgestalt, sie sind erkannt,
Die Allebendigen, die Kräfte der Götter.   [2:119]

And as a fire gleams in the eye of the man when he plans something
exalted, thus anew by the signs, the deeds of the world, a fire now
is ignited in the souls of the poets. And what before happened but was
scarcely felt is now manifest for the first time, and those who had smilingly tilled our field in the forms of slaves, they are recognized, the all-
living ones, the powers of the gods.

The poet here returns to the third person, "die Dichter" rather than
"ich," thus marking a more generalized, less crucially "engaged" style
of thought. The strophe's only first-person is the plural "uns," merging
the speaker's identity with that of poets in general. Moreover, the poet
again resorts to simile: just as a fire gleams in the eye of any man who
plans something exalted, so now such a fire is gleaming in the "souls"
of poets, ignited by the recent "signs, the deeds of the world." The
thunderstorm is again the controlling image. The "signs" (the cataclysmic events of the Revolution and wars, the "Waffenklang" of the
previous strophe) are the indications of divine will. The deeds themselves are charged with God's fire, the creative-destructive lightning
bolts of divine vehemence. The poets' souls have now "caught" this
deific energy, and are aflame with holy inspiration; thus, they are more
profoundly aware of divine presences in external reality.[11] All forces in
Nature are revealed as "powers of the gods," the "all-living" manifestations of all-unitive Life. Through this new awareness, the poets can
again consciously participate in divine Life.

The "spirit" of these deific powers is to "waft in song." This "song"
("Lied"), which is to embody divine Spirit in living (breathing) form,
will be "the Holy," just as the poet's word would become if he could
name Nature. The rest of the fifth strophe and the first lines of the
sixth recount the conditions for a successful genesis of inspired song
("Lied"), identical with that song ("Gesang") called "the work of
gods and men" in the sixth strophe. The song ("Lied") is to "grow
out of"[12] three divine powers: "the sun of the day," "warm earth,"
and "storms." The storms ("Wettern") however are differentiated as
"those in the air" and "others." These latter are the "thoughts . . . of
the communal Spirit" ("Des gemeinsamen Geistes Gedanken") or,
in the prose sketch of the poem, "thoughts . . . of the divine Spirit"
(Gedanken . . . des göttlichen Geistes").[13] These thought-storms

which "wander forth between heaven and earth and among the peoples" are "more prepared in the depths of time, and more problematical, and more perceptible to us." In their involuted turbulence they perhaps resemble the self-composing clouds of "Heimkunft." Their energy, however, exceeds human capacity for total participation, and in this dangerous transcendence they are threatening and potentially destructive. Yet, as thoughts of all-unitive communal Spirit they are harmonious in themselves. Here is another instance of a recurring paradox: All-Unity is in itself, absolutely, a state of perfect harmony and peace; and yet, insofar as it surpasses our participation, it poses a threat to our finitude. While this transcendent intensity may assume the form of volcanic fire (as for Empedokles) it can also appear as the thunderbolt of supernal Zeus.

This strophe also provides an instance of the correspondence of style and thought between this poem and the Manes Scene of *Empedokles*. There, the thunderstorm was a manifestation of the wrath of the "Lord of Time" over the menacing anarchy; his lightning bolt "illuminated" the night, but this merely exacerbated mortal unruliness. Here the storms are signs of general divine energy and vehemence.[14] In both cases the divine turbulence of heaven corresponds to mortal turbulence on earth, the "deeds of the world." In this poem, however, the storms are more fully developed as symbols. Compared to merely phenomenal storms these are better "prepared" ("vorbereiteter") in the depths of time, manifesting more profoundly the will and ordinance of time's Lord, and more indicative of divine providence to us. They wander forth, mediating divine will "between" Heaven and Earth and "among" the peoples; however, despite their evident fury, the storms are finally subsumed, "quietly terminating" ("stillendend") in the soul of the poet. They end there after finishing their work in the world.

One might conclude that any momentous thought, after having its effect on history, is destined to become subject matter for poetry. However, in these lines, although the thoughts end quietly, they are still charged with divine Life. And they do not become mere stuff for literature, but in their godlike vitality have a disquieting effect on the poet's soul:

Dass schnellbetroffen sie, Unendlichem
Bekannt seit langer Zeit, von Erinnerung
Erbebt, ...   [2:119]

So that she, quickly struck, familiar with the Infinite for a long time,
trembles with memory, ...

The soul's act of memory ("Erinnerung") has strong connotations of
inwardness and hence self-confrontation. When the soul is entered by
thoughts of the divine communal Spirit she is shaken not only by
remembrance of all former experiences or intimations of "infinite," all-
unitive Being, but also by an awareness of innermost participation in
it. The following lines present this experience as a procreative act:

... und ihr, von heilgem Stral entzündet,
Die Frucht in Liebe geboren, der Götter und Menschen Werk
Der Gesang, damit er beiden zeuge, glükt.   [2:119]

... and to her, inflamed by the holy beam, there succeeds the fruit born
in love, the work of gods and men, song, that it might bear witness
to both.

The soul conceives her child (the ultimate "song") of the holy lightning bolt, the potent instrument of Zeus that "inflames" her. The
divine storms previously seen as "thoughts" which "quietly end" in the
soul are now regarded as the advances of an overpowering divine lover.
The "song" born of this union, "die Frucht in Liebe geboren," will be
a demigod, the offspring of a divine father (Zeus the Thunderer) and
a human mother (the poet's soul). It will thus be the "work of gods
and men." This extraordinary song comes to the soul that it might
"give witness to both" the divine and the human.

The degree of parallelism between this poem and the Manes Scene
should now be fully evident. We have noted how the dominant image
if the thunderstorm is present in a similar function in Manes' speech.
The main point of similarity, however, is in symbolic action. The
"song" here is seen as the product of "sun," "warm earth," and
"storms." In Manes' speech, the "new Savior" is engendered by these
same divine forces:

... denn wie die Rebe
Von Erd' und Himmel zeugt, wenn sie getränkt

Von hoher Sonn' aus dunklem Boden steigt,
So wächst er auf, aus Licht und Nacht geboren.   [4:135]

        . . . for as the vine bears
witness to Earth and Heaven when, imbued by the high Sun, it emerges
from the dark ground, so does he grow up, born of Light and Night.

Both the "song" and the "Savior" are born of "sun" and "earth," of
"light" and "night." Both, as demigods, "give witness" to their dual
parentage—the same verb ("zeugen") is used in both cases. Both have
need of the divine lightning bolt: song in its conception, and the
Savior in assuming his role as mediator ("der neue Retter fasst   /
Des Himmels Stralen ruhig auf" [. . . the new Savior calmly seizes
upon the beams of heaven; 4:136]). Finally, both resemble the dionysian "grapevine" in origin and effects. While the trees in the opening
strophe here are compared explicitly to poets, the grapevine (cf. "Der
Weinstok") becomes the figure for ultimate song. All three—song,
Savior, and their common image—are alike in genesis from sun, earth
and storm, and in their mediating, conciliatory effects on mortals.

A fourth term in the symbolic equation, the winegod Bacchus, is
introduced at the end of the fifth strophe. The poet again returns to
simile here, this time in the form of allegorized myth:

So fiel, wie Dichter sagen, da sie sichtbar
Den Gott zu sehen begehrte, sein Bliz auf Semeles Haus
Und die göttlichgetroffne gebahr,
Die Frucht des Gewitters, den heiligen Bacchus.   [2:119]

So fell, as poets say, when she desired to see the god visibly, his lightning
on Semele's house, and the divinely-struck bore the fruit of the
thunderstorm, the holy Bacchus.

The myth is offered as an analogue to the conception of song by the
poet's soul. In the myth's primary version Zeus destroyed Semele in
procreation, though the child Bacchus was saved from his mother's
body; however, at this moment in the poem Semele's own fate is not
mentioned, only the fortunate birth of her child.[15] Still, implicit in
the myth itself (despite its allegorical adaptation) is a warning that
such visitation might possibly be destructive to the poet's own soul.

The mediating, conciliatory function of the winegod establishes a functional similarity to a Savior as well as to grape and song. This similarity is developed in Hölderlin's "Brot und Wein." Here, Bacchus is seen as the bringer of divine joy in the safely mediated form of wine: "Und daher trinken himmlisches Feuer jezt / Die Erdensöhne ohne Gefahr" (And therefore the sons of earth now drink without danger heavenly fire) [2:119]. While such divine fire in the form of the thunderbolt is possibly dangerous to the parent vine (and fatal to Semele), in its modified form of wine it gives euphoric comfort. This act of mediation requires a mediator, who can receive the divine lightning and transform its dangerous fires into the harmless, beneficent gift. This is now the work of poets:

> Doch uns gebührt es, unter Gottes Gewittern,
> Ihr Dichter! mit entblösstem Haupte zu stehen,
> Des Vaters Stral, ihn selbst, mit eigner Hand
> Zu fassen und dem Volk ins Lied
> Gehüllt die himmlische Gaabe zu reichen.   [2:119–20]

> Yet for us it is fitting, you poets, to stand with bared heads beneath God's
> storms, to grasp the Father's beam, itself, in our own hand and to
> extend to the people the heavenly gift wrapped up in song.

In an analogous situation, the ideal Savior in *Empedokles* was to take the Father's lightning bolts quietly unto himself, to the harmony of his own soul; here, the bolt is to be enclosed in a linguistic construct, the "Song." The song is the "holy Word" which names divine All-Unity and is infused with "all-living" Spirit.

But in this strophe the means of achieving ultimate song are described in altered (even simplified) terms. In the sixth strophe, the poet's soul must receive the thunderbolt, submit wholly to its power, and itself be thoroughly "shaken" and reminded of the inward resources of its own life if it is to bear this song as its child. The song is thus considered equally the work of the god and of the poet's own soul. In the seventh strophe, however, the poet does not admit the lightning into his soul, but literally keeps it at arm's length, grasping it in his hand. He does not here give of himself as a mother to her infant, but engages in detached handicraft, encasing divine fire into song as an outer protective covering. It is true that the poet must still expose himself to danger, standing with "bared head." But his "soul" or inner being is no longer fundamentally involved in the inception. Still, his hands must be "guiltless" and his heart as "pure" as a child's:[16]

Denn sind nur reinen Herzens,
Wie Kinder, wir, sind schuldlos unsere Hände,
Des Vaters Stral, der reine versengt es nicht
Und tieferschüttert, die Leiden des Stärkeren
Mitleidend, bleibt in den hochherstürzenden Stürmen
Des Gottes, wenn er nahet, das Herz doch fest.   [2:120]

For if we are only pure of heart like children, if our hands are innocent,
the Father's beam, the pure, will not singe, and deeply shaken,
suffering with the sufferings of the Stronger, the heart will stay firm in the
storms, rushing upon us from on high, of the god when he nears.

The poet's "heart" is thus subjected to the same kind of violence as his "soul" has been. There is here, however, a more significant difference than that of the probable differentiation of heart (seat of emotion and sentiment) and soul (principle of autonomous being). The soul's experiences in the earlier strophe are themselves essential to the genesis of song, conceived and born as a child, while the heart's sufferings here are presented as intense, yet only incidental to inception. Though the poet's heart may suffer heroically in the process, the actual work of preparing the song is done exclusively by the poet's hands. In this context, guiltlessness of the hands and purity of heart are important primarily for the personal security of the poet.

By an analysis of the prose drafts, Pete Szondi has clearly shown the transitional stages (omitted in the poetic version) of the fragment's last lines of verse.[17] In the manuscript version usually considered final, the poet's change of attitude is signalled by spaced, broken lines: "Doch weh mir! Wenn von / . . . / Weh mir! / . . . / Und sag' ich gleich, / . . ." [2:120]. The last completed lines read:

Ich sei genaht, die Himmlischen zu schauen,
Sie selbst, sie werfen mich tief unter die Lebenden
Den falschen Priester, ins Dunkel, dass ich
Das warnende Lied den Gelehrigen singe.   [2:120]

I might approach to look upon the Heavenly, they themselves, they
throw me deep beneath the living, the false priest, into the darkness, that
I might sing the warning song to those willing to learn.

The poet here anticipates a hypothetical situation in which he might himself "approach" the gods, instead of waiting for deity to approach him as in the eighth strophe ("wenn er nahet"). The gods would react to the impertinent behavior of such a "false" (bogus) priest by casting him into the abyss, a place of darkness far from divine presence. There he might sing a song warning others to avoid his mistake.

The poet's own improper initiative towards the gods is given here as the only reason for punishment. However, as Szondi notes, the prose version offers greater detail. The unrevised transitional passage reads:

Aber wenn von selbstgeschlagener Wunde das Herz mir blute,
und tiefverloren der Frieden ist, u. freibescheidenes
Genügen, Und die Unruh, und der Mangel mich treibt zum
Überflusse des Göttertisches . . .   [2:669–670]

But when my heart is bleeding from a self-inflicted wound, and peace
is deeply lost, and freely-allotted contentment [is lost], and unrest and
want drive me to the superabundance of the gods' table . . .

The poet himself may be driven by his own unrest and his need to become an uninvited guest at the gods' feast. Such impertinence is not arbitrary or whimsical but motivated by a real desperation; and yet it is not free of guilt, since the heart's wound is "self-inflicted." This culpable self-wounding might be the chief (and perhaps ultimate) motive for his blasphemous approach. It is akin to the motive which Manes first attributes to Empedokles' suicidal resolve, when he calls him a "sacrificial beast" [4:135].

Here, the poet's approach to the gods as a "false priest" may be a mere hypothetical possibility or, as Szondi insists, the metaphor of the poetic speaker's actual disposition.[18] But even the possibility might have been so frightening as to occasion the abandonment of the poem at this point. Even the chance that the poet might behave as a "false priest" would seem to preclude any further statements here on the functions of poetic priesthood; for after the third strophe, the poem is essentially hypothetical, telling how the poet would act if certain conditions were present. Conditions concomitant with the epiphany of All-Unity are anticipated as imminent, and thus the present indicative is generally used; but it is strictly an anticipated present. After a rush of optimistic hypotheses, the very possibility (expressed in the subjunctive) of a disastrously false priesthood is apparently enough to discourage further speculation. The poem disintegrates in the dire misgivings dialectically generated by its hypothetical lines of thought.

Actually, the basic difficulty of this crucial poem inheres in the intricate, often confusing structure of its dialectic. The dialectic is initiated by a major problem experienced by the poet in confronting All-Unity: poetic convention, and language itself in its very structures, presuppose a distinction between subject and object, consciousness and thing. Given this situation, it may seem virtually impossible for a poet to speak authentically of cosmic unity; the linguistic medium is fundamentally antithetical to what it should convey. The structure of the hymn is that of the workings of this essential conflict between intention and language. An analytical summary of the poem in terms of this dialectic may therefore lead to a clearer understanding of the poem's ultimate significance in the development of Hölderlin's poetry.

The poem begins with an extended simile; a simile, perhaps more than any other figure, representatively embodies the opposition of subject and object. Here, the basic comparison is between a landscape under certain weather conditions and a mode of poetic consciousness. This simile does not explicate the basis of the comparison; however, the rest of the poem might be considered its interpretation and commentary. The parallel-opposition between external nature and poetic consciousness continues in the second part of the second strophe, where Nature is no longer viewed as phenomenal, external physical reality but as its noumenal Life Force, endowed with sympathetic consciousness.

Then, suddenly in the third strophe, the separation between subject and object, consciousness and substance, is momentarily abolished. The life-principle behind objective landscape seems to burst forth as the all-unitive force of the entire cosmos. Both poet and object are forgotten, and no distinction is made between the inspired consciousness of the individual and the "all-creative" inspiration of the universe. This absolute consciousness is not opposed to any object but is at the center of all things, the sentient unitive force of reality structured "according to fixed law." The poet's finite self-consciousness is thus fleetingly abandoned in his lucid participation in all-unitive absolute awareness.

The poet then endeavors to tell how "we" (poets) should respond to this revelation. But to think of a response is to be self-conscious, and self-consciousness always entails the consciousness of an other, as object. Hence, in telling how "poets" should respond to a vision of All-Unity, the speaker is necessarily compelled to consider himself (as poet) apart from this All-Unity. This description of his response thus inevitably falsifies both the vision and the function of its participant, who is now reduced to subjective viewer and actor. Then, as noted earlier, the poet deserts the literalness of the third strophe and returns to simile. He now (as a reflective consciousness) confronts the deeds of the world and the divine powers as objects. All-Unity is still presumed to be operative behind these objects; and yet, of course, All-Unity cannot be realized within the terms of subject-object dualism.

The situation by the fifth strophe is thus quite evidently confused. The song is here said to "grow" from sun, earth, and storms; yet, in the following strophe, it is treated as the product only of storms (the thunderbolt) and the poet's soul. The statements cannot be wholly reconciled without forcing some arbitrary distinction between "Lied" and "Gesang." Sun and earth are simply disregarded in the second account of the genesis; yet we can see the dialectics of this confusion. The first account regards song as a merely "natural" product in which the poet's role is disregarded. The second concentrates on the subjective factor, the "soul," and considers only the divine Life in and behind Nature, not its phenomenal variety. The mediating term, with its embroiled syntax, is the distinction between "storms in the air" and "other" storms which are actually figures of the Spirit's thoughts. Figurative language is self-alienating. The original vision of All-Unity is thus itself torn apart into the subjective and objective components of its description.

The poet's resort to mythical allegory in the story of Zeus and Semele is a final instance of this separation. The simplifications in this story distort matters, converting three unlike entities (divine immediacy, the poet's soul, song) into three uniformly anthropomorphic personages (Zeus, Semele, Bacchus). The allegory thus makes the situation more graphic but also more opaque. The objective aspect has become dominant in the attempts to describe the vision. Prompted by the sexual metaphor for the subjective aspect of poetic inception, the poet has now translated even aspects of consciousness into visualized mythic figures. What remains of this poem is thought out in opaque, physical images. This physicality may account for the perhaps excessively vivid tableau of the poet standing bareheaded in a thunderstorm, catching a lightning bolt in his hand, and encasing it in a song which can then be safely delivered to the "Volk." It seems unlikely here that Hölderlin is consciously seeking the baroque effect of a metaphysical conceit.

It is this physical (no longer clearly allegorical) mode of thought which is perhaps responsible for the poem's woeful termination. To think of divine realities in graphically anthropomorphic terms such as Zeus the Lover is not only crude (and regressive) but ultimately self-defeating, since the mode of thought will ultimately triumph over its intended "content." As Hegel observed, Greek polytheism died as its gods became excessively (though inevitably) humanized.[19] Perhaps the crude and regressive mode of consciousness at the poem's end— which permits the poet's temptation—is a function of a naively physical mode of expression. As noted, the prose sketch supplies the poet's motivation for approaching the gods. The single line of the final version describing this action, however, is perhaps even more significant: "Ich sei genaht, die Himmlischen zu *schauen* . . ."—"I might approach to *look upon* the Heavenly." Here the danger inherent in the poet's chosen mode of expression becomes manifest; the terms of the expression themselves tempt the poet to believe that he can "see" the gods as if they were physical entities. And it is perhaps the dominant physicality at the end of the poem that suggests to the poet the "self-inflicted wound" of the prose version, the primitive bloody self-sacrifice. This is the atavistic sin that marks the false priest.

In the earlier versions of *Empedokles* the protagonist might also be guilty of self-desecration; as noted, in the third version Manes ridicules him as a sacrificial beast. But it is only in this version that Empedokles seems destined to go beyond that mode of sacrifice to become something like Manes's "der neue Retter." As previously mentioned, this is a major point of correspondence between this poem and *Empedokles*—the poet here sees the danger of becoming a "false priest" like the earlier Empedokles, sacrificing himself in his personal anguish to attain a private ecstasy of divine immediacy.[20]

And yet, it has been shown that the most fundamental relationship between these works is in their terms of affirmation. The poet here ardently hopes that his "song" will have the effect of reconciling men with gods, rescuing them as does Manes's "Savior." The image for both song and Savior is the grapevine; both are engendered of sun, earth, and storms; both are demigods of divine and human parentage; and both bear witness to ("zeugen") the human and the divine. There remains, however, the fundamental difference that "der neue Retter" is a person, an individual who lives on earth and must die; the "song" of the hymn is an articulation of language.

We have seen how this fragmentary prelude to Hölderlin's major hymns develops formally and thematically out of *Empedokles*, just as the elegies developed out of the Frankfurt Nature poems. The following chapters will trace the dialectic of attempted solutions to the poetic problems that emerged and were unresolved here.

10. "Der Rhein"

Any analysis of "Der Rhein" might well begin with Hölderlin's own cryptic annotation, a marginal note specifying the "law" or developmental pattern of the hymn:

> Das Gesez dieses Gesanges ist, dass die zwei ersten Parthien der Form [nach] durch Progress und Regress entgegengesezt, aber dem Stoff nach gleich, die 2 folgenden der Form nach gleich dem Stoff nach entgegengesezt [sind] die lezte aber mit durchgängiger Metapher alles ausgleicht.   [2:731]

> It is the law of this song that the first two parts are opposed in form through progress and regress, but are alike in matter, [and that] the two following [parts] are alike in form [but] opposed in matter, but the last [part] settles everything with a pervading metaphor.

As Bernhard Böschenstein points out in his detailed study of the hymn,[1] there are five "parts" to the poem, and each part is a triad, a group of three strophes. The "matter" ("Stoff") of the parts poses relatively little difficulty. The first two triads (1–3 and 4–6) are "alike" in matter, as both treat of the Rhine. The second two triads are unlike in matter, since one (7–9) deals with rebellious, titan-like blasphemers (opposed to the Rhine) and the other (10–12) speaks of Rousseau. It is generally agreed that the "metaphor" of the concluding triad (13–15) concerns the figure of the Bridal Feast between men and gods.

The major difficulty in Hölderlin's note is what he means by "form." The sense in which Hölderlin uses the term "form" can be most simply understood as directional movement of thought.[2] The first two triads are thus "opposed" in form through "progress and regress," with the direction of thought in strophes 1–3 simply reversed in 4–6. Walter Hof applies Hölderlin's complicated theory of tonalities in designating the first strophe as "naive" or calmly descriptive, the second as "heroic" or narrative of conflict, and the third as "ideal" or reflective, expository.[3] This "progress" or development is "regressed" or reversed in the following three strophes, as the fourth could be considered "ideal," the fifth "heroic," and the sixth again "naive." The two following triads would then be "alike in form," since their strophes show parallel rather than opposing developments. Since the "metaphor" of the closing triad is to "settle everything," it presumably resolves tension of form as well as matter, and acts as a settlement for the entire poem. How this is achieved is perhaps the major question to be asked in interpreting the poem as a whole. First, however, we might examine the individual structure of each designated part or triad, noting the various particulars of "form" and "matter."

The first triad recounts the circumstances of the poet's initial perception of the Rhine's destiny, offers an awestruck but sympathetic account of its rebellion, and tells of the poet's reflections upon it. Unlike most of Hölderlin's major poems, the first strophe here begins with the focus on the speaker: his location, what he perceives, and what happens in his soul at the moment of perception. He is described as sitting "in dark ivy, at the portal of the woods"—near an opening in the forest, where he can behold unmediated sunlight without leaving the shade.[4] What he sees is the noonday sun above the Alps, about to decline along steplike slopes to visit the "source," the fountainhead of the Rhine. The strophe then turns from description to explain what the Alps mean. According to the "opinion" of the Ancients, they are divinely built, "the fortress of the Heavenly." They remain graphic intersections of land and sky, citadels the gods may inhabit and points where they may conveniently visit earth. The "golden noonday" descends on these slopes to visit the river's source, for the Alps are yet the place "where . . . in secret many things decisive still may reach men."

The "decisive" things are earthly destinies; the poet "unsuspectingly" perceives such a destiny. Here, as elsewhere, the optimal figure for any destiny is the river. A destiny is the course of a finite consciousness engendered by the divine principle into earthly, resistant actuality, what may be termed the "inert." Although born of a moment of unity between heaven and earth, it always experiences disunity and alienation, for what is divine in it will always be opposed by what is inert in this world.[5] A destiny is impelled by desire to escape the pains of alienation and conflict; the desire is what drives it onward. And yet it must encounter other, more painful forms of conflict and frustration. Likewise, for Hölderlin, the river is born of union between earth and the heavenly fire.[6] The sunlight, in "visiting the source" ("Den Quell besuchend") is returning to the site of a former erotic union to recreate the act of engendering. Once born, however, the river finds itself in deepest seclusion from paternal sunlight and encounters earth as an obstacle. And the river, like the destiny of consciousness, feels frustration and rage as it tries to overcome alienation—and driven onward, yet blocked by land, it encounters only more obstruction and frustration.[7]

We have necessarily anticipated the following strophes in order to clarify what "destiny" the speaker perceives. The strophe's concluding lines indicate how this perception occurs. The poet, sitting in "warm shade," feels his soul, eloquently "speaking to itself of many things," imaginatively transported to Italy "and far away to the coasts of Moreas" or Greece. Here, as in "Brot und Wein," "dark ivy" suggests the quiet serenity of the Dionysian priest, as does the poet's shaded location. Poets in the elegy were urged to envision past and possible future moments of divine immediacy while contenting themselves with the present. Yet here the shade is "warm," and the poet begins to feel the intensity of the sunlight outside the forest. With such warmth infiltrating from the divine source, the mood reverts to that of the enthusiastic third strophe of "Brot und Wein," as heat of inspiration produces an intense desire for its fulfillment. The poet's soul desires to return to the locus of greatest possible divine enthusiasm, ancient Italy and, finally, the holy land of Greece. The poet thus perceives the destiny typified by the Rhine even as his soul experiences temptation to return to the ancient world. This is appropriate, for the Rhine is itself impelled to take that direction: to the south and east. The Rhine does not represent the poet's own destiny, nor the destiny of any particular person, nation or civilization. It embodies a certain archetype or pure possibility of destiny. The destiny here perceived is described and reflected upon in the following five strophes.

The second strophe, a single sentence, describes the river's violent early phase and local reactions. The poet hears the raging lamentations:

Jezt aber, drinn im Gebirg,
Tief unter den silbernen Gipfeln
Und unter fröhlichem Grün,
Wo die Wälder schauernd zu ihm,
Und der Felsen Häupter übereinander
Hinabschaun, taglang, dort
Im kältesten Abgrund hört'
Ich um Erlösung jammern
Den Jüngling   [2:142]

Now, however, there in the mountains, deep beneath the silver peaks and beneath the cheerful greenery, where the woods tremulously look
down upon him, and the heads of rocks, one upon another, look down all day long, there in the coldest abyss I heard the youth as he wailed for redemption . . .

The river as a young man is no longer at immediate origin, but already developed in strength. He is far removed from fires of divine Life; yet he violently desires release from earthly confinement. Although his parents, "Mother Earth" and "the Thunderer," hear his raging accusations and pity him, they are not able to help him now, for once a destiny is begun it must fulfill itself. Yet the river is not resigned, and the "rage of the demigod" is horrible enough to frighten "mortals" from the place; the anguish of a finite consciousness wholly mindful of divine origins cannot be faced by ordinary men.

The third strophe ("ideal" or reflective in tone) gives the poet's interpretation of what he has just described. The Rhine is "the noblest of streams" and is "free-born," engendered in the absolute freedom of divine immediacy. Unlike his more servile "brothers," the Ticino and the Rhone (who dutifully follow courses of least resistance), he is determined to realize the freedom of his birth. His regal soul thus impels him towards Asia Minor, the area of Hellenic civilization and the historical site of greatest divine presence.[8] The strophe finishes with generalizations on the river's significance:

Doch unverständig ist
Das Wünschen vor dem Schiksaal.
Die Blindesten aber
Sind Göttersöhne. Denn es kennet der Mensch
Sein Haus und dem Thier ward, wo
Es bauen solle, doch jenen ist
Der Fehl, dass sie nicht wissen wohin?
In die unerfahrne Seele gegeben.   [2:143]

Yet wishing is foolish in the presence of destiny. But the blindest are sons
of gods. For the man knows his house and it occurs to the animal
where it should build, but for them the defect that they do not know
where to go is instilled in their inexperienced souls.

Confronted with destiny, any wishing is senseless. Destiny arises from the conflict between desires and circumstances, and there is no sense in wishing to escape the results of one's own desires. Yet, those most blind to their situations are "sons of God"—demigods like the Rhine whose awareness of divine origin is intense enough paradoxically to obscure the inevitability of obstacles. A man without such awareness at least "knows his house," recognizes his allotment in life and adapts to it; the "animal" also knows instinctively where to build its nest or lair. But a demigod obsessed with divine origin has in his "inexperienced soul" the "defect" that he does not really know where to go.

Thus, by the end of the third strophe the poem has "progressed" from calm description through an account of heroic action to reflections on the Rhine and demigods in general. The moment of greatest ideality or conceptual generality has been reached, and will be continued in the first half of the fourth strophe, the beginning of the second triad. Now that this stage of reflective awareness has been attained, the development of the second triad will reverse or "regress" that of the first, returning through more particularized comments on the Rhine to another consideration of heroic action (fifth strophe) and finally to the calm, "naive" descriptiveness of the sixth.

The beginning of the fourth strophe continues the general reflections:

> Ein Räthsel ist Reinentsprungenes. Auch
> Der Gesang kaum darf es enthüllen. Denn
> Wie du anfiengst, wirst du bleiben.   [2:143]

> A riddle is the pure in origin. Even song can hardly reveal it. For as you begin so you shall remain.

Whatever is of "pure origin" and has kept the purity or radical truth of this origin (the consciousness of a demigod) is yet a "riddle" even to itself. Even inspired "song" (itself proceeding from pure consciousness) is scarcely able to disclose its mystery. The nature of one's origin determines the course of one's destiny: "for as you begin you will remain." Though unable to solve the riddle, the speaker thus asserts the decisiveness of originary force and the primacy of "birth" over environment. The Rhine is engendered "from a favorable height," the mountain peaks where waters originate, the abode of his divine Father. He is born "from holy womb," the cavernous depths of his mother Earth. Thus fortunate in birth, he seems destined to remain happy in joyous awareness of the strength and legitimacy of his own desires. He accordingly wills "to remain free his entire life," supremely justified in "fulfilling his heart's wish, alone"—self-realization of the godhead he considers his birthright.

The fifth strophe narrates the results of the river's will to come into his estate. From the first, "his word is a jubilation." The Rhine does not "like to cry in swaddling clothes like other children," helpless and dependent. Rather, he resembles Hercules, whose first heroic deed was to kill the snakes sent to destroy him.[9] Like these snakes, the river's banks are deceptive in approach, feigning interest in the child's welfare. But the young stream soon realizes they want to prevent the fulfillment of his destiny, and he already is strong enough to defeat them. Thus, "where the crooked banks first creep to his side, and thirstily wind about him, the [yet] unsuspecting one, and desire to draw him and guard him well within their own teeth, he laughingly tears up the snakes," joyfully conscious of power, "and dashes off with the booty." It seems then that he cannot be stopped, that he may force his way through mountains blocking his path to the east, and "like the lightning" split Earth itself. This would be an Oedipal rape with the child assuming his father's role (as God's thunderbolt) and forcefully returning into the body of his mother.[10] Such violence would destroy the ordered structures of Nature itself. For the demigod to prevail would be universally catastrophic, with "bewitched" forests and "collapsing" mountains following the river into an abyss of chaos. Someone "greater" must "tame" him to preclude this.

Thus, once the river has overcome his initial obstacle he is forced by his own divine Father to yield to the whole opposing presence of Earth itself. The sixth strophe describes the results of this intervention. The heavenly Father wishes to spare his "sons" their "life" of godlike desires hastening to self-destruction.[11] Paternally benevolent, he is unmoved but "smiles" indulgently when streams such as the Rhine, "incontinent but restrained by the holy Alps," rage against him in the deep.

The speaker has now come to understand the scene described in the second strophe. The "Thunderer" was not (as it seemed) indifferent to his rebellious child, but was benignly frustrating its potentially fatal desires for immediacy. The imposed suffering transmutes the Rhine's will into something "pure" like a swordblade on a forge. The will is not broken but tempered, made healthier and stronger in self-mastery. In the harshness of discipline the river has learned to confine his desires to the possible. Also, as in the grand tradition of the "Bildungsroman" from *Wilhelm Meister* to *Der Grüne Heinrich,* he has learned to apply himself to useful, constructive tasks:

Und schön ists, wie er drauf,
Nachdem er die Berge verlassen,
Stillwandelnd sich im deutschen Lande
Begnüget und das Sehnen stillt
Im guten Geschäffte, wenn er das Land baut

Der Vater Rhein und liebe Kinder nährt
In Städten, die er gegründet.   [2:144]

and it is beautiful how henceforth, after he has left the mountains, he
contents himself quietly wandering in German land and stills his
longings in good activities, when he cultivates the land as Father Rhine
and nourishes dear children in cities which he has founded.

This strophe thus anticipates the German "Biedermeier" mood or the
English "Victorian compromise" expressed in *Sartor Resartus* and
novels like *David Copperfield*. The river leaves the Alps and, now a
teutonic *paterfamilias*, sublimates his surviving desires into productive
energies; his controlled impulses have been tempered into something
more "pure."[12]

The first two parts of the hymn thus constitute a unit recounting
the story of the Rhine (it might be argued that the poem's title relates
directly only to these six strophes). We have noted the "material" and
"formal" patterns of the two triads; however, another developmental
structure also emerges here,[13] the dialectic between what may be
termed "unitive Life" and "the inert." In the first strophe, the poet
feels an impulse to divine immediacy and perceives a destiny where
such unitive impulse (despite conflict with the inert) is most fully
expressed. The ensuing five strophes trace the dialectic of this destiny.
In the second, the consciousness of the demigod is shown in heroic violence without a conceptual or mythical framework to make the violence intelligible. A conceptual framework is provided by the third and
fourth strophes, which reflect on the conflict between innate desire
for unitive Life and the resistant inertia of earthly actuality. Desire is
ultimately the dominant factor in the Rhine's destiny. On the basis of
conceptual understanding, the fifth and sixth strophes can now supply
mythical (narrative) contexts for the scene in the second strophe. The
fifth tells of the stream's early childhood and the early triumph of his
unitive impulse until it becomes a threat to Earth herself. Knowledge of
the threat fosters awareness of the Father's motive in frustrating the
stream's desire. The end of the sixth strophe presents the effect of the
tempering process: the stream now directs his energy to help form the
structured mode of life which he had once threatened to destroy. The
dialectical conflict between unitive Life-impulse and inert actuality is

thus resolved, with unitive Life mediated (and earthly actuality vitalized) in this world.

Yet the river's momentary violence has raised a problem needing further consideration. The following strophes therefore examine the case of "defiant" men ("die Trotzigen") who seek violently to overcome the necessary inequality between themselves and gods.

The first strophe of this part begins with reference to the Rhine. Although settled into a seemingly permanent state of tranquil cheer, the Rhine "never, never forgets" what he was before his tempering into domestic life. A demigod *must* never forget "the origin and the pure voice of youth." It would be better to destroy the day's sweetness and light, the culture he has built as Father Rhine, to demolish everything rather than renounce the memory of divine origin or the ultimate justice of the deific impulse. The Rhine may be tamed, but not emasculated; his desires may be moderated, but never wholly extinguished. Even total destruction must be preferable to self-betrayal. The remainder of the strophe speculates on an historical case of such destructiveness. The "bands of love" ("Liebesbande") are relationships which hold together the participants of any communal structure. However, these mediating relationships may lose their effective, voluntary quality, hardening into "fetters" that bind men against their will. Such degeneration is fairly common in history: a once-voluntary constitution may become oppressive, a religion of love perverted into an autocratic church.[14] The poet does not know "who" is responsible for these developments; he can only contemplate the inevitable revolt against the oppressive structure, and the excesses that rebellion may produce. In an unspecified past instance some "defiant" men, no longer able to tolerate the fetters of compulsion, had "mocked at their own rights, certain of the heavenly fire."[15] Their rights were possibly an essential part of the old constitution, yet they were rejected along with all components of order. But destruction of any mediating system of life involves confrontation with immediacy, exposure to "heavenly fire." Men's own divine freedom, absolutely realized when life's structures are destroyed, can itself consume men in their nihilism. In such a moment of absolute freedom men sought "to become like the gods," as "for the first time, despising mortal paths, they chose [a course of] foolhardy audacity." These men were destroyed by their own intense zeal.[16]

The eighth strophe, seeking to understand this suicidal wish, begins by reflecting upon the proper relationship between gods and men:

> Es haben aber an eigner
> Unsterblichkeit die Götter genug, und bedürfen
> Die Himmlischen eines Dings,
> So sinds Heroen und Menschen
> Und Sterbliche sonst. Denn weil
> Die Seeligsten nichts fühlen von selbst,
> Muss wohl, wenn solches zu sagen
> Erlaubt ist, in der Götter Nahmen
> Theilnehmend fühlen ein Andrer,
> Den brauchen sie;   [2:145]

> But the gods have enough with their own immortality, and if the
> Heavenly need anything, it is heroes and men and other mortals. For be-
> cause the most blessed ones feel nothing of themselves, another
> must (if it is permitted to say such a thing) participatively *feel* in the
> gods' names. Him they need.

The gods "have enough" with their own immortality, their deathless-ness and lack of need for reflective self-consciousness. They simply *are*: they have no feeling of selfhood. They exist in All-Unity. For mortals, self-consciousness stems from the need for self-protection. Our self-consciousness, then, results in differentiation of the self from other selves and from the undifferentiated all-unitive Life of the gods. The unreflective, unfeeling gods "have need" of "heroes, men, and other mortals" that their being may be reflected in finite but self-conscious minds. Though Hölderlin is naturally hesitant to attribute any deficiency to the gods, he here avers that they require some mortals to "participate" in their being as mediated through their "names" and reflectively to "feel" this participation.[17] Since the gods are truly present in men's souls, our reflective feelings of the gods' presence can give them a momentary sensation of their own being. Thus all gods traditionally demand that men should give honor and glory to their names. And yet they react violently when mortals go beyond such participation and seek divine status. Such "enthusiasts" ("Schwärmer") are men so enraptured by participatory feelings that they desire to be "like" gods in immediacy of all-unitive Life.[18] The raving destructiveness of the defiant enthusiasts here is quite similar to what Empedokles saw among his own people:

Und wenn, indess ich in der Halle schwieg,
Um Mitternacht der Aufruhr weheklagt,
Und suchend durchs Gefilde stürzt, und lebensmüd
Mit eigner Hand sein eignes Haus zerbrach,
Und die verlaideten verlassnen Tempel,
Wenn sich die Brüder flohn, und sich die Liebsten
Vorübereilten, und der Vater nicht
Den Sohn erkannt, und Menschenwort nicht mehr
Verständlich war, und menschliches Gesez,
Da fasste mich die Deutung schaudernd an:
Es war der scheidende Gott meines Volks!   [4:137]

And when, while I was silent in my hall, at midnight the rebellion raised
its lamenting cry, and they rushed seeking through the fields and,
weary of life, demolished their own houses and their repugnant, abandoned temples, when brothers fled one another, and the dearest
ones passed by one another in haste, and the father did not recognize his
son, and human language was no longer intelligible, or human law:
then the meaning, shuddering, took hold of me—it was the departing
god of my nation!

Empedokles perceives that when a nation's "god" departs, chaos and violent conflicts break out. This god was the principle of communality, the implicit nexus of all "bands of love." The god's departure then turns love-bands into fetters, and violence ensues from the destruction of these now intolerable conditions. As in "Der Rhein," a man destroys his own house and all enclosing structures of his earthly life.

The eighth strophe reflects on such instances of destructiveness. Yet, we recall, the seventh strophe's example of defiant violence is itself presented rhetorically as an alternative which, however fearsome, would still be preferable to a complete "forgetting" of divine origin. Between the two extremes of forgetfulness and destruction there is a *via media*, in which desires arising from participation are moderated. This blessed moderation is exemplified by the Rhine in his final phase.

The ninth strophe elaborates on such holy contentment. The Rhine typifies the life of a man who, after tumultuous youth, has "found a well-allotted destiny" in later years when he can still think back on "wanderings" and even "sufferings," whose memory is "sweet" because he knows the fortunate outcome. The implicit viewpoint here is no longer that of the river itself, but of someone standing on the "safe shore" while his memories are the waters now sonorously rushing past. Destiny is here regarded as completed, a fixed place on land, not moving like the river of the previous strophes. Such destiny is no longer progress toward a goal, but the goal itself. And from the vantage of one safely arrived on shore it is possible to survey the region "up to the border which God had designated for his dwelling-place when he was born." The younger Rhine "did not know where to go," but now he knows where he belongs. And "then he rests blissfully contented" in possession of "everything that he wanted." This is "the Heavenly," not unmediated divine fire but happily mediated divine presence. As a youth the Rhine's destiny had violently and boldly striven for divine immediacy and had attempted to force mergence with it. Now, however, the divine presence "smilingly" and freely "embraces the bold one as he rests."

As noted earlier, the third and fourth sections of the poem are "like in form" but "opposed in matter." The "matter" of the third part is the "defiant" men or, more precisely, the opposition of these to the elder Rhine, who has overcome his earlier temptations to violence. The "form" of the triad may be the progression of tones or rhetorical modalities from "heroic" through "ideal" to "naive."[19] Or the form may be regarded as a logical dialectic: statement of opposition as a problem (seventh strophe), analysis of the problem (eighth), and overcoming of the problem (ninth).

The fourth part's formal resemblance to the third may be seen in the progression of modalities: unreflective presentation of action ("heroic") in the tenth strophe, reflective interpretation ("ideal") in the eleventh, and naive description in the twelfth. The logical dialectic is also similar: opposition and posing a problem in the tenth strophe, analysis of the problem in the eleventh, and resolution of the problem in the twelfth. The matter of the fourth part is clearly the destiny of Rousseau; he seems to be contrasted to the defiant enthusiasts, though this opposition is not total. The antithesis between the parts is clearer if we take the matter of the third part to be the radical unlikeness of the Rhine and the enthusiasts: Rousseau as one person experiences both the enthusiasm of the destroyers and the serenity of the later Rhine. The stated opposition in matter may thus be between the either-or presentation of modes in the third part and the both-and presentation in the fourth—between antithetical alternatives and individual synthesis.[20] The synthesis Rousseau achieves is not merely particular, like the Rhine's attained harmony, but universal, since he appears to introduce the "Bridal Feast" between mortals and gods in the final triad.

In the tenth strophe, however, Rousseau is first presented in seeming distinction to "demigods" as an enigmatic figure. The speaker is currently thinking of demigods such as the Rhine himself. The Rhine, like other demigods, represents a desirable possibility for the poet, since he differs from most mortals only in his impelling consciousness of the divine source. Any demigod's life must therefore "move" the soul of a poet seeking his own authentic mode of fidelity to origin. But the speaker is then reminded of the problematical case of Rousseau. He does not yet know what to call him: "how do I name the stranger?"

Rousseau's strangeness seems to inhere in his somewhat puzzling achievement. His "strongly enduring" soul had become "unconquerable" while he, despite a variety of persecutions, remained unyielding in his vision of truth. This vision was itself the product of a "sure mind" endowed with "sweet gifts to hear" the quiet voices of the gods. He also had a gift to "speak so that, out of holy fullness like the Winegod, he foolishly, divinely, and lawlessly dispenses . . . the language of the most pure." The "most pure" are the gods whose words Rousseau lavished on the multitude without regard for decorum or consequence. In his indiscriminate promulgation of divine mysteries Rousseau resembles the earlier Empedokles, as condemned by Hermokrates:

Hinweg mit ihm, der seine Seele blos
Und ihre Götter giebt, verwegen
Aussprechen will Unauszusprechendes
Und sein gefährlich Gut, als wär es Wasser,
Verschüttet und vergeudet . . .   [4:97]

Away with him who exposes his soul and her gods, who insolently wishes to express what is not to be expressed and spills out and squanders his dangerous blessing as if it were water. . . .

In "Der Rhein" Hölderlin himself speaks in like terms of Rousseau's imprudence, yet with no marked disapproval. Though Rousseau may be "foolish," he is morally innocent in uncontrolled revelation of divine truths. What he says is "intelligible to the good" who can understand and respond properly to inspired words. And when Rousseau's writings instigate trouble (as perhaps in some phases of the French Revolution) the fault lies not with Rousseau or his words but with those unable or unwilling to interpret them properly. His utterances are thus said "rightfully" to "strike with blindness" the "desecrating slaves" who misapplied them. His indiscretions were due solely to the "holy fullness" of his inspiration and his resemblance here to Hölderlin's benevolent Dionysus.[21] And yet, the speaker admits, Rousseau remains a "stranger" not easy to "name."

In an attempt to resolve this strangeness, the eleventh strophe begins with general reflections and then applies them to the particular case:

Die Söhne der Erde sind, wie die Mutter,
Allliebend, so empfangen sie auch
Mühlos, die Glüklichen, Alles.
Drum überraschet es auch
Und schrökt den sterblichen Mann,
Wenn er den Himmel, den
Er mit den liebenden Armen
Sich auf die Schultern gehäufft,
Und die Last der Freude bedenket.... [2:146]

The sons of the Earth are, like the mother, all-loving, therefore they also,
tirelessly, the happy ones, are receptive to All. Thus it also surprises
and frightens the mortal man, when he considers the heaven which with
loving arms he has heaped on his shoulders, and the burden of joy.

The "sons of the Earth" are mortals true to the human condition and to the demands of earthly existence.[22] They take full responsibility for their own finitude. (They are not actually opposed to demigods, since the demigods themselves, like the later Rhine, must ultimately acknowledge sonship to Earth as well as to their heavenly Father.) The Earth is all-loving because, as basis of all finite life, she affectionately supports all living beings within her embrace and is inexhaustibly responsive to the Heaven above her. Any mortal (her child) may aspire to her generosity even if his own finitude dooms him to failure. As in "Brot und Wein," each mortal has his "measure" or limit of how much all-unitive Life he can endure, and soon comes to awareness of this limit. But a man with the "strongly enduring" soul of Rousseau may not at first be strained by his receptivity to divine Life. He may almost unknowingly come to the point where his capacity is reached and nearly exceeded. He is then shocked to discover he has taken on himself more than he can bear of participation in All-Unity, and may feel its transcendence pressing down on his shoulders with the full weight of Heaven. Upon such realization "it often seems best to him to be in almost complete forgetfulness there where the light-ray does not burn, in fresh greenness in the shadow of the woods by Lake Bienne." What "seems" best for him may of course be what *is* best. And Rousseau may have done what was best when after his persecutions he retired for a while to the tranquility of that lake.[23] One might repose, protected from the intensity of the sun, in a state of almost complete forgetfulness. Yet this forgetfulness is never total, though all consciousness may fade except for what Rousseau himself calls pure "sentiment de l'existence," an unreflective awareness of mere Being undistracted by external things. Rousseau speaks of this rarified sense of Being as an experience analogous to the self-sufficiency of God.[24] "Almost complete" oblivion might thus be a moment when Rousseau realizes his own destiny as demigod—one like the Rhine who would "never forget" origin.

And Rousseau does not remain idle even in this repose, when reality appears virtually reduced to a green thought in a green shade. He reverts instead to a naive mode of consciousness and language, for it here seems "best" to him, "unconcernedly poor in musical notes like beginners, to learn from nightingales." In contemporaneous aesthetics the naive poet is one who, ideally uncorrupted by excessive reflection, sings of elemental "human nature" attuned to the nonhuman "natural" world.[25] This concept is altered somewhat by Hölderlin, who regards the naive tonality merely as one recurring moment in a poetic dialectic. The naive mode of poetry may follow and in turn be followed by more energetic or sophisticated modes, as in the case of Rousseau, who in the previous strophe had possessed a dangerous literary eloquence. The new form of composition corresponds to Rousseau's new mode of consciousness, with temporary abandonment of attention to All-Unity as a problem, and a release from the cares which (in "Heimkunft") must often plague the singer. The poetic resources of Rousseau's new, naive mode of speech may be "poor," but he is also "unconcerned" ("sorglos"). He might thus emulate the untroubled spontaneity of "nightingales."

We now see the continuity between the tenth and eleventh strophes. The lives of demigods move the poet, but he is astonished by the power of Rousseau's words and his capacious soul. Puzzlement at Rousseau's strangeness leads to a more generalized reflection. Rousseau is not alien to humanity but realizes mortal sonship to Earth in most exemplary fashion. Like Earth herself he takes on his soul the onus of "all," enduring as much as any man the burden of participating in divine All-Unity. Rousseau, viewed primarily as poet, thus actually accomplishes the poet's task of the "Feiertag" hymn: he endures the dangerous presence of Deity, which he mediates poetically to other men. However, while not yet destructive, divine presence exceeds even Rousseau's strength. He thus modulates into a simpler and safer mode of consciousness and language, not out of irresponsibility but from virtuous prudence before God. The situation he then seeks, a place of protective shade, is very like the poet's situation in the opening strophe. Rousseau's "strangeness" for Hölderlin is thus the uncanniness a poet must experience in another man who ultimately projects his own destiny. Paradoxically, Hölderlin views Rousseau, a writer of prose, as the man who most clearly anticipates the poetic fulfillment he himself desires.[26]

This attitude is clearly shown in the earlier ode "Rousseau," where Rousseau is figured as a "tree" like those of the "Feiertag" hymn.[27] The tree is about to bear "fruit," a consummate realization of all-unitive Life like the grape ("Frucht in Liebe geboren") of the other poem. Rousseau enjoys such expectations because he has lived to anticipate approaching gods and has hearkened to their voices:

> Vernommen hast du sie, verstanden die Sprache der Fremdlinge,
>> Gedeutet ihre Seele! Dem Sehnenden war
>>> Der Wink genug, und Winke sind
>>>> Von Alters her die Sprache der Götter.
> Und wunderbar, als hätte von Anbeginn
>> Des Menschen Geist das Werden und Wirken all,
>>> Des Lebens Weise schon erfahren,

Kennt er im ersten Zeichen Vollendetes schon.
 Und fliegt, der kühne Geist, wie Adler den
 Gewittern, weissagend seinen
  Kommenden Göttern voraus, [2:13]

 You have heard them, understood the speech of the strangers,
interpreted their souls! A sign was sufficient for the yearning man, and
signs have for ages hence been the language of the gods.
 And marvelously, as if from the beginning the man's mind had already
learned all process and action, the way of life, ...
 he already knows completion in the first sign, and flies, the bold spirit,
like eagles before the storms, prophetically in advance of his approaching gods.

In "Der Rhein" the arrival of these gods ("Fremdlinge") is seen as a
gentler epiphany, and Rousseau now appears to lead us to a festive
reunion with them.

In the twelfth strophe, then, he arises from his afternoon rest. His
slumber had been specifically a "holy sleep," probably trance-like Rous-
seauvian "reverie" of rarified awareness and pure "sentiment de l'existence." "Awakening" from this repose in the "coolness of the woods,"
he would then find it "splendid ... now in the evening to go towards
the milder light. . . ."[28] Paradoxically, the nearer the sun (of divine
presence) approaches the earth, the more safely it can be encountered;
God's presence is more threatening in pure transcendence than in any
refracted immanence on the level of earthly life. "The Day" thus benevolently "declines towards today's earth finding more good than
evil" there. In the first strophe the speaker had beheld "golden noonday" descending the "steps of the Alps" in full transcendent glory.
Now in the calm of evening, the Day assumes the function of "shaper"
("Bildner") and the earth is his satisfactory "pupil" ("Lehrlingin").
The Day, "who had built the mountains and designated the paths of
the streams" and had "also, smiling, directed the busy life of men ...
with his breezes," is now resting from his labors. No longer viewed as
harsh, Providential direction is now seen as a gentle breathing upon
the lives of mortals. Moreover, the divine principle is "declining" not
in anything like tragic *Götterdämmerung*, but freely and generously
disposed to confer the benefits of his visitation.

The thirteenth strophe (and the hymn's concluding section) thus
begins:

Dann feiern das Brautfest Menschen und Götter,
Es feiern die Lebenden all,
Und ausgeglichen
Ist eine Weile das Schiksaal.   [2:147]

Then men and gods celebrate their bridal feast, all the living celebrate, and destiny is settled for a while.

An earlier version of the previous strophe had clarified this transition, referring to Earth not merely as "Schülerin" but as "Braut," and terming Day not merely "Bildner" but "Pygmalion."[29] In its fullest scope, then, the "Bridal Feast" is between the Day-god and the Earth he has moulded and endowed with Life. The divine principle of all-unitive Life is reconciled with the particulars of earthly reality. When such reconciliation occurs, "all the living celebrate" in all-unitive joy. The bridal celebration will also involve all aspects of divinity and all finite, conscious beings—"humans and gods." And "destiny," the consequence of conscious separation from the divine source, will be "settled for a while," since mediated unity with Deity has always been the goal and motive force of destiny for all men.

The following lines tell how various types of men will respond to the advent of this Feast. Four categories are listed: "fugitives," the "brave," "lovers," and the "unreconciled." The fugitives who previously had found no place in an unsettled world and the brave who had struggled to maintain visions of justice are both now entitled to lodging or "sweet" rest, since a new peace has resolved the world's disorders. "The lovers, however, are what they were." Like the earlier Hölderlin and Diotima in "Menons Klagen," the lovers inhabit a private world of joyous harmony and divine presence, dwelling on blessed "islands" of light. Those who preserve such beatitude in themselves find nothing new or remarkable in the Bridal Feast, merely universalization of their own condition. The lovers are always "at home" in harmonious peace, and simply remain at home when peace and harmony become general.[30]

However, not all men have lived in such concord: many remain "unreconciled." These are now "transformed" and moved to face one another, hastening to extend hands in friendship while there is still time: "before the friendly light goes down and the night comes."[31] For, as indicated, this evening bridal of Earth and Sky is not a permanent state—human isolation is only resolved ("ausgeglichen") temporarily. The kindly light of universal friendship will then be followed by "night," a time of realized divine absence as in "Menons Klagen" and "Brot und Wein." The latter's historical myth may thus seem altered—here we are not dwelling in night and looking forward to a new day, but living in the afternoon of a civilization and anticipating the momentary glories of its consummation. Yet this does not revise Hölderlin's fundamental view of history. It simply reverses the day-night metaphor of the elegies, enabling the poet to view the same historical process from a different perspective. Hölderlin's consistency is not in images but in basic ideas, and he will occasionally reverse images to present these ideas from new points of view.[32]

The following strophe contemplates the transiency of the Bridal Feast and the meaning of the reconciliations. Though the Feast is a universal occurrence, it is not uniform; the preceding strophe told how various types of men would react to it. Now we learn that this all-unitive experience will not be of the same duration for everyone: "Yet for some this will pass over quickly; others will keep it longer." The following lines explain: "The eternal gods are full of Life at all times; but even a man can preserve the Best in his memory until death, and then he experiences the Highest. Only everyone has his measure. For it is difficult to bear misfortune, but [good] fortune [is] more difficult [to bear]." Unlike the gods, mortals (as stated in "Brot und Wein") can endure the fullness of divine Life only at times:[33]

Nicht immer vermag ein schwaches Gefäss sie zu fassen,
Nur zu Zeiten erträgt göttliche Fülle der Mensch.   [2:93]

Not always is a weak vessel able to hold them, only at times does man endure divine fullness.

While divine absence is painful, it is even more difficult to withstand the beatitude of divine presence. And everyone has his own "measure" ("Maas") of how much Life he can endure. Hölderlin here rephrases what was said in the elegy:

Fest bleibt Eins; es sei um Mittag oder es gehe
  Bis in die Mitternacht, immer bestehet ein Maas,
Allen gemein, doch jeglichem ist auch eignes beschieden,   [2:91]

> One thing remains certain: whether it be at midday or whether it goes
> into midnight, a measure always exists, common to all, yet
> everyone is also allotted his own.

But while "Brot und Wein" generally emphasizes mankind's universal measure, the present poem stresses the individual's particular capacity, just as it observes the diversity of guests at the feast and explains how an individual can possess his capacity at various hours of "day" or "night." One preserves a memory of the "Best," one's most intense personal experience of all-unitive divine Life. This memory is maintained until "death"—"And then he experiences the Highest." Here the Best is the remembered *summum bonum* and the Highest is the vital experiencing of it.[34] But these lines need not literally mean that the ultimate is always experienced at actual, physical death. Rather, the wording ("bis *in* den Tod") suggests that one always projects the ultimate experience of divine Life into (or beyond) death itself. The futurity of this individual anticipation is precisely analogous to the universal expectation of the Bridal Feast: the glorious end of historical day corresponds to the glory awaited at the end of individual life.

Each individual thus can "maintain" ("behalten") his personal experience of the universal Feast and anticipate a final, personal consummation of this experience (the Highest) in death. Ideally, the capacity for this difficult joy might be preserved through the entire night of privation that follows the Feast for most:

> Ein Weiser aber vermocht es
> Vom Mittag bis in die Mitternacht,
> Und bis der Morgen erglänzte,
> Beim Gastmahl helle zu bleiben.   [2:148]

But a wise man was able, from noon to midnight and until the morning gleamed, to remain clearheaded at the banquet.

As noted in the lines from "Brot und Wein," a man's "measure" may subsist from "midday all the way to midnight." Here, the "wise man" is Socrates, who in the *Symposium* ("*Gastmahl*") remains bright and lucid all night while other guests have fallen into drunken somnolence.[35] He perseveres in his private experience of the Best, discoursing on cosmic Love, throughout a night of general forgetfulness "until the morning gleams," itself typifying a new historical day of abiding, universal divine presence.

The hymn's final strophe turns from Socrates to a contemporary, Hölderlin's friend Issak von Sinclair. As a political revolutionist, Sinclair could be numbered among the "brave" ("die Tapfern") who dedicate their lives to the harmonious justice the "Brautfest" will achieve, and are therefore rewarded with "sweet slumber." However, in this present time of waiting the hero's situation is comparable to the poet's. Like the poet in the first strophe (and like Rousseau) Sinclair here keeps to the shade. Yet he is also prepared for action, whether on a "hot" path beneath alpine pines, where divine fire is indirect but intensely felt, or in the "darkness" of a German oak forest. In either situation God may appear to him "wrapped in steel," armored like the medieval Lord of Crusaders, the God of heroes. Or, because Sinclair is a visionary, his God might appear in "clouds" as a private vision of transcendence. Either mode of divine apparition would be appropriate for Sinclair: he "knows" God because he "youthfully knows the power of the Good." It is God's power ("Kraft")which, in youthful ardor, he most acknowledges; like the Rhine and the unnamed heroes earlier, Sinclair is implicitly a demigod, a true son of the divine Father, and as revolutionist he seeks to implement the Father's will on earth. He is always able to perceive the approving smile of the "Ruler" and respond to his wishes. His perception of Deity remains clear at all times: "by day, when the Living appears feverish and chained-up, or also by night when everything is mixed without order and age-old confusion returns." The "Living" is all-unitive Life, which is not now generally manifest to men as divine all-presence. Day is here a disquieting time of inauthenticity and arbitrary structures that repress divine vitality in the world. The amorphous divine substance may alternatively appear as a nocturnal chaos, "age-old confusion" of Old Night antedating divine imposition of order. Regardless of whether Sinclair perceives the world as chaos or as feverish repression, he can always recognize and serve the God who rules time.

Although the entire poem is dedicated to Sinclair, this concluding strophe might appear to be an afterthought.[36] Yet, it succeeds in resuming the poem's dominant topic of heroic destiny and provides an actual, contemporary example of heroism. As the alpine setting here is reminiscent of the poem's beginning, it might be thought that Sinclair's destiny could possibly be similar to the Rhine's. More important, Hölderlin's own remarks (in the note) seem to insist that this strophe be considered an essential part of the concluding triad. The last triad is said to "settle everything with a pervasive metaphor." The "metaphor" is presumably the figure of the Bridal Feast. How then, does it "settle" things?

In the poem, of course, the Feast is said to "settle destiny" for a "while": "Und ausgeglichen / Ist eine Weile das Schiksaal." The same word (ausgleichen) is used in the note. The festive reunion of men and gods momentarily resolves the mortal "destiny" impelled by their separation; this destiny is "balanced out" by a temporary equalizing of relationships. However, Hölderlin's wording suggests another form of settlement within the poem itself, an overcoming of tensions between "form" and "matter." We recall that the first pair of triads were "like in matter but opposed in form," while the second pair were "opposed in matter but like in form." We have already analyzed in some detail the significance of this statement for the first twelve strophes. But there remains the question of how the "metaphor" settles all this.

Böschenstein observes that for this poem, Hölderlin probably uses the term "Metapher" to mean the fundamental idea realized in the work, the intellectual import ("Gehalt") or "unifying component" that gives the work coherence.[37] Aside from the previously noted alternation of tones, the "formal" aspect of the first twelve strophes can also be conceived of as the dialectic of the mediacy or immediacy of divine presence. Thus, the first two parts are opposed in form because the first triad begins with mediacy, approaches immediacy, and then reflects upon the conflict of this approach, while the second triad reverses the process. Similarly, parts three and four are alike in form because each triad begins with a consideration of an enticement to immediacy, reflects on this, and then ends with a celebration of mediated existence. The various "matters" of the first twelve strophes can, accordingly, be conceived as exemplary destinies: the river in the first two parts, the opposed instances of the "defiant" enthusiasts and the Rhine in the third part, and the harmonious instance of Rousseau in the fourth. These destinies vacillate between approach to immediacy

and contentment with the mediate; even in the case of the defiant enthusiasts such contentment is suggested as a lost condition or as an
alternative, such as the Rhine's. Each "matter" may thus embody the
mediacy-immediacy dialectic which is also presented formally in diverse sequences.

But the Bridal Feast "settles everything" as a pervasive metaphor
harmonizing matter and form. The material and formal components
of the closing triad are fused and subsumed in the "content" or meaning, the final poetic statement. The Bridal Feast is the appropriate
figure of this statement. Unlike the static states of strophes six and
nine, the image of mediation presented in the thirteenth strophe is of
a dynamic process. The reflections in strophe fourteen are not mere
generalizations (as in earlier "ideal" strophes) but specifications, de-
tailing how the process of mediation will work. Finally, the "heroism"
of the concluding strophe is not as "defiant" as that of the Rhine or
the enthusiasts or as dangerous as that of Rousseau in his momentary
approach to immediacy. Rather, Sinclair in his responsive obedience
keeps a proper relationship to (and distance from) the God he serves.
Thus, in these strophes, the usual formal dialectic of mediacy-reflection-
immediacy is kept within bounds, held to the dialectical process of the
Bridal Feast itself rather than permitted to range between extremes.

The matter of the concluding triad is likewise presented differently
than in the previous sections. The earlier parts depict destinies vacil-
lating between euphoric mediation and dangerous nearness to the immediate. The present section, however, presents not destinies but
figurae—archetypal instances of modes of coping with the process of
mediation. Thus, the thirteenth strophe presents a number of types,
not in their entire lives but in the single, crucial moment of reconciliation. The fourteenth depicts one ideal example of festive endurance,
Socrates, and the fifteenth presents Sinclair, not yet involved in the
Feast but anticipating it through his own appropriate relationship with
Deity. Thus the matter (like the form) of this concluding triad is at
once more differentiated and more homogeneous. Matter and form are,
as Hölderlin indicates, equalized or settled in the mediating process
represented by the "metaphor" of the Feast—just as on the plane of
historical myth, the Bridal Feast is said to "settle" momentarily the
"destiny" of all men. The poem thus aspires to be a formal model for

resolving that dialectic of mediacy and near-immediacy experienced by all seeking a viable mode of relating themselves to divine All-Unity.

"Der Rhein," like other major hymns, clearly anticipates a future moment when men will be reconciled with Deity. However, unlike two other principal hymns, "Friedensfeier" and "Patmos," this poem foresees a transient rather than ultimate reconciliation. Also, "Der Rhein" is not at first obviously engaged in the project specified in the "Feiertag" hymn—the search for an appropriate poetic name for divine All-Unity—although this concern is not wholly absent. Thus, the Rousseau who walks toward the Bridal Feast is primarily Rousseau the seer and "poet" who has just relearned the art of poetry. The specific form of the Bridal Feast (although perhaps as inevitable as sunset) seems to be virtually a result of Rousseau's mediation. Poetry must serve as the instrumental cause of the Feast's occurrence, since the very possibility of the Feast must be proclaimed if it is ever to be real. Finally, "Der Rhein" itself might stand as a model of reconciliation among conflicting attitudes toward All-Unity, anticipating the Bridal Feast both in message and in poetic form.

11. "Friedensfeier"

Unlike "Der Rhein," but like "Wie wenn am Feiertage" and "Patmos," "Friedensfeier" is directly concerned with the project of suitable articulation of All-Unity; more is said on the topic here than in any other poem. "Friedensfeier" is also the most optimistic of Hölderlin's great hymns, for it views divine return as imminent. The celebration which is the objective correlative of all-unitive comprehension is about to begin; the poet awaits only the unitive principle himself, the "Prince" of the Feast. In the second strophe, he seems to "see" this personage already. The goal of Hölderlin's entire poetic project appears almost within sight.[1] While it is possible to understand "Friedensfeier" as an occasional poem written to commemorate the 1802 Peace of Lunéville, Hölderlin's poem is much greater in scope than its occasion would seem to justify, situating the event in the contexts of poetry, history and even eschatology. Hölderlin sees the new peace as instigating a millennium of manifest divine presence and perfect harmony among men, the beatitude foretold in "Brot und Wein" where life becomes a dream of the gods: "Traum von ihnen ist drauf das Leben" ("Thereupon life is a dream about them") (2:93).

After an introductory preface to the public,[2] the first strophe begins by setting the scene for an anticipated Feast:

Der himmlischen, still widerklingenden,
Der ruhigwandelnden Töne voll,
Und gelüftet ist der altegebaute,
Seliggewohnte Saal; um grüne Teppiche duftet
Die Freudenwolk' und weithinglänzend stehn,
Gereiftester Früchte voll und goldbekränzter Kelche,
Wohlangeordnet, eine prächtige Reihe,
Zur Seite da und dort aufsteigend über dem
Geebneten Boden die Tische.
Denn ferne kommend haben
Hieher, zur Abendstunde,
Sich liebende Gäste beschieden.   [3:533]

Full of heavenly, quietly resonating, calmly wandering tones, and aired is the anciently built, blissfully accustomed hall; the cloud of joy is fragrant about green carpets, and there stand glistening afar, full of ripest fruits and chalices wreathed in gold, well-arranged, a splendid order, rising on the side here and there above the levelled ground, the tables. For hither, coming from afar, at the hour of evening, loving guests have arrived.

The opening strophe of the poem may apparently be descriptive either of a feast hall or of a landscape.[3] As the wording is somewhat ambiguous, it may help to examine its syntactical structure. The grammatical subjects of the three clauses in the first sentence are "Saal," "Freudenwolk" and "Tische." The first image is of a festive room, although the second subject indicates that this image might not be taken literally. The first real indication that this is no ordinary hall comes in the second clause: a "cloud of joy" hovers fragrantly about "green carpets." A landscape is suggested, with vapors floating above green fields. The music can be understood as the sounds of nature after a rain. The next clause, however, again presents the image of a hall: the tables, a "splendid order," are standing well arranged. Yet these are also said to be "gleaming afar" and "rising on the side here and there above the leveled ground," which suggests that the "tables" might be mountains rising above the green field-carpets of the preceding clause.[4]

The concluding lines of the strophe offer an explanation ("denn") both for the hall's arrangement and for its recognition. It is precisely because "loving guests," various forms of deity, are about to assemble here from "afar" at the "evening hour" of our civilization, that we are now permitted to see an old, accustomed landscape as the festive hall it was always meant to be. The storms of history are now past, and the landscape-hall appears for the first time in its fullness of beauty and significance for us. Its function is akin to that of the Greek landscape in "Brot und Wein," "designed solely" for festivities.

Now that the guests have begun to arrive, the poet in the second strophe thinks he "already" can see the "Prince of the Feast":

Und dämmernden Auges denk' ich schon,
Vom ernsten Tagwerk lächelnd,
Ihn selbst zu sehn, den Fürsten des Fests.   [3:533]

And with dim eyes already I think, smiling from his earnest day's labor, to see him himself, the prince of the feast.

The identity of the Prince has been the principal focus for the poem's controversy, and much critical difficulty has come from a tendency to posit the actuality of a mythical or historical person existing beyond and prior to the poem.[5] We might do better to inquire about the identity of this figure as constituted wholly by the words of the poem itself.

The Prince is first seen indistinctly by the speaker, ambiguously "smiling from the serious day's work" now completed. The "day" is the era of Western civilization now coming to its close, as in "Der Rhein." The Prince of its concluding feast has had a major part in its "work" as indicated in the following lines:

Doch wenn du schon dein Ausland gern verläugnest,
Und als vom langen Heldenzüge müd,
Dein Auge senkst, vergessen, leichtbeschattet,
Und Freundesgestalt annimst, du Allbekannter, doch

Beugt fast die Knie das Hohe. Nichts vor dir,
Nur Eines weiss ich, Sterbliches bist du nicht.
Ein Weiser mag mir manches erhellen; wo aber
Ein Gott noch auch erscheint,
Das ist doch andere Klarheit.   [3:533]

Yet even if you like to disown your foreign land, and as if tired from the
long heroic march, you let your eyes drop, oblivious, lightly shaded,
and take on the form of a friend, you who are known to all, yet
such majesty almost forces the knee to bend. I know nothing before
you, I know only one thing, that you are not mortal. A wise man might
illuminate much for me; but where a god also appears there is yet
another kind of clarity.

The Prince would willingly deny his "foreign land," his status as a
stranger among men.[6] He now assumes the form of a "friend" to us, in
modesty and fatigue as if "tired" from long heroic exploits, and casts
his eyes down forgetfully, "lightly shaded." Despite his modest de-
meanor, the Prince is hailed as one "known to all" whose exaltation
almost in itself causes knees to bend before him. Yet, the speaker is
still uncertain about this Prince whose nature remains unspecified; he
only knows that the Prince cannot be mortal. This he discerns from
the Prince's effects on him: although a mere man of wisdom might
"illuminate much," when a deity appears there is yet another kind of
"clarity." The divinity of the Prince is thus shown in the clarity he
creates. As in Hölderlin's earlier poetry, any experience of comprehensive lucidity can only be in a moment of divine vision.[7] (Such is the
illumination anticipated in the Tübingen hymns, proclaimed in the
poem of love for Diotima, and tenuously achieved in a private audience
with God in "Heimkunft.") Now this luminosity is about to be universally established through the mediation of a deific Prince at the all-
unitive feast.[8]

Yet the identity of the Prince is still indeterminate. In the third
strophe, the poet can only recount the Prince's rôle in heroic activities:

Von heute aber nicht, nicht unverkündet ist er;
Und einer, der nicht Fluth noch Flamme gescheuet,
Erstaunet, da es stille worden, umsonst nicht, jezt,
Da Herrschaft nirgend ist zu sehn bei Geistern und Menschen.
Das ist, sie hören das Werk,

Längst vorbereitend, von Morgen nach Abend, jezt erst,
Denn unermesslich brausst, in der Tiefe verhallend,
Des Donnerers Echo, das tausendjährige Wetter,
Zu schlafen, übertönt von Friedensläuten, hinunter.   [3:534]

But not of today, not unproclaimed is he; and one who did not shy from
flood nor flame astonishes now that it has become quiet, not in vain,
for sovereign authority is not to be seen anywhere among spirits and men.
That is, they hear the work long being prepared from morning to
evening now for the first time, for immeasurably rages, down into sleep,
fading away in the depths, the echo of the Thunderer, the thousand-
year storm, drowned out by the sounds of peace.

The Prince is not merely "of today," nor is he "unproclaimed." He has
participated in extensive warlike action, avoiding neither "flood nor
flame."[9] He "astonishes" us now perhaps because his previous belliger-
ent activity is ended and he appears paradoxically as the Prince of a
peace celebration. The peace itself may also amaze us because it has
brought about a complete abolition of authority in heaven and on
earth. The various deities can now approach us as equals, and the once
dominating Prince will himself come to us quietly as a friend.

The "day's work" of the second strophe is the total action and accomplishment of the historical day of our civilization. This makes explicit the temporal analogy implied in the twelfth and thirteenth
strophes of "Der Rhein." Here, however, the day of civilization is an
era of protracted storm, "das tausendjährige Wetter." And this figure
of the historical storm (developed in *Empedokles* and the "Feiertag"
hymn) is fully elucidated here. The storm is the medium of civilization's "work" and the form of its long progress "from morning to evening." The work is now "heard" for the first time, just as the sound of
the storm itself, "immeasurably" raging, reverberating into the depths,
is laid to sleep, finally superseded by "sounds of peace." The harmonies
of peace are thus implicitly equated with the sounds of the storm's
achievement; peace itself is the ultimate work or product of the war-
ring storm. The storm was the theater of the Prince's heroic actions
and the "flood" and "flame" of the earlier strophe are the storm's
torrents and lightnings. The storm is called the "echo of the Thunderer," Zeus as Father God and Lord of Time: it is the reverberation
of divine will and is finished only when this will has been consum-

mated. The Prince, as the protagonist or genius of the storm, is thereby identified as the executor of divine will.

After this explanatory digression, the third strophe concludes in a mood of joyous expectancy. The poet urges "days of innocence," moments of innocuous openness to divine presence like those of children and lovers, to contribute their joys to the feast. The "Spirit" of joy is also to be present, "blossoming" with naive exuberance in the evening quietness. The poet exhorts his "friends" (presumably fellow-poets), even if their locks are "silver-gray," to disport themselves like joyous "eternal youths," attendant priests at the celebration. The mood at the end of this strophe thus corresponds to that of the first, for the hymn's first triadic unit is clearly devoted to ardent anticipation of the Feast.[10]

But though all men and gods are implicitly called to the Feast, the speaker in the fourth strophe explicitly invites one individual as guest of honor. It is the major crux of the poem whether this guest, here clearly recognizable as Christ, is to be considered identical with the Prince.[11] Before confronting this problem, however, we should first look at the details of this triad, devoted to Christ and his historical function.

The fourth strophe's first sentence is blurred in syntax:

Und manchen möcht' ich laden, aber o du,
Der freundlichernst den Menschen zugethan,
Dort unter syrischer Palme,
Wo nahe lag die Stadt, am Brunnen gerne war ...   [3:534]

And many I would invite, but O you, who, in friendly seriousness inclined towards men, there under Syrian palms, where the town lay nearby, liked to be by the well ...

While the poet would like to invite "many" to the Feast, he singles out the special guest addressed simply as "du." But the narration begun in the following lines breaks the syntactical pattern, as the original intent of the sentence is apparently abandoned; the poet does not here specify why the "du" has been called or what function he will serve at the Feast. The hymn's controlling image is itself ignored until the ninth strophe, when the reasons for the invitation are made clear. In the above lines, the reference to the "well" is generally thought to refer to Christ's encounter with the Samaritan woman, an instance of his combined "friendliness" and "seriousness."[12] This episode occurs in a place of shady coolness and repose:

> Das Kornfeld rauschte rings, still athmete die Kühlung
> Von Schatten des geweiheten Gebirges ...   [3:534]

> The cornfield soughed round about, the coolness breathed quietly from
> the shadow of the sacred mountains ...

The motif of cool shadowing is continued figuratively in the following lines:

> Und die lieben Freunde, das treue Gewölk,
> Umschatteten dich auch, damit der heiligkühne
> Durch Wildniss mild dein Stral zu Menschen kam, o Jüngling!
> Ach! aber dunkler umschattete, mitten im Wort, dich
> Furchtbarentscheidend ein tödtlich Verhängniss. So ist schnell
> Vergänglich alles Himmlische; aber umsonst nicht;   [3:534]

> and the dear friends, the loyal cloud, also shaded you about, so that the
> holy-daring, your beam, came mildly through wilderness to men, O
> youth! Ah, but more darkly, in the midst of speech, fearfully decisive, a
> deadly fate enveloped you in its shade. Thus everything Heavenly
> is quickly fleeting, but not in vain;

The "dear friends," Christ's disciples, constituted a "faithful cloud": Christ's message and divine personality could not reach others directly, but only through the interpretation of his disciples, their Gospel accounts and preaching. Their mediation served as clouds or overgrowth in diffusing the original intensity of Christ's words and presence, making the light milder and (though weaker and somewhat compromised) more tolerable. It is clear Hölderlin does not completely regret this providential moderation of Christ's "holy daring": even as Christ was shaded from the sun, so have his later followers been shaded from the primal intensity of his light. And yet shading can be of a different sort. For the fatal doom of Christ's own death more darkly overshadowed him in the midst of speech before he had fully articulated his divine vision. His doom thus "fearfully" decided not only his own life, but the entire course of the religion and civilization he founded. This overshadowing constitutes a total darkness of opacity and silence, the opposite extreme from the similarly fatal glare of unmediated light—the death of God is no better for man than the destructive immediacy of total presence. And yet (the strophe concludes) even though "heavenly" presence here is "quickly fleeting," it is not "in vain."

The fifth strophe shows the actual benefits accruing from transiency of divine visitation:

> Denn schonend rührt des Masses allzeit kundig
> Nur einen Augenblick die Wohnungen der Menschen
> Ein Gott an, unversehn, und keiner weiss es, wenn?
> Auch darf alsdann das Freche drüber gehn,
> Und kommen muss zum heiligen Ort das Wilde
> Von Enden fern, übt rauhbetastend den Wahn,
> Und trifft daran ein Schiksaal, aber Dank,
> Nie folgt der gleich hernach dem gottgegebnen Geschenke;
>
> [3:534–535]

> for sparingly, at all times conscious of the measure, only for a moment a
> god touches the dwellings of men, unforeseen, and no one knows
> when. Thereupon also the insolent may pass over it, and the savage must
> come to the holy place from ends far away, and, crudely touching,
> exercise his delusion, and thereby encounter a destiny, but gratitude,
> never does it follow immediately after the god-given gift;

A god of course knows what measure of divine intensity a man can bear and, unlike man himself, is aware of the best (safest) moment for epiphany. But once a place has been visited by Deity, it must be encountered by the "insolent" and the "savage." The "insolent" are perhaps self-willed men lacking any openness to divine presence (thus ignoring the holy place) while the "savage" are the spiritually barbarous, obtuse yet capable of some crude response. The former may be those wholly unconcerned with the particulars of Christ's visit, while the latter may include the typical historical Christians whose muddled piety darkened and blurred Christ's original presence.[13]

The following statement is more general: "but gratitude, never did it follow immediately after the god-given gift; it [the gift] is to be grasped only by profound testing." The "gift" is exemplified here by Christ's brief stay on earth as a "moment" of divine visitation. Such a benefice may be ignored or crudely misinterpreted, but it never meets at once with appropriate thanks. Gratitude is the only fitting response to divine epiphany (as in "Heimkunft"), yet the response cannot occur until the gift itself is comprehended or "grasped" by man. And such comprehension can occur only after extensive "testing" of the gift through deep reflection on our imperfect and confused experience of it—here, our two thousand years of puzzlement at Christ and his words.[14] Throughout this time, man's gratitude for Christ's visit has been deficient. And yet, Hölderlin concludes, this lethargy of reaction has been beneficial:

> Auch wär' uns, sparte der Gebende nicht,
> Schon längst von Seegen des Herds
> Uns Gipfel und Boden entzündet.   [3:535]

> Also, if the giver were not sparing, our rooftops and floors would have been set afire by the blessing of the hearth long ago.

This blessing is the sacred fire bequeathed as a divinely given gift at the god's momentary visit to the "dwellings of men." As hearth-fire it is the source of warmth and light, vivifying our lives. Yet if this presence becomes too intense it will rapidly destroy the structure of life itself. Hence the god is "sparing" in his visitation of men. The context suggests that providence uses our own incomprehension as a further means of sparing us; if we had earlier realized the full intensity of Christ's divine presence and words, this realization in its unchecked ardor would have destroyed the entire structure of Christian civilization. The stupidity of Christendom has been providential.

The sixth strophe then recounts the *mediated* forms of divine presence granted us. We "received much of the divine" in the sensory forms of natural elements. "Flame" (actual fire) is "given into our hands," as are "shore and ocean floods," the elements of earth and water. For Hölderlin, all of these powers are deific (as is the fourth element of air or Aether beyond our hands' reach) and "alien" to us in their divine efficacy, acknowledged in the "Feiertag" hymn as "Die Allebendigen, die Kräfte der Götter" ("the all-living ones, the powers of the gods"). Yet, paradoxically, they are intimate with us "in more than human fashion," and our familiarity with them helps us to maintain rapport with the Infinite. The element of heavenly fire performs a somewhat different function:

Und es lehret Gestirn dich, das
Vor Augen dir ist, doch nimmer kannst du ihm gleichen.   [3:535]

And you are taught by the constellation that is before your eyes, but never
can you resemble it.

The primary lesson the constellation "teaches" is that we can never
"resemble" it. The eternal stars are immutable and transcendent, and
serve to admonish man of his own transiency and finitude. Thus while
the earthly elements facilitate a mediated rapport with divine Life, the
constellations impress us with our limitations.

However, the concluding lines of the strophe indicate that the now
transcendent Deity may soon become more accessible to us:

Vom Allebendigen aber, von dem
Viel Freuden sind und Gesänge,
Ist einer ein Sohn, ein Ruhigmächtiger ist er,
Und nun erkennen wir ihn,
Nun, da wir kennen den Vater,
Und Feiertage zu halten
Der hohe, der Geist
Der Welt sich zu Menschen geneigt hat.   [3:535]

But of the All-Living, from whom there are many joys and songs, one is a
Son, a calmly powerful one is he, and now we recognize him, now that
we know the Father, and to hold holidays the high one, the Spirit
of the world, has inclined to men.

These lines might seem to allude to the three persons of the Trinity:
"Vater," "Sohn," and "Geist." Yet the latter is not "der Heilige Geist"
but "der Geist der Welt," the World-Spirit of secular idealism; Hölderlin's consistently idiosyncratic use of Christian *topoi* and ideas should
make us wary of interpreting such references in orthodox terms. The
"Father" is not the traditional Christian God but specifically the All-
Living or All-Vivifying ("Allebendigen"), the divine principle of All-
Unity. Since the presence of Deity is perceived optimally in inspirational joy, he is the source "from whom there are many joys and songs."
While the Father may have a number of sons, only one is mentioned
here, a "calmly powerful" one, presumably Christ.[15] And we "now"
can "recognize" this son, since the shadings and distortions of Christian tradition are finally abolished in the second strophe's all-renewing

"clarity." For we now "know the Father" himself clearly as the "All-Living" rather than as the customary authority figure of orthodoxy. Accordingly, the relationship between Father and son is clarified. And the son is fully recognized when "to celebrate holidays the High One, the Spirit of the World, has inclined to men." In the twelfth strophe of "Der Rhein" the same verb (sich neigen) is used to describe the Day's visitation to the earth: "Zur heutigen Erde der Tag sich neiget" ("to today's earth the Day inclines.") Both passages refer to divine visits after the formative activity of history has been completed. The "Spirit of the World" is thus the world's vivifying, structuring divine force, not a "person" distinct from the Father but that dimension of the all-living God active within the historical world.[16]

The seventh strophe (and the subsequent development of the triad) elaborates upon the process and result of the Spirit's operations:

Denn längst war der zum Herrn der Zeit zu gross
Und weit aus reichte sein Feld, wann hats ihn aber erschöpfet?
Einmal mag aber ein Gott auch Tagewerk erwählen,
Gleich Sterblichen und theilen alles Schiksaal.   [3:535]

For long was he too great to be Lord of Time and his field extended afar, but when has it ever exhausted him? But for once a god may also choose a day's work, like mortals, and share all destiny.

God's transcendence has itself prevented God from functioning optimally as the impelling Spirit of time. The "field" of historical operations has always been vast, yet too much of his divine Being has remained unengaged in the process. Thus until now the divine Spirit has seemed too great ever to take part exhaustively in the workings of history. But now that God is manifesting himself more fully in immanence, he appears more involved in human affairs. This is the moment that initiates the poem's festivities. Divine condescension is here effected not through Christ but through the Spirit, and involves not a literal incarnation but an immersion in history, a "sharing" in the totality of human affairs. The image implies God's manlike willingness to do a day's work in the field. Yet this field is explicitly that of historical "time," and God descends in order to take charge of it as "lord." The Deity simply foregoes radical transcendence to achieve a more immanent involvement in destiny.

The ultimate intent of destiny is announced next:

Schiksaalgesez ist diss, dass Alle sich erfahren,
Dass, wenn die Stille kehrt, auch eine Sprach sei.   [3:535]

The law of destiny is this, that all must get to know one another, so that,
when the silence returns, there may also be a language.

This edict is clarified by the next strophe's assertion that throughout
history "we have been a conversation and have heard from one another,
but soon we will be song" ("Seit ein Gespräch wir sind und hören
voneinander, / . . . bald sind wir aber Gesang") (3:536). We are
finite beings whose determining characteristic is our ability to com-
municate, and our essential history is the history of our participation
in a centuries-long "conversation." The law of destiny decrees that
through conversation we should achieve total knowledge of ourselves.
When we have learned all there is to know about the totality of our
possibilities as men, and have caught up with whatever has been said
about these possibilities, then finally there will be no further need for
talk. The "silence" that preceded all debates of historical consciousness
will "return." This will not be a mere communicative vacuum, but the
harmonious expression of the unified, total awareness that is the goal
of our conversational self-discovery.[17] We shall *be* song as we *were*
conversation. Then we shall realize our being as clear participants in
All-Unity, and the joyous harmony which is the cohesive essence of
All-Unity will pervade our communal being.

The conclusion of the seventh strophe details how this (yet unspecified) harmonious "silence" is to be achieved:

Wo aber wirkt der Geist, sind wir auch mit, und streiten,
Was wohl das Beste sei. So dünkt mir jezt das Beste,
Wenn nun vollendet sein Bild und fertig ist der Meister,
Und selbst verklärt davon aus seiner Werkstatt tritt,
Der stille Gott der Zeit und nur der Liebe Gesez,
Das schönausgleichende gilt von hier an bis zum Himmel.

[3:535–536]

But where the Spirit is active we are also along, and dispute what indeed
the best might be. So to me the best seems now, now when his image
is completed and the master is finished, and himself transfigured by it

steps out of his workplace, the quiet god of time, and only the law
of love, the beautifully settling, holds good from here on up to
heaven.

The Spirit has now become totally involved in historical process. Yet
his work engages us as participants; we are also involved and "dispute"
just what the "Best" might be. Our conversational existence is the
medium of this dispute, through which we meet one another and constitute our communal being in discourse. The controlling topic of the
epochal debate is the determination of the Best. This view is indeed
historically accurate, for the abstract problem of the *summum bonum*
has been a central question of philosophical discourse since Plato. As
the ultimate point of men's contention, it has occasioned a continuous
dialogue wherein each man could know himself and others. The Spirit
itself has been the ultimate impelling force in our struggle for truth.

Now, however, this dialogue is about to cease as the moment of absolute clarity approaches. The poet may thus hail the moment itself as
the much-disputed Best: not as an Idea but as an historical event. The
Best is, finally, its own epiphany. Looking again to the following
strophe for explanation, we learn that the "image" is a "Time-Image"
("Zeitbild"). The divine Spirit of the World, now effectively "Lord
of Time," is revealed as an artist who has fashioned the entire temporal process into one unified, simultaneous image: the product is a
perfect depiction of the process that brought it into being. We are
able to achieve a unified total perception of historical process only
when its picture is complete; the process culminates precisely in its own
illumination. The true goal of history is thus our absolute comprehension of it. Here, of course, Hölderlin is fairly close to his former school-
mate Hegel, for Hegel's mysterious Absolute may be nothing other
than the mind which has achieved total self-comprehension through
comprehensive awareness of its own development, as detailed in the
Phänomenologie des Geistes.[18] And, as with Hegel, the realization of
unified totality will constitute an era of peace, for historical dialectic
will then be completed. The "law of destiny" ("Schiksaalgesez")
which regulates dialectical interaction is superseded by the "law of
love" ("der Liebe Gesez"). As in "Der Rhein," human "destiny" with
its opposition and suffering is "settled."[19] Here, however, the settle-

ment seems not transient but definitive, and valid for the entire cosmos: it prevails "from here on up to Heaven," and men are harmoniously united with supernal gods.

The eighth strophe (necessarily anticipated in explicating the seventh) clarifies the harmony thus achieved:

Viel hat von Morgen an,
Seit ein Gespräch wir sind und hören voneinander,
Erfahren der Mensch; bald sind [wir] aber Gesang.
Und das Zeitbild, das der grosse Geist entfaltet,
Ein Zeichen liegts vor uns, [das] [dass] zwischen ihm und andern
Ein Bündniss zwischen ihm und andern Mächten ist.[20]   [3:536]

Much, from morning on, since we have been a conversation and hear from one another, has man learned; but soon we are song. And the Time-Image which the great Spirit unfolds, it lies before us as a sign which between him and others is a pact between him and other powers.

We have been a "conversation" and have heard from one another since the dawn of our present civilization. Soon, however, harmony will replace contentious discourse.[21] The "others" here are numinous forces such as the powers of Nature in the sixth strophe.[22] The image of human time necessarily depicts the deific presences of the natural world, because man has always appraised and shaped them in the terms of his own progressive consciousness. The Time-Image evolved by the impetus of divine Spirit within history is therefore a "sign" established between the God of history and other interacting divine forces; as such, it functions as a "pact" ("Bündniss") establishing this unitive alliance. The sign is both a token of harmonious relationships and their actual confirmation, making them explicit:

Nicht er allein, die Unerzeugten, Ew'gen,
Sind kennbar alle daran, gleichwie auch an den Pflanzen
Die Mutter Erde sich und Licht und Luft sich kennet.   [3:536]

Not he alone, the Unbegotten, Eternal are all knowable in this, just as in the plants the Mother Earth and Light and Air are known.

All primal (uncreated), eternal divine powers can be recognized as constituents of the Time-Image just as the traditional elements of earth, light and air are all recognizable in plants. This analogy is appropriate in its complexity. Elements are knowable in plants not only as components but as metaphorical attributes. Similarly, divine forces have not only assisted in the composition of the image, but are recognizable in the image itself. The total image of history must incorporate all divinities ever acknowledged or worshipped by man, for his varied responses to these deities have helped to determine the composition of the final picture.

Yet, the Time-Image is not itself the definitive figure for the imminent all-unitive harmony—its controlling image is still the Feast:

Zulezt ist aber doch, ihr heiligen Mächte, für euch
Das Liebeszeichen, das Zeugniss,
Dass ihrs noch seiet, der Festtag,
Der Allversammelnde, wo Himmlische nicht
Im Wunder offenbar, noch ungesehn im Wetter,
Wo aber bei Gesang gastfreundlich untereinander
In Chören gegenwärtig, eine heilige Zahl
Die Seeligen in jeglicher Weise
Beisammen sind, und ihr Geliebtestes auch,
An dem sie hängen, nicht fehlt;   [3:536]

But yet at last, you holy powers, there is for you the sign of love, the
witness that it is still you, the feast day, the all-gathering, where Heavenly
ones are not manifest in miracles, nor unseen in the storm, but where
hospitably with one another in song, present in choruses, a holy
number, the blessed ones are together in every way, and their most
beloved too, to whom they cling, is not missing;

The Feast must finally take precedence over other metaphors of harmony; it is the "sign of love" ("Liebeszeichen") that constitutes in itself the love it signifies, unlike the Time-Image which (though more lucid) is merely the sign of a formal pact.[23] The Feast Day reassures the gods that they are still individuated, appreciated and dear to us, for this day will "assemble" all gods with men. The "heavenly ones" will not merely be "manifest in miracle," as in Biblical times, or "unseen in the storm" as in the centuries of Christian tumult, but will instead be "hospitably" responsive to one another. The interrelationships of the gods will be made wholly clear in this moment of all-unitive vision.

Their guest of honor is Christ. Because he is most beloved, he has been summoned in glory to the banquet:

> denn darum rief ich
> Zum Gastmahl, das bereitet ist,
> Dich, Unvergesslicher, dich, zum Abend der Zeit,
> O Jüngling, dich zum Fürsten des Festes;   [3:536]

... for therefore did I call, to the banquet that is prepared, you, unforgettable one, you, at the evening of time, O youth, you to the Prince of the feast;

The use of the past tense ("rief") reminds us that Christ was tentatively called by the poet at the beginning of the fourth strophe, but the evocation was interrupted by the long digression just concluded here. Pieced together with all parenthetical matter removed, the call would read: "Und manchen möcht' ich laden, aber o du . . . dich rief ich zum Gastmahl. . . ."[24] He would "like to invite many," but he especially "called" Christ to the banquet. Christ is hailed three times here in this magniloquent invitation.

And here again is a major crux of interpretation. The problem is authentically crucial, since the meaning of the entire poem is contingent on one's interpretation of these lines. Most simply stated, the syntactical difficulty lies in the ambiguity of the verb phrase. Thus, the clause "rief ich . . . dich zum Fürsten des Festes" can have two possible meanings. It can mean "I called you *to* the Prince of the Feast" as one person is called upon simply to meet another person. Or, it can mean "I called you to *be* the Prince of the Feast." In the first case, the youth and the Prince are two distinct persons. In the second, they are the same person.[25]

As regards circumstantial evidence in the poem, there are several similarities in the descriptions of the Prince and Christ.[26] From these, it is quite clear why so many perceptive critics have considered Christ and the Prince identical. Yet, the larger contexts of the poem would tend to discourage such a reading. First, it must be recalled that the chief agent in the preceding strophes is not Christ, but the Spirit. It is the Spirit who is inclined towards men to "celebrate holidays," ("Feiertage zu halten"), principally the ultimate Feast at the end of his work. There is nothing in the sixth strophe to suggest that the Son should be regarded as simply identical with this Spirit. If anything, the Spirit could possibly be considered ultimately a function of the Father-God.[27] The Spirit is here termed "Der hohe" ("the High One"), a term Hölderlin elsewhere reserves for the Father; the titles "Herr der Zeit" or "Gott der Zeit," here applied to the Spirit, are likewise designations of the Father (or Zeus) elsewhere in Hölderlin's poetry.

But we must once again recall that for Hölderlin, God (considered conceptually) is the principle of All-Unity. "Father" or "Father Aether" are simply names given that divine manifestation having greatest meaning for us. Thus, in the sixth strophe, the Deity is named first as the "All-Living"; he is said to have a Son, and only then is he named (in function of this relationship) as Father. And the Spirit (regardless of its phenomenal identity or non-identity with the Father) is essentially the all-living or all-enlivening divine force operative within the process of history: he composes the Time-Image; he is the vivifying impetus of contentious discourse ending in all-unitive song; he has condescended to his "day's work" ("Tagwerk") in the "field" of time. The latter function corresponds directly to what is said of the Prince in the second strophe: "vom ernsten Tagwerk lächelnd."[28] Likewise the Prince's denial of his "foreign land" corresponds explicitly to what is said of the Spirit in the sixth and seventh strophes. The "clarity" ("Klarheit") occasioned by the "god" of the second strophe corresponds to the radiant transfiguration ("verklärt") of the "God of Time" in the seventh. Finally, it is evident from the overall context that the Prince's function as (former) warrior, suggested in the second strophe, or participant in the storms of history, as inferred from the third, are simply further alternative metaphors for the Spirit's involvement in the historical argument that is ultimately resolved in the harmonies of peace—the "Friedenslauten" of the third strophe, the "Gesang" of the eighth and ninth. In summation, then, we can conclude from both thematic and structural considerations that the Prince of the Feast and the divine Spirit of the World (who comes to us specifically to "hold" such a Feast) can best be understood as identical in this poem.[29]

The question then remains, what is Christ's function here? The Prince, we recall, is already seen (though dimly) at the opening of the second strophe, and is seen *as* Prince of the Feast; his function is dis-

cerned before his actual identity. The poet confesses then that he
"knows nothing" before this Prince except that he must be a god; the
identity of the Prince as Spirit of the World becomes evident only in
the third triad. Christ, however, is not immediately seen by the poet,
who must *invite* him to the Feast. The mere identity of Christ is
clearly known from the Bible and tradition—which, however, had
tended to obscure the true character of his divinity and his historical
function. We cannot "re-cognize" ("er-kennen") Christ until we
"know" ("kennen") the Father, until the Spirit has come to earth to
hold festivities where all deities are invited; and we cannot *know* Christ
in himself until we see him in relationship to the other divine forms at
the all-unitive Feast, not as its instigating Prince but as its guest of
honor. It is suggested that in this capacity he will become the cynosure
of all guests: "their most beloved, on whom all depend." He may perhaps, as focal point, assume some figurative attributes of the spiritual
Prince.[30] And yet, there is no clear indication that his identity is simply merged at this point with that of the Spirit who convenes and maintains the Feast. For Hölderlin, Christ is but one of the mythic-historical revelations of divine all-presence.

Hölderlin's view of Christ's relation to other forms of deity is indicated in the concluding lines of the ninth strophe:

>   und eher legt
> Sich schlafen unser Geschlecht nicht,
> Bis ihr Verheissnen all,
> All ihr Unsterblichen, uns
> Vom eurem Himmel zu sagen
> Da seid in unserem Hausse.   [3:536]

> . . . and our race will not lie down to sleep until all you promised ones, all
> you immortal ones, to tell us about your heaven, are here in our
> house.

While Christ may be the most beloved of the "immortals," he is one
among many invited to the Feast the Spirit convenes. The returning
gods have been long "promised" us, and we are now to realize the
prophecy enunciated in "Brot und Wein." For now the Father ("Vater

Aether") will be universally recognized through his manifestation as the Spirit of the World. We can therefore serenely expect all forms of deity to assemble in one grand visitation of our earthly "house." In our present confidence we will not rest at this evening of time until the vision of All-Unity is granted us.

The concluding triad, then, is pervaded by a mood of serene expectation. It does not substantively further the poem's main argument, but is something of an idyllic afterthought like the fourth act of *Prometheus Unbound*. The tenth strophe presents a naive, bucolic picture of our anticipation of the gods. Its opening lines depict a landscape like that at the poem's beginning: the air refreshed by a thunderstorm, the "gently-breathing" breezes, the valley "smoking" with mists. These amenities are viewed as heralding the approach of gods, and people respond to the scene with joy: "Yet hope reddens the cheeks" of those living now, "and before the door of the house sit mother and child, and look upon the peace." "And few seem to die," for "an anticipation, sent by the golden light, holds back the soul, a promise holds the oldest" from death. The hopes and presentiments fostered by the last light of time's evening encourage souls to cling to life until the promise has been fulfilled and they can "lie down to sleep."

The eleventh strophe provides conceptual elaboration of this mood, leading to mythical interpretation. The strophe opens with generalization: "Indeed difficulties, prepared and also carried out from above, are the spice of life." Our varied troubles, all providentially ordained, make life more piquant. After the difficulties of the stormy age, we now especially cherish simple joys: "for everything pleases now, but most of all what is ingenuous." Our anticipated experience of total euphoria is viewed mythically as the fulfillment of an Hellenic prophecy: "For the long-sought, the golden fruit, fallen from an ancient stem in battering storms, but then as dearest possession protected with tender weapons by holy destiny itself, it is the form of the Heavenly Ones." This golden apple of the Hesperides was previously mentioned in the concluding strophe of "Brot und Wein":

Was der Alten Gesang von Kindern Gottes geweissagt,
  Siehe! wir sind es, wir; Frucht von Hesperien ists!   [2:95]

What the song of the ancients foretold of the children of God, see, we ourselves are they; it is the fruit of Hesperides!

The vague promise of the earlier poem is here enunciated in greater detail. The golden fruit is "the form of the Heavenly Ones," the visible actuality of the gods' presence. This visible form was of course present to the Greeks, then lost to men for nearly two thousand years. The apple was originally connected to the "ancient stem" of the tree of all-unitive Nature, just as religious awareness had once been "naturally" a part of the organic totality of Life. It was then blown off in the "storms" of history, the metaphysical violence of the Christian era. Since then, however, it had been protected with "tender weapons" by destiny as its "dearest possession." And now, as we come into inheritance of this gift, the gods will be visibly present to us again. The tender weapons that had protected it from previous generations were perhaps their faint misperceptions of deific form. These failures of recognition were themselves providential, like Christendom's inability to perceive and acknowledge the true significance of Christ: "Aber Dank, / Nie folgt der gleich hernach dem gottgegebnen Geschenke; / Tiefprüfend ist es zu fassen" ("But gratitude, never does it follow immediately after the god-given gift; by deep testing is it to be grasped"). But now the gift is recognized and appropriated in gratitude, for we perceive Christ integrated into our unified perceptual image or "Gestalt" of all heavenly gods. This comprehensive religious vision is itself the long-promised fruition.

The mysterious concluding strophe of the poem is perhaps best understood as a detailed meditation on the previous metaphor:

Wie die Löwin, hast du geklagt,
O Mutter, da du sie,
Natur, die Kinder verloren.
Denn es stahl sie, Allzuliebende, dir
Dein Feind, da du ihn fast
Wie die eigenen Söhne genommen,
Und Satyren die Götter gesellt hast.
So hast du manches gebaut,
Und manches begraben,
Denn es hasst dich, was
Du, vor der Zeit

Allkräftige, zum Lichte gezogen.
Nun kennest, nun lässest du diss;
Denn gerne fühllos ruht,
Bis dass es reift, furchtsamgeschäfftiges drunten.   [3:537–538]

Like the lioness did you lament, O Mother, when, Nature, you lost them,
your children. For, all too loving one, your enemy stole them from
you when you had almost taken him in like your own sons, and associated
the gods with satyrs. Thus you have built much and buried much, for
it hates you, that which you, all-powerful, prematurely raised to the light.
Now you know, now you abandon this; for gladly rests without feeling, until it is ripe, what is timidly busy below.

The poet is now addressing himself to "Nature," the all-unitive Life
force. Nature brings all things into individuality and receives them into
oblivion at their demise. As the principle of generation, she is called
"Mother": all particular entities, gods, men, and other creatures, may
be regarded as her "children." But it is difficult to identify the offspring
intended in the opening lines. It may be debated whether these particular children of Nature are mortals or gods. Nor is the matter wholly
clarified in the following lines. This passage suggests that her "sons"
are "gods" inadvertently exposed to bad company. Yet, the problem is
here complicated by the question of the identity of the "enemy." Some
critics interpret this enemy as a cosmic evil force opposing the goodness of Nature, but such a reading cannot be justified here or in the
larger contexts of Hölderlin's work, which is purely innocent of moral
dualism. More probably, it is man himself in his individualistic, defiant
hatred of divine All-Unity who steals Nature's "children," the manifest
forms of the gods.[31] Such theft was possible because unitive Nature is
"all-too-loving" and had nearly accepted man in his anti-natural mood
as her true child. But men in their perverse egotism are like "satyrs,"
and their association with gods would defile the gods' purity. When
gods (such as the Olympians) are treated with contemptuous familiarity they cease to be gods.[32]

But Nature, like D. H. Lawrence's "god-stuff," has been the mother
of many different forms of God: "Thus you have built much and
buried much." Each new generation of deities (and indeed every transient form of spirituality) has been denied and thereby abolished in
turn by that which unaccountably "hates" Life. This negative force,

again, is the insolent rational mind which Nature herself had fostered into awareness before history, only to be opposed by its willful egotism. But now, as history is drawing to a peaceful close, Nature recognizes how pointless were her previous contentions with negativity. She now realizes that ultimate fruition will appear only when time is wholly matured. The spirit of enmity in man has been vanquished by the new Peace. Nature has ceased her frantic production of new beings because she no longer contends with any negative principle. The final lines are given as the reason ("Denn") for her new quietude. Their effect is reassuring. That which is anxiously busy is not evil, but good;[33] it is about to ripen into fruition, and its anxiety is due to its vulnerability while it is still "busy" in the delicate process of growth. The image of the fruit in the preceding strophe has been altered to that of a nascent seed or root. What is "anxiously busy" cannot achieve its full "Gestalt" until it has attained "feeling" or sentiment of existence through human recognition of it.[34] Until then it must remain unrecognized and "without feeling," while Nature contentedly awaits the time for fulfillment. Human "destiny" has now been settled, the anti-Life principle within man made innocuous, and we need only anticipate the ultimate fruition of history in the Spirit's all-unitive Feast.

We can now see how the poem as a whole is constructed. There are twelve strophes, comprising four parts of three strophes each. Most simply, they present first the scene of expectation and some hints about the Prince of the Feast (first triad), a digression offering historical explanation for what is expected, focusing on the beginning and end of our epoch (second and third triads), and a concluding section (fourth triad) which provides an organic myth for expectancy itself. The characteristic preoccupation with futurity is thus more fully developed in "Friedensfeier" than in any of Hölderlin's other hymns. In its ecstatic optimism "Friedensfeier" remains (though such parallels are inexact) Hölderlin's equivalent of *Prometheus Unbound*.

Also, probably to a greater extent than in any previous hymn, the theme of All-Unity pervades "Friedensfeier."[35] The topic functions fully and explicitly here as the controlling idea. We might briefly recount its contrapuntal development in the hymn. In the first triad we are informed that the unspecified Prince of the Feast is "known by all" ("Allbekannter"), and that his appearance occasions the "clarity" associated with all-unitive insight. In the second triad, after speculating on Christ's destiny and our receptivity to divine forces in Nature (their comprehensive unity is not yet recognized), the poet designates God as the "all-vivifying" ("Allebendigen"), the all-unitive Life principle of Being. Because we now realize God's essence and his Spirit is now inclined to Earth, we are at last able to recognize God's Son. The third triad then explains the Spirit's workings and their triumphant result. The Spirit comes "to share all destiny" and become its integrative force. The law of this destiny is "that all should come to know one another" and know themselves as one in this experience. Once communal self-knowledge is achieved, the law of destiny is superseded by the all-unitive law of love ("der Liebe Gesez"). The Spirit composes a Time-Image, bringing all moments of history into perceptual unity. This image itself functions as a unitive bond between the Spirit and "other" divine forces because "all" divine powers are knowable in and through this image ("kennbar alle daran"). However, the most appropriate figure of this unitive vision of the gods is still the Feast Day, the "all-gathering" occasion. All gods will be present there constituting a number "holy" in completeness ("eine heilige Zahl"). Christ will be present among them as their most beloved, the unifying nexus of love for the entire assembly. The poet concludes this triad with a grandiose declaration that he expects "all you promised [gods], all you immortal ones" to be present in loving unity at this celebration of Peace. The concluding fourth triad tells how in anticipation "everything pleases now" ("Alles gefällt jezt"), especially simple things, as we now trust in an ultimate unitive order beyond all finite complexities. The golden fruit we are ready to possess is the all-unitive "form of the Heavenly." The hymn's final strophe is addressed to Nature as the "all-too-loving" and "all-powerful" ("Allkräftige") Life force soon to find its ultimate fruition in perfect articulation.

"Friedensfeier" thus constitutes Hölderlin's most intensely affirmative statement of hope for the objective realization of All-Unity. The Feast is ultimately a metaphor of poetic accomplishment: harmonious "Song" is to compose our being through an ideal "language" that will be found when our present existence as conversation has attained its proper conclusion. But of course the hymn is an evocation, not the Feast itself. It remains within discourse despite its triumphant anticipation of Song. And its affirmation, according to the laws of discourse, is itself subject to dialectical negation. Its hope is soon put into question, and as its promised all-unitive vision recedes further into the future the poet discovers that we may be compelled to choose those aspects of Deity which appear to us and neglect others. Thus we may be limited to an awareness of God merely through particular—and incomplete—manifestations. But any such partial awareness is a denial of God's unitive essence. These difficulties arise and are considered in a hymnic attempt soon after "Friedensfeier," the fragmentary and inconclusive poem "Der Einzige."

12. "Der Einzige"

"Der Einzige" exists in three unfinished versions.[1] In all three versions, the first four strophes are substantially the same. Beginning with the fifth strophe, however, the versions are radically dissimilar. What the versions have in common is obsession with a central problem: the poet's relationship to Christ within the context of the Hellenic pantheon. Although intriguing, the hymn is not itself a major poetic achievement; each version reaches an impasse. Yet it is a significant document in the development of Hölderlin's poetic thought, a transitional moment of doubt between the affirmation of "Friedensfeier" and the synthesis of "Patmos." We will here examine the first version of "Der Einzige" as indicative of the problems Hölderlin had to confront after "Friedensfeier."

The first strophe begins with a question: "What is it that binds me to the old, blessed shores, so that I love them still more than my fatherland?" The ancient shores are those of Greece, "blessed" for gods once present there. Of course, Hölderlin has consistently revered Greece as a sacred place of divine visitation; it is a Holy Land. Yet the assurances of "Brot und Wein" and "Friedensfeier" should have pacified any obsessive nostalgia for the ancient world, since they foretell an arrival of gods in contemporary Europe; present concerns should therefore be devoted to one's own part of the world. Nevertheless, in "Der Einzige," the poet confesses that his previous attachment to Greece has now intensified to spiritual bondage:

Denn wie in himmlische
Gefangenschaft verkaufft
Dort bin ich . . .   [2:153]

For as if sold into heavenly captivity, I am there . . .

The poet is now at the mercy of the gods he seeks. And yet this captivity is voluntary, even somewhat euphoric—he is now, after all, where he most desires to be: "I am there where Apollo went in the form of a king and Zeus condescended to innocent youths and the High One begat sons in holy fashion and daughters among men." In Greece, the god Apollo appeared as king especially among poets,[2] and the Father-Deity himself descended visibly to earth to beget demigods.

The second strophe further celebrates the immediacy of revelation and spiritual engendering among the Greeks. "Many high thoughts" have "sprung from the Father's head, and great souls have come from him to men." The Greeks understood inspiration not as a psychological phenomenon but as the personal communication of a god; men's highest thoughts came directly from the Father's mind.[3] Likewise, greatness of soul was transmitted directly from the Father in the form of concrete participation in his own divine Being. The poet then lists several places in the Hellenic world that are associated directly or indirectly with Greek heroism (athletic or martial prowess) and thus with one type of "great soul" engendered by Zeus.[4] As they are further associated with the highest forms of poetry, the Pindaric hymn and the Homeric epic, they are also reminiscent of the divinely inspired "high thoughts." The poet's spiritual visitation of these places may thus indicate a desire to share in their inspirational intensity.

The third strophe suggests that the poet's attempted participation has not been completely fruitless:

Viel hab' ich schönes gesehn,
Und gesungen Gottes Bild,
Hab' ich, das lebet unter
Den Menschen, . . .   [2:153–154]

I have seen much that is beautiful and have sung the image of God that lives among men, . . .

These lines may refer to Hölderlin's poetry in general.[5] As noted elsewhere, the "beautiful" is always a manifestation of all-unitive divine Being.[6] The poet has "sung" many instances of its manifestation which constitute an "image" of God. The poet's singing might thus represent an approach to the spirit of Greek poetry and some acquaintance, however distant, with its source and object, the Hellenic deities. And yet one particular divine epiphany has been denied to the poet:

. . . aber dennoch
Ihr alten Götter und all
Ihr tapfern Söhne der Götter
Noch Einen such ich, den
Ich liebe unter euch,
Wo ihr den lezten eures Geschlechts
Des Hausses Kleinod mir
Dem fremden Gaste verberget.   [2:154]

. . . but nonetheless, you old gods and all you brave sons of gods, I still search for one whom I love among you, where from me, the foreign guest, you conceal the last of your race, the jewel of your house.

The poet cannot find the last of their divine race, the beloved one whom the others seem to "hide" from him as too precious to behold.

This, the fourth strophe indicates, is Christ:

Mein Meister und Herr!
O du, mein Lehrer!
Was bist du ferne
Geblieben?   [2:154]

> My Master and Lord! O you, my teacher! Why have you stayed far
> from me?

The phrase "Mein Meister und Herr!" is taken directly from the Gospel.[7] The poet is following convention by addressing Christ in his traditional rôles as ruler, instructor, and model for emulation. The first
question addressed to him sounds like a conventional expression of
religious desire: "Why have you stayed far from me?" A second question, however, betrays radical unorthodoxy: "and when I inquired
among the ancients, the heroes and the gods, why did you remain
missing?" As in "Brot und Wein," Christ is the final and most perfect
representative of Hellenic divinities, the "jewel" of their "house."
What might surprise us here is not that Hölderlin again affirms the
kinship of Christ to Greek gods, but that he cannot experience this
relationship personally. Although he has conceptually avowed how
Christ is related to the others as diverse manifestations of divine Life,
he now confesses his existential inability to achieve any unitive vision
of Christ among them. The speaker thus addresses Christ by names
familiar from his Christian upbringing though generally foreign to his
poetry: "Master," "Lord," and "Teacher." Such names serve only to
emphasize Christ's distance from him; he remains personally "far."
Now, in sad perplexity, he senses that the gods themselves would hin-
der any apprehension of Christ in his Hellenic contexts:

> Und jezt ist voll
> Von Trauern meine Seele
> Als eifertet, ihr Himmlischen, selbst
> Dass, dien' ich einem, mir
> Das andere fehlet.   [2:154]

> And now my soul is full of mourning, as if, you Heavenly ones, you your-
> selves were zealously insisting that if I serve one I must be without
> the other.

Here as elsewhere, "Trauer" ("mourning") designates a profound
spiritual disorientation. The ancient deities now reveal themselves to
be as zealously possessive as Jehovah, and they appear to insist on a
clear choice, "service" either to themselves or to Christ, frustrating
the poet's desire to serve both in song. Since Hölderlin is totally com-

mitted to an all-inclusive comprehension of divinity, nothing could dishearten him more than a compulsion to exclusive choice. If Deity is essentially All-Unity, then to exclude any aspect of Deity is blasphemy. The gods themselves thus seem to insist on a heinous violation of divinity's very nature, as the poet's perception of the gods now appears in hopeless conflict with his most fundamental belief.

The fifth strophe begins with an attempt to analyze the impasse:

> Ich weiss es aber, eigene Schuld
> Ists! Denn zu sehr,
> O Christus! häng' ich an dir,
> Wiewohl Herakles Bruder . . .   [2:154]

> But I know that it is my own fault. For too much, O Christ, I cling to you, although you are Hercules' brother . . .

The gods themselves are not to blame if he cannot find Christ among them; it is not their jealousy but his own partiality that prevents him. The poet's excessive devotion to Christ precludes any general vision that would rank Christ merely equivalent to other divinities. He is thus unable to achieve a unified and balanced view of Deity. But he cannot renounce Christ, although he is not proud of the force of his attachment. Instead, he explicitly confesses it as a weakness, a culpable fault ("Schuld"); his aim is not personal salvation but unitive vision.

In the remainder of this strophe the poet, seeking assurance that such vision is still possible, recounts the mythical facts of Christ's begetting by the Father-God. Zeus and Jehovah are of course equivalent names for the same paternal Deity, and all demigods are half-brothers.[8] Thus Hercules is brother to Christ, though of a different mother and of different character.[9] Of closer spiritual kinship is Dionysus ("Evius"): "And boldly I confess that you are also brother of Evius, who yoked the tigers to his car and down to the Indus, offering friendly service, founded the vineyard and tamed the rage of the nations." Critics have frequently noted that these lines can be read in conjunction with the opening strophe of the ode "Dichterberuf":[10]

> Des Ganges Ufer hörten des Freudengotts
>   Triumph, als allerobernd vom Indus her
>   Der junge Bacchus kam, mit heilgem
>   Weine vom Schlafe die Völker wekend.   [2:46]

> The banks of the Ganges heard the triumph of the God of joy as, conquering all, the young Bacchus came hither from the Indus, waking the nations from sleep with holy wine.

As in "Brot und Wein," Dionysus has the function of comforting men with quiet, holy joy, helping them better endure the absence of other deities. These two passages emphasize different aspects of this activity. The lines from "Dichterberuf" speak of Dionysus' triumphant awakening of peoples from spiritual apathy to holy joy; the present poem emphasizes his rôle as restrainer and comforter of men violently unhappy at the gods' absence. The yoking of tigers' wrath symbolizes his "taming" the "rage" of nations: in teaching men to make wine, he urges them to euphoric service of himself. Christ as "brother" of Dionysus shares this function, teaching men in the Eucharist to join with one another in holy remembrance. The functional likeness of Christ and Dionysus suggested in "Brot und Wein" is thus made explicit here. Yet their murky identity as the "stiller Genius" of the elegy is here differentiated into two distinct mythical personalities performing approximately the same rôle. Such deviation from the Christian tradition is what the speaker "boldly" confesses ("kühn bekenn' ich") in his present clarity of insight.

And yet, despite this bold declaration, something still troubles the poet in his assertions:

> Es hindert aber eine Schaam
> Mich dir zu vergleichen
> Die weltlichen Männer.   [2:155]

> But shame hinders me from comparing the worldly men to you.

"The worldly men" is usually understood to refer to other demigods, men in this world distinguished by awareness of divine paternity.[11] Assuming this, we might ask why the poet would feel a "shame" in comparing Christ with them despite his conceptual certitude that all demigods are equally sons of the Father. The following lines seem about to raise this question: "Und freilich weiss / Ich, der dich zeugte, dein Vater, / Derselbe der . . . [2:155]." The sentence is not completed. It begins, "And indeed I know, he who begat you, your Father, the same who . . ." Following these lines, the strophe breaks off, leaving a space blank as if for later completion. The only remaining words here are: "Denn nimmer herrscht er allein" ("For he never reigns alone"). Any logical connection can merely be inferred: "er" presumably refers to the Father, not Christ, who heretofore has been addressed in the second person. Striving perhaps to overcome his existential "shame," the poet begins an elaboration of what he "knows" conceptually. The meditation seems to be concerned with the Father who "begat" the three demigods, and with consequent reaffirmation of their brotherhood. Perhaps the strophe was never completed because the poet could not resolve the conflict between shame and theoretical certitude.

The remaining strophes of the hymn function as a reflective postscript to explain the poem's failure; they also return inconclusively to problems raised earlier. The seventh strophe begins: "Es hänget aber an Einem / Die Liebe . . ." ("But Love hangs on One" [2:155]). This statement seems to resume a thought initiated in the fifth strophe: "Denn zu sehr, / O Christus! häng' ich an dir." Love will always tend to attach itself exclusively to one object, such as Christ. The following lines show that the statement could refer also to the poet's experience in writing this poem: "Namely, this time the song has proceeded too much from my own heart; I will make good the fault if I sing still other [songs]." His excessive love for Christ, blamed in the fifth strophe for his inability to achieve unitive vision, is here responsible for this particular poetic failure. The poem paradoxically achieves a type of success as an embodiment of the spiritual impasse it proclaims. But such an ironic triumph does not please the poet; the speaker resolves upon greater detachment in treating the problem in later poems, thereby "making good" the present failing. And yet he acknowledges the difficulty of success on such an emotional topic: "I never hit upon the measure as I wish to do." Here "measure" (or "moderation": "Maas") specifically refers to the balance of objectivity that the poet must achieve between excessive devotion and contemptuous neglect; but more generally it designates the limits of mortal participation in divine presence, as in "Brot und Wein" and "Der Rhein."[12] The exclusiveness of attachment to Christ is thus also a "failing" in the poet himself, as it impugns the law of mortal finitude, the necessary distinction between human and divine. An excess of participation in divine Life is as bad as a deficiency and more immediately dangerous, since it threatens our own destruction.[13] If participation in divine Life is mediated only through one figure (Christ) rather than many (as in polytheism), the resulting concentration of divine presence in a single focal point poses great danger.

Although this poem may be about Christ, it is thoroughly un-Christian in attitude. Its title, "Der Einzige," suggests a problem, not an answer. The given attachment to Christ is viewed as a threat not only (explicitly) to poetry but (implicitly) to the poet. Again, the only type of salvation the poet seeks is a unified vision of all forms of God and its adequate articulation in language; such an ultimate Song would be the "Best" that he wishes.

The concluding strophe of "Der Einzige" attains a kind of thematic resolution in relating the poet's own problems to those faced in this world by Christ and other demigods ("heroes"); it thus establishes an analogy between Christ, heroes and poets: "For as the Master moved on earth [as] a captive eagle, and many who saw him were afraid,[14] while the Father did his utmost and actually effected his best among men, and also the Son was very troubled until he ascended towards heaven in the breezes: like him the soul of the heroes is captive." The souls of Christ and other demigods were "captives" in this world. Christ is here indeed compared with "worldly" men, and the basis of the comparison is in their "worldliness"—not fatuous involvement in transitory things, but the earthly bondage of a soul whose origin is in transcendence. As in "Der Rhein," a demigod who remembers the divine source must always experience worldliness (Heideggerian "being-in-the-world") as frustration and conscious alienation. On earth, Christ was thus troubled or obscured to himself ("betrübt") like a "captive eagle" nostalgic for his native sky. But by means of Christ's divinely-ordained bondage the Father effected his "Best" ("sein Äusserstes")— a perfectly lucid and concrete outward manifestation of divine presence. And yet (as in "Friedensfeier") men did not immediately recognize this presence, and this failure of recognition must have "troubled" Christ and intensified his alienation. The souls of heroes or other demigods also feel alienated and trapped on earth, obsessed by remembrance of their divine source and longing for escape. This feeling of worldly captivity constitutes a major similarity between Christ and other heroes.

But poets are also condemned to captivity here: "Die Dichter müssen auch / Die geistigen weltlich seyn" ("The poets must also, the spiritual ones, be worldly" [2:156]). The true poet is always "spiritual" ("geistig") in creative response to the workings of the Spirit on earth.[15] As suggested in "Friedensfeier," poets do the Spirit's work by striving through imperfect discourse towards all-unitive Song. In responsiveness to Deity, the true poet's soul thus resembles that of the demigods; like them, the poet must also experience alienation from earthly life. The poet's "worldliness" also consists in a feeling of entrapment. In this respect the poet can seemingly without shame compare Christ to "worldly men," including even himself. The special sense of "heavenly" captivity to Greece in the first strophe is here replaced by a more general sense of "worldly" captivity shared by all doing the Spirit's work.

The unfinished hymn "Der Einzige" in its first version is thus more personal and uncertain than any previous hymn we have considered. The poet's "I" is prominent throughout; and its voice is personal and experiential, not prophetic. The poem's excessive subjectivity is due to the same exclusive devotion to Christ responsible for its impasse; it achieves only tenuous resolution to one of its problems, the kinship of Christ to other demigods. As later versions attest, the major problem remains unresolved: whether the poet, given the partiality and radical subjectivity of his current attitude, can ever achieve the all-unitive vision proclaimed in "Friedensfeier." The poet must seek a new, revised assessment of the problem itself in "Patmos" before any new resolution can be attained.

13. "Patmos"

In "Patmos" the problem of All-Unity is confronted with a penetrating analysis achieved in no other poem.[1] This confrontation is principally determined by the inner logic of Hölderlin's poetic development. Considering the hymn in context, we see that the question of All-Unity had to be thoroughly reconsidered after the ecstatic hopes of "Friedensfeier" had been thwarted by the virtual hopelessness of "Der Einzige." "Patmos" attempts to find a way out of this impasse through a fundamental reappraisal of the problem. The previous major hymns had optimistically assumed that time was ripe for all-unitive manifestation of Deity and had encouraged the poet to articulate the objective vision in song. "Patmos," however, begins with an acknowledgment that such optimism is no longer possible. It graphically states the difficulties of the present situation and proceeds to a complex analysis of how the situation might be remedied.

The opening strophe is one of the most difficult passages in Hölderlin's work. Part of its difficulty derives from its construction. It begins with two general statements (lines 1–4), then depicts a landscape (5–8), gives the poet's interpretation of the landscape (9–12), and finally expresses a desire for symbolic action within the landscape itself (13–15). Thus, marking the divisions:

Nah ist
Und schwer zu fassen der Gott.
Wo aber Gefahr ist, wächst
Das Rettende auch.

Im Finstern wohnen
Die Adler und furchtlos gehn
Die Söhne der Alpen über den Abgrund weg
Auf leichtgebaueten Brüken.

Drum, da gehäuft sind rings
Die Gipfel der Zeit, und die Liebsten
Nah wohnen, ermattend auf
Getrenntesten Bergen,

So gieb unschuldig Wasser,
O Fittige gieb uns, treuesten Sinns
Hinüberzugehn und wiederzukehren.   [2:165]

Near is the god and difficult to grasp. But where danger is, grows also
that which saves. In darkness dwell the eagles, and the sons of the Alps go
fearlessly over the abyss on lightly-built bridges. Therefore, since the
pinnacles of time are heaped all around, and the dearest ones
live near, perishing on most separated mountains, then give us innocent water, O give us wings, most loyal in mind to go over and to return.

The opening lines are most enigmatic. The relationship between the first two sentences is not immediately apparent; however, the notion of "danger" serves as an obvious focal point. Some critics assume that, because of frequent warnings of divine fire in Hölderlin's later work, the "danger" must consist in the *nearness* of the God.[2] Others, rejecting such statistical arguments, insist that "danger" lies in the poet's experience of *difficulty* in "grasping" Deity, since the strophe's remaining lines depict a state of fragmentation and separation.[3] They point out that the "danger" experienced by separated lovers is relatable not to any nearness of Deity, but to alienation from one another and (presumably) from the God they find difficult to grasp in unison, to comprehend. While the first four lines may have autonomous meaning, the remainder of the strophe seems to suggest that the danger here refers principally to the difficulty in apprehending the God.

But we might also consider these lines in the larger context of Hölderlin's work. The Deity is to be understood essentially in all-unitive terms as the all-living ("all-lebendig") and the all-present ("all-gegenwärtig"). In all-presence it is always "near" to us, and this nearness is felt with greatest intensity when we are most intensely aware of divine presence.[4] And yet God's totality is inevitably experienced as "difficult to grasp," and the sense of difficulty increases as divine presence is more intensely (and threateningly) felt in actuality and nearness. Most generally considered, the "danger" consists both in nearness and in difficulty. The nearness of God is dangerous whenever it threatens to consume us in the divine fire of its unmediated intensity. The difficulty of comprehension is likewise dangerous if it discourages us from further efforts to relate to Deity, inclining us to godless lives of resigned alienation. The ultimate source of danger here (as elsewhere in late Hölderlin) is our inability to find proper balance or "measure" between the two extremes of neglect for All-Unity or impatience for unmediated union.

And yet, "where danger is, grows also that which saves." Salvation from the dilemma emerges organically in the very situation where nearness and difficulty are greatest, and the opposing temptations to immediacy or neglect most extreme. "That which saves" would thus achieve a finite but adequate "grasp" of all-unitive divine Life. Such comprehension of Deity would be the achievement of "Song," the ultimate poem that "Friedensfeier" holds to be our coming mode of existence: "Bald sind [wir] aber Gesang" (3:536). The "Feiertag" hymn has already viewed this Song's attainment as a form of autonomous "growth."[5] In "Patmos" its emergence is viewed not merely as a blessing but also as salvation from the difficulty of its own achievement. In the opening statements, however, the form of salvation is yet unspecified and the danger itself remains unclear. It must be inferred from the landscape of the following lines. The high mountains with deep gorges between them suggest danger. Yet the eagles are signs of hope and chosen messengers of Zeus;[6] although they dwell here in darkness, they suggest the feasibility of living with peril, as do the "sons of the Alps" who cross between mountains on their fragile bridges.

The landscape's symbolic functions are then presented. The mountain peaks are allegorized as "peaks of time." Those who live on the peaks love and are "near" one another, since the distance across the gorges is not great. Yet the mountains are "most separated" by intervening depths, and the loving ones are effectively kept apart. In enforced separation they grow weak ("ermattend") despite close mutual awareness. As the poet implicitly projects himself into this situation, the strophe's concluding lines take the form of supplicating prayer. With "wings" or "water" one could cross over the abysses to neighboring peaks and reunite the separated lovers. Such action would be accomplished "loyally," mindful of poetic obligations. The wings, of course, would enable us to fly between peaks; the function of the water is somewhat unclear. Its "innocence" or sobriety (as opposed to wine) might refresh us and keep us in holy lucidity; also (more obviously) the water might join the peaks so that we could cross over by boat.[7]

A somewhat more serious problem is posed by the phrase "peaks of time" ("Gipfel der Zeit"). Since we generally think of time as linear, a directionally horizontal line running from past to future, we may be inclined to regard those peaks simply as points on such a line, like peaks on a graph—as something like "high points" of history.[8] However, there is little in Hölderlin to encourage such an interpretation, since his mature view of history and of time itself is clearly non-linear. As seen in "Friedensfeier," time is regarded as a dynamic process, impelled by an immanent force (the Spirit) towards a goal (the Feast or "Zeitbild"). The "Peaks" of such a process would therefore be moments when human time seems to be nearing its consummation. Hölderlin's usual symbolic reading of the Alps is thus strongly suggested here: the peaks of time are precisely those moments when our mortal existence is closest to God. It is only in this sense that they could be considered moments of achieved "height" in the historical process.[9]

The speaker of the opening lines may himself be situated on one of these temporal peaks where "we" are spiritually growing weaker through want of authentic contact with the near, yet elusive, deity. The principal danger is that we may perish through inability to relate ourselves to God. Yet, our desire is not only for God but for one another. If achieved, the reunion we seek would foster our union with the all-unitive Deity we all wish to grasp. Because we are finite, our religious comprehensions can never be adequate to their infinite object, only to ourselves. The fullest comprehension must be achieved through an authentic community, which fuses diverse subjectivities in collective apperception. The ultimate comprehension of God can be achieved only through the greatest, most perfect, and most comprehensive community, an image of the All-Unity it seeks to grasp. Thus the poet in "Heimkunft" is compelled to return home to seek a broader, authentically communal basis for his new religious awareness; the Greeks in "Brot und Wein" were enabled through their perfect community to achieve their lucid vision of gods; and, in "Friedensfeier," mankind as constituted harmoniously in "Song" will again attain all-unitive vision of the forms of Deity. In the present strophe, going back and forth between peaks would therefore serve to unite "lovers" not only to one another but to God in communal apprehension. By helping to unite those on peaks of time the poet can thus assist them (and himself as part of their community) in overcoming the "danger" and "difficulty" of the opening lines. The poet would thereby remain "most loyal in mind" ("treuesten Sinns") to others and to himself, but also to Deity and to his own fundamental conception of God as all-unitive Life. Moreover, the poet is cognizant that to bring men into communion with one another and union with God would in effect restore them to the joyous lucidity of divine presence known by the Greeks and (finally) by the disciples of Christ. The rest of the poem resolves these implications.

The second strophe, then, gives the poet's reaction to an unexpected result of his prayer for transport between the peaks of time: "So I spoke, when a genius abducted me from my own house, more quickly than I had expected and afar, where I had never thought to come." Though he had wished to remain true to his present historical situation or standpoint, his prayer to cross over is abruptly answered when he is torn away from his own "house" to a place where he had had no desire or expectation to go. Moreover, the only "wings" here would be those of an uncontrollable spirit or "genius." His flight is involuntary, compelled by an alien force whose intent he cannot surmise, and he can only report with awed amazement on what he sees during flight: "There glimmered in twilight as I went the shadowy woods and the yearning brooks of [my] homeland; I never knew the lands; yet soon, in fresh glistening, mysteriously in golden smoke, there blossomed, growing quickly with the steps of the sun, fragrant with thousand peaks, Asia upon me. . . ." The strophe's initial setting was still presumably the Alpine landscape, the general region of the poet's "Heimath." Its salient features are "shadowy woods" and "yearning brooks," aspects of landscape given full poetic treatment in "Der Rhein." Here, also, they represent a native situation of restraint and frustrated desire. The time is the twilight before dawn, a moment of troubled, uncertain expectation. In his rapture the poet is unable even to recognize these "lands"; he can only stare on them as pure forms. But his flight is now approaching a realm he does recognize and where (as in "Der Einzige") he feels compelled to be. Flying eastward he encounters the rising sun, seemingly dawning at unusual speed. "Asia" (Ionia) seems to blossom up towards him in accelerated "steps of the sun," emerging like a flower in rapid evolvement, in the "fresh glistening" of early morning (as in Greece's prime) yet also "mysteriously in golden smoke," likely the haze of myth and legend shrouding the Hellenic world for us in its own mystery.[10] Asia's thousand peaks are "fragrant" in the morning air, flowerlike and redolent with perfect sacrifices to the gods. The Hellenic East is encountered literally as a morning-land (*Morgenland*) and the poet is compelled to relive its sacred dawn. The "blossoming" celebrated in "Brot und Wein" is reexperienced here: Ionia "blooms up" at him as at the beginning of the Greek era. The poet's flight and his ecstatic stupor have effectively abolished all historical perspective.

The third strophe elaborates on the poet's helpless, awestruck bewilderment. Although he had wished to unite those living on peaks of time, he is now where he cannot help others, or even himself. The first strophe's wish has not been fulfilled, but thwarted. Forcibly returned to the ancient world, the poet can do nothing to establish community in his own time. Asia here is not simply a "peak of time" now willingly attained, but a place of virtually atemporal "heavenly captivity," as in "Der Einzige." The poet can only seek to escape from this enchanted but undesirable situation.

Upon first arriving, however, he is "blinded" by the excess of unaccustomed light, the abiding radiance of divine presence; as in the later versions of "Der Einzige," he stands in "flaming air" (2:157). Disoriented, he feels impelled to seek something known, for everything there seems strange. Yet at first he is simply awestruck by the beauty of the region: everything has the glorious freshness of a dream and his previous imaginative visitations there seem forgotten, as he is even "unaccustomed" to the place where Hyperion had once climbed Mount Tmolus.[11] He merely notes the Pactolus bearing "gold" (emblematical of divine virtue) and the garden of flowers that constitutes a "quiet fire" of divine presence in intense yet calmly mediated form. While this vegetative fire blooms at the base of the cliff, "silver snow" is also said to "bloom" on the peaks in its own flowerlike mode of holiness. Other holy vegetation, ivy (an emblem and even witness of immortal life),[12] grows "inaccessible" on the cliffs themselves. The trees by the cliffsides further suggest present inaccessibility of divine presence, for the "palaces" they support remain distant in grandeur. Everything seen and described here serves to alienate the poet, though such scenes were once dear to him. The presently unsettling results of his daemonic nostalgia have apparently estranged him now from its customary objects.

In the fourth strophe, then, the poet "sought . . . something that I knew." He goes to the Ionian Coast and beholds the beckoning "streets" or sea-lanes unshaded from the glare of light, going forth almost at random. Already baffled, the poet is now further confused by the maze of possible routes. But he is reassured by a sailor who knows the "islands." For Hölderlin, islands are generally places of friendly asylum. In both "Menons Klagen" and the second version of "Der Einzige," for example, islands offer individuals solace in a fragmented and predominantly hostile world.[13] Yet they remain, literally, places of isolation. While offering security, they do not encourage attempts to remedy the general situation. Clearly analogous to the peaks in the first strophe, they are sites of authenticity and nearness to

God, but also of helplessness and even slow death. Though the speaker of the first strophe may have requested water to help him join peaks, he is here incapable of uniting these outposts; he merely chooses one as a refuge for himself. The poet's spiritual condition has thus regressed to a state inferior to that of the first strophe's prayerful resolve.[14]

The islands here are those of the Greek archipelago. In the long poem "Der Archipelagus," they are the "blossoming" daughters of the sea, themselves "mothers" of Greek heroes.[15] Now, however, all heroes are dead; and, despite their beauty, the vitality and abundance of most of these islands make them unattractive to the alienated poet. But the knowledgable "sailor" tells him about Patmos: "And when I heard that one of the nearby [islands] was Patmos, I very much desired to turn in there and to approach the dark grotto." The poet hopes he can find there something "known" and sympathetic to his present mood. And what he particularly seeks on this most Christian of Greek islands is the "dark grotto," a place of withdrawal and seclusion from the overpowering intensity of daylight. The grotto is thus a site of religious darkness and inwardness, proper both to Christianity and to Hölderlin's own fundamental awareness of divine absence. Unlike the mainland's deific radiance, the grotto's secluded darkness would be something the poet "knows" which might foster his return to self-awareness. But paradoxically he is also attracted by the poverty of the island.[16] The strophe concludes with negative praise: "For not, like Cyprus, rich in spring or [like] one of the others does Patmos dwell splendidly. . . ."[17] The other islands' abundance of divine vitality now alienates the poet, who prefers kindred desolation.

The fifth strophe further explains Patmos' attractiveness in terms of its "hospitality." While nearly all islands can appear hospitable, Patmos is noted for its sympathetic responsiveness to shipwrecked "strangers." The land itself groans and splits under the effects of intense sunlight and drought, in apparent commiseration with wretched visitors. The island thus provides the ideal objective correlative for the poet, a stranger who, now exiled from his home in spiritual shipwreck, must lament his fragmented world and his estrangement from others. Yet as is evident from the strophe's concluding lines, the designation "stranger" can especially apply to the island's most famous guest, the shipwrecked evangelist St. John:

                    So pflegte
Sie einst des gottgeliebten,
Des Sehers, der in seeliger Jugend war

Gegangen mit
Dem Sohne des Höchsten, unzertrennlich, . . .   [2:167]

So once she cared for the man loved by God, the seer, who in blissful
youth had walked with the Son of the Highest, inseparably, . . .

The sympathy Patmos now gives the poet had once been accorded
John as he mourned the loss of his own homeland and his "departed
friend," Christ. Hölderlin here follows the tradition that John the
beloved disciple is identical with the visionary who wrote the Book
of Revelation on Patmos.[18]

The rest of the sixth strophe (the hymn's pivotal moment) moves
from the poet's situation to John's recollection of his nearness to
Christ, especially at the Last Supper:

                    . . . unzertrennlich, denn
Es liebte der Gewittertragende die Einfalt
Des Jüngers und es sahe der achtsame Mann
Das Angesicht des Gottes genau,
Da, beim Geheimnisse des Weinstoks, sie
Zusammensassen, zu der Stunde des Gastmals,
Und in der grossen Seele, ruhigahnend den Tod
Aussprach der Herr und die lezte Liebe, denn nie genug
Hatt' er von Güte zu sagen
Der Worte, damals, und zu erheitern, da
Ers sahe, das Zürnen der Welt.
Den alles ist gut. Drauf starb er. Vieles wäre
Zu sagen davon. Und es sahn ihn, wie er siegend blikte
Den Freudigsten die Freunde noch zulezt,   [2:167]

. . . inseparably, for the bearer of thunder loved the simplicity of the
disciple and the attentive man saw clearly the face of the god
when, at the mysteries of the grapevine, they sat together at the hour
of the banquet, and in his great soul, calmly surmising, the Lord pronounced death and the last love, for he never had enough of words
to speak of goodness then, and to cheer, when he saw it, the raging of the
world. For All is good. Thereupon he died. There would be much to
say about this. And the friends saw him, the most joyous one as
he gazed victoriously, still at last,

As their situations are now alike, the poet has assumed John's memories and appropriated the disciple's past to his own present condition. The remainder of the poem will posit the relevance of this past with its remembrance of Christ and Christ's departure. In seeking refuge on Patmos, the poet takes upon himself the Christian traditions associated with that island. This poem thus marks a decided shift in Hölderlin's historical perspective. The moment demanding interpretation is still the end of the ancient world, the culmination and dissolution of its all-unitive vision. But this vision is now appraised chiefly in Christian contexts, as the glaring Hellenic radiance has forced the poet to a more privative, ascetic site of memory. The memory of the vision is no longer linked with a nostalgic desire to recapture the past, because the past is considered irretrievably gone. The poet is now chiefly concerned with Christ as the culminative focus of divine presence, and with the consequences of his demise. The hymn will conclude that it is only through interpretive recall that our present situation of helplessly fragmented being can ever be remedied.[19]

The sixth strophe accordingly recounts John's last clear memories of Christ. Since Hölderlin still thinks of Christ among Hellenic deities, Christ is designated here as bearer of storms or thunder, purveyor of authoritative power in a form traditionally appropriate to Zeus. Yet Christ is said to have loved the "simplicity" of his youngest disciple, as such ingenuousness ("Einfalt") is characteristic of unreserved openness and receptivity to divine presence.[20] Because of his privileged position and attentiveness, John could clearly discern the manifest divinity in Christ's face at the Last Supper, the "banquet" ("Gastmahl") where disciples were convened for the "mysteries of the grapevine."

By his use of the word "Gastmahl"—the same word used for the Platonic "Symposium" in "Der Rhein"—Hölderlin again suggests an identity of Greek and Christian ceremonies. The supra-Christian character of this love feast is even more clearly shown by reference to "Geheimnisse des Weinstroks," which is also appropriate to rites of Dionysus; moreover, Dionysus (as son of Zeus and Semele) could share the title "der Gewittertragende." We thus recall the deliberate vagueness of the closing strophes of "Brot und Wein," where the "stiller Genius" could be Christ, Dionysus, or both, and the rites of bread and wine could refer to liturgies of Dionysus and Ceres as well as to the Christian Eucharist. Christ and Dionysus were left undifferentiated there, identical in function as comforting spirit. In "Der Einzige," of course, Christ and Dionysus were differentiated as brothers. But here it might seem that the functional identity of the rites is again implied, as if Christ might again be identified with the other demigod.

But the following lines indicate new significance. Aside from Christ's proclamation of the commandment of love and his own death,[21] there may also be a reference here to the words consecrating the bread and wine (Matt. 26:26–29), because their conversion into Christ's body and blood and distribution among the disciples could only imply (or be tantamount to) Christ's own death and dismemberment. He thus pronounces his death and ultimate love at the same moment, indicating he is about to die for the disciples, giving them his body to eat and blood to drink for their comfort and strength. The present symbolic dismemberment is a necessary precondition for their future remembrance of him; and he must be divided among them in spirit if they are to remain spiritually united in him, the "branches" with the "vine."[22] Calmly anticipating his actual death the following day, Christ could not find words enough to convey his full vision of divine goodness and benevolence, since he had now, in the face of his death, attained his own awareness of God's love and all-unitive power. He then sought words to "cheer" or pacify with holy joy "the raging of the world," the furious dissonance of a time when the divine center cannot hold and anarchical confusion is loosed among men.[23] Like Manes' envisioned Savior in *Empedokles*, he would calm the storm of the world's contentious turmoil;[24] for the divine all-unitive "benevolence" (or "goodness": "Güte") that he proclaims has the virtue of bringing all things into joyous concord. The pronouncement "All is good" can be read both as an utterance by Christ at the Last Supper (heard by John) and as a statement of absolute validity in itself.

This is the most radical formulation of Hölderlin's own belief that all things are pervaded by the unitive divine force of Goodness.[25] Since Hölderlin attributes the expression of this belief to Christ at the Last Supper, we may assume that the poet holds to the idea of All-Unity as firmly here as in the Tübingen poems. But the context here shows that the idea is no longer tainted by the facile optimism of Tübingen.

In the face of death itself, Christ proclaims universal goodness against raging violence. Confronted with ultimate hatred, Christ is capable of ultimate love, perfectly articulated in his pronouncement that "all is good." This pronouncement cannot be made except by one in whom such ultimate love has been fully realized. One such as Christ who grasps the omnipresent love of God recognizes this love as the unitive force of goodness in creation. John witnesses this moment of greatest realization of divine truth. But, as Hölderlin notes in "Friedensfeier," the disciples were unable to comprehend the import of this essential divine revelation.[26] They could only watch in bewilderment as Christ sustained his joy of awareness into death: "And the friends saw him still at last as he, the most joyous one, looked in victory. . . ." Christ's realization of goodness survived even the world's final negation of Life.[27]

Yet, the seventh strophe continues, the disciples remain bewildered:

Doch trauerten sie, da nun
Es Abend worden, erstaunt,
Denn Grossentschiedenes hatten in der Seele
Die Männer, aber sie liebten unter der Sonne
Das Leben und lassen wollten sie nicht
Vom Angesichte des Herrn
Und der Heimath. . . .   [2:167]

And yet they mourned now that it had become evening, astounded, for
the men had what was greatly decisive in their souls, but they loved
the life under the sun and they did not want to leave the face of
the Lord and their homeland.

The opening lines of the strophe may refer to the risen Christ's encounter with two disciples on the road to Emmaus.[28] Unrecognized, Christ asks them why they are so "sad"; later when he is about to depart they beg him, "Abide with us: for it is toward evening, and the day is far spent" (Luke 24:29). More generally, however, "evening" here signifies the close of the ancient day of divine presence, now consummated with the death of Christ. The disciples now go into an intense "mourning" ("trauern") that perplexes and cripples them. They are confused and upset about Christ's abrupt departure and its meaning for their lives. The disciples had in their souls the "greatly decisive" awareness of Christ that was to decide their own lives as missionaries and profoundly affect the history of the world through them. And yet, for a while after Christ's death they remained attached to "life under the sun," their still present memories of living in light of divine presence. These memories had been indelibly burnt into them, "driven into [them] like fire in iron," and they were still glowing with ardor. Moreover, in explicit allusion to Emmaus, "the shadow of the dear one went by their side"—not the actual living (or bodily resurrected) presence of Christ, but his "shade" or *manes*, the recalled image of the dead. In later versions of the strophe, Hölderlin stresses the noxiousness of this shade, and the unhealthiness of the disciples' devotion to personal remembrance.[29] They had succumbed to an unwholesome nostalgia which threatened to waste their lives in quietistic inertia, a morose dwelling in the past.

And "therefore," so they could overcome this malaise, "he sent them the Spirit, and indeed the house trembled and the storms of God rolled thundering far over their apprehensive heads, when the heroes of death were assembled, gravely pondering, now that he in departing appeared to them once again." This of course refers to the coming of the Holy Spirit at Pentecost:

> And when the day of Pentecost was fully come, they were all with one accord in one place. And suddenly there came a sound from heaven as of a rushing mighty wind, and it filled all the house where they were sitting. And there appeared unto them cloven tongues like as of fire, and it sat upon each of them. And they were all filled with the Holy Ghost, and began to speak with other tongues, as the Spirit gave them utterance.
>
> [Acts 2:1–4]

In Hölderlin's interpretation, the Spirit is sent by Christ himself, presumably the prophetic "Spirit of Truth" promised the disciples in John 16:12–13. Pentecost is thus the moment when Christ bids farewell by appearing as giver of the Spirit, the vital force which will impel them to proclaim Christ's truth and enable them to live authentically the gospel already received.

The Spirit appears like a mighty wind from heaven that initiates tempests, "the storms of God," dispatched by "der Gewittertragende" to roll over the disciples' heads and thunder far off into the future.

These presumably will collectively evolve as the great thunderstorm of history impelled and managed by the Spirit himself; Pentecost is thus the inception of the "tausandjähriges Gewitter" of "Friedensfeier."[30] The disciples become the first active participants in the Spirit's tempestuous workings. The Pentecostal experience has converted them from mourners to zealously activistic "heroes of death," who share Christ's triumphantly defiant attitude toward mortality. Christ's final apparition in sending them the Spirit helps them overcome their former devotion to his memory.

The eighth strophe offers a meditation on their new activism. The syntax of this strophe is somewhat unclear, but the first complete sentence might be translated as follows: "For now the Royal One extinguished the sun's day and broke the straight-beaming, the scepter, divinely suffering, of himself, for it shall return again at the right time." "Der Königliche" is God as ruler of history, "Herr der Zeit" of "Friedensfeier." At the death of Christ he extinguished the day of divine presence in the ancient world. He thereby broke his "scepter," emblem of universally recognized authority directly conveyed, "straight-beaming" as light itself.[31] Divine authority is unambiguous and clearly knowable only when divine presence is objectively manifest; in time of divine absence each man must live by his own light, if not in darkness. The moment of extinction of divine light and authority is marked by "divine suffering," the agonizing death of God to the world. And yet the Deity ordained this extinction through his own will, knowing that manifest presence and rule would return "at the right time," the moment he himself chooses.[32] The divine rule could not have been maintained past the time of Christ: "It would not have been good, later, and abruptly breaking off, disloyal, the work of men. . . ." If human acknowledgment of divine authority continued after the divine presence itself had disappeared, it would actually be a work of human self-deception, with men "disloyally" making laws for themselves under delusion that such laws were ordained by God. And, when the deception is finally discovered, the spurious divine rule would be "abruptly broken off" and God's honor would suffer, for the credibility of all forms of divine control would then be questioned. God therefore wisely broke the scepter of his power in holy fashion, and at the proper moment.

Moreover, man's subsequent life in darkness was not without consolations: "and it was a joy from now on to live in loving night and to preserve unswervingly in simple eyes abysses of wisdom. And living images are also greening deep on the mountains. . . ." While night may be a time of objective absence, it can be a "loving" time for those who subjectively maintain memory of divine presence. The disciples turned inward towards abysmal depths of wisdom preserved in profound, abiding responsiveness to Christ. With such inner riches the disciples remained serenely indifferent to desolations of the outer world, and could perceive even in night some "living images" of organic life and mediated divine presence.[33]

And yet (as the ninth strophe continues) such inner joys were threatened by the violence of outward events and the woeful destinies of the disciples themselves. While the Spirit after Pentecost was willing, the disciples were weak and discomfited by their compulsion to go forth and teach all nations. The divine will was experienced as violent: "Yet it is fearful, how here and there, infinitely afar, God disperses the Living." This has a certain universal validity, as it tells of the breakup of all human community and of vital, unitive cohesion ("das Lebende"). In immediate context, however, the community disrupted is specifically that of the disciples. The strophe continues: "For even to leave the face of the dear friends and go far away over the mountains alone where Heavenly Spirit was twice recognized and univocal [einstimmig]. . . ." It was "fearful" for the disciples to abandon their friends and the Holy Land, where the divine Spirit had been "twice" recognized (once as the living Christ and then as the Holy Spirit at Pentecost); they were reluctant to leave this holy place even though the Spirit itself had commanded their departure.

Yet they were soon forcibly, even violently, compelled: "and it [their departure] was not prophesied, but seized [them] by the hair, [suddenly] present. . . ." There are Biblical references to people being seized and carried off by the hair of their heads;[34] the poet's own experience in the second strophe is perhaps a latter-day equivalent. The disciples' abduction occurred "when the God, hastening away, suddenly looked back at them, and they, conjuring him to halt, henceforth bound as on golden ropes, naming evil, reached out their hands for one another—." The "god" here is presumably Christ. As he left the world, he unexpectedly looked back one last time at the disciples. At this moment the disciples were forcibly removed from their place and separated from one another. It is unclear whether the "golden ropes" here bind the disciples (in spirit) to one another, or separately to the departing god.[35] The latter seems more plausible in the context, with its emphasis on separation rather than union. But however they are bound, they extend hands to one another from that moment, possibly reaching out in vain while being drawn farther apart. And as they reach out, they "name evil," to be understood contextually as their growing condition of separation and the general breakup of divine community. For if All-Unity is absolute Good, "evil" must be whatever would oppose or disrupt participation in unitive Life. Christ was able to affirm that "all is good" only in a moment of comprehensive vision; whatever might prevent this comprehension (which alone can deny evil) must be a phenomenal experience of evil for us. The awareness expressed here corresponds to an implicit perception of evil as human fragmentation preventing grasp of Deity. The ninth strophe thus describes the inception of the process which leads to our present desolation.

The tenth strophe is a single complex question about this process.[36] Its first clause summarizes the poet's interpretation of Christ's death: "But when he died to whom beauty adhered the most, so that there was a wonder in his form and the Heavenly Ones pointed to him. . ." Christ's "beauty" is probably the aura of divine presence, possessed so perfectly by Christ that his "form" appeared to men as a "wonder."[37] Christ also was the center of attention for all heavenly gods as in "Friedensfeier" ("ihr Geliebtestes auch, / An dem sie hängen"); here, the others "point" to him as the quintessence of the divinity all possess. The question's second clause resumes the situation at the end of the last strophe, where, though physically separated, the disciples still dwelt together in communal memory of Christ's love. The next section is longer and more complex: "And [when] it does not merely take away the sand or the willow, and seizes the temple, when the honor of the demigod and of his [disciples] blows away and the Highest himself averts his face, because there is not anything immortal to be seen any more in Heaven or on the green earth. . . ." The implicit image here is of a torrential storm that tears away both natural and human structures. Of particular significance is the destruction of the temple (perhaps that of Jerusalem), an event indicating the collapse of social modes of religious mediation.[38] Even the honor of the demi-god Christ and his disciples is blown away in this wind. Ultimately God himself averts his face, utterly abandoning the now shattered world and withdrawing divine presence from the heavens and "the green earth," so that both immanent and transcendent divine presence are now hidden from man. In the final words of the strophe ("Was ist diss?"), the poet is moved to question the meaning of the historical process leading to this catastrophe.

The eleventh strophe attempts to answer:

> Es ist der Wurf des Saemanns, wenn er fasst
> Mit der Schaufel den Waizen,
> Und wirft, dem Klaren zu, ihn schwingend über die Tenne.
> Ihm fällt die Schaale vor den Füssen, aber
> Ans Ende kommet das Korn,
> Und nicht ein Übel ists, wenn einiges
> Verloren gehet und von der Rede
> Verhallet der lebendige Laut,
> Denn göttliches Werk auch gleichet dem unsern,
> Nicht alles will der Höchste zumal. . . .   [2:169]

> It is the toss of the sower when he seizes the wheat with his shovel and tosses it into the clear, swinging it over the threshing-floor. The husks fall before his feet, but the grain comes to the end, and it is not an evil if some gets lost and the living sound dies away from the speech, for divine work also resembles our own, the Highest does not want everything at once.

The historical process amounts to the winnowing of grain. The reference is to John the Baptist's words about Christ, ". . . whose fan is in his hand, and he will thoroughly purge his floor, and gather his wheat into the garner; but he will burn up the chaff with unquenchable fire" (Matt. 3:13). Characteristically, Hölderlin departs from the traditional interpretation of this biblical passage, referring the image instead to his concern for All-Unity. The analogy is thus between the wheat to be winnowed and the all-unitive "speech" ("Rede") perfectly articulated by Christ at the Last Supper: "all is good."[39] The process of history is the winnowing of this visionary message, the separation of essential from inessential components. The shovelful of wheat is tossed upward into the "clear," the sky or open area free of structured relationships. While corresponding to the painful divisions within the Christian community after Christ's death, this breakup of the primal unitive vision is necessary to separate the fundamental truth from subsequent distortions of Christ's teachings, the "cloud" in "Friedens-feier." The disintegration of the Christian vision and community, la-mented in the previous strophes, is now shown to be ultimately bene-ficial; in the process the husk of error falls away while the grain of essential truth is left, arriving at the end. Moreover, the poet declares, there is nothing bad in the loss of some of the grain or some of the meaningful resonance of the words of Christ. The projected all-unitive vision may emerge (at first) somewhat incomplete; yet such transient, accidental deficiency may itself be a part of the divine plan, "for the Highest does not want everything at once." Resuming the analogy found in "Friedensfeier" between human and divine modes of accom-plishment, the poet states that the "divine work" of purging Christ's vision and restoring its original truth may "also resemble" our own work in its imperfection. Yet, despite the calamities of history, the ultimate restoration of all-unitive vision and the reestablishment of human community are inevitable.

The concluding lines of the strophe tell of a conjectured response to the muted hopefulness of the present. Having means available, the poet could form a vivid image of Christ through which to foster re-membrance and hope. The image could thus (and more effectively) comfort us like the gifts of bread and wine. But there is also danger involved in constructing a divine likeness in time of expectation. The opening lines of the twelfth strophe pose a hypothetical event: "But if one spurred himself on and, talking sadly, on the way, when I was defenseless, attacked me, so that I was astounded, and a slave wished to imitate the image of the god—."[40] The poet fears that, while on the way to poetic fulfillment, unarmed, he might be overtaken by another traveller who is aggressively impatient because sadly distraught ("trau-rig") and desperate at divine absence. Such a man might "attack" the poet and force from him the "image of the god" he had made. Then, while the poet stood by dumbfounded, the other might as a "slave" seek to "imitate" this divine image. This would not be authentic *imitatio Christi,* as the imitator would set himself at two removes from reality, making himself into a mere copy of a copy; he would falsify both Christ and himself in distorting their true identities. He becomes a "slave" through such false imitation, binding himself to a dead object and making his soul a static, unfree thing in emulation, no longer open to all divine influences.

At this point Hölderlin breaks off the hypothetical narrative in horror of its possible consequences and recounts a previous experience of divine anger. "I once saw the Lord of Heaven visible in wrath, not that I should *be* anything, but to learn."[41] This divine admonition suggests that one must not (like the slave in his misuse of the image) seek a particular and fixed identity that would restrict one's responsiveness to divine presence. One should instead "learn," maintaining an open receptivity to God.[42]

The warning then continues in detail: "Benevolent are they [the heavenly gods] but what they hate the most, as long as they rule, is the false, and then [in the case of falsehood] the human would no longer have any validity among men." The gods are generally beneficent, although their full goodness has not yet been revealed. However, as long as they reign in transcendence, they hate falsification of the human or the divine, which might result in devaluation of what is merely (and authentically) "human." If mortals then sought to become supermen, the gods would violently punish such *hubris,* for the distinction between them and mortals must be reverently observed. If men will be patient, all gods will once again become immanent (as in "Der Rhein" and "Friedensfeier"): "For they [men] are not in charge, but the destiny of the Immortals is in charge, and their work moves of itself, and it proceeds in haste to its end. That is, when heavenly triumphal procession goes higher, there will be named, like the sun, by the strong, the jubilant Son of the Highest. . . ." The "destiny" of the gods rules history. The historical process is the gods' autonomous "work"; regardless of what men think or do it moves rapidly towards its own goal. When this preordained "triumphal procession" reaches its ultimate point, the gods will be manifest again to men, and Christ will appear as at the banquet of "Friedensfeier." He will then be named in his sunlike radiance by the "strong," those who (as in

"Brot und Wein") can endure the intensity of divine epiphany, and can grasp it in an appropriate "name."[43]

The thirteenth strophe tells how this naming may be accomplished. The naming of Christ (implicitly in relation to other gods) will be a "pass-sign" giving release and deliverance. The power of song will be as a staff ("Stab des Gesanges") summoning gods and beckoning them "down" to earth for festive visitation. We can now recognize that nothing is "common" ("gemein") or trivial, for everything now reveals its intrinsic value as a potential component of All-Unity. The staff of song will have power to "awaken the dead," at least those who are free of corruption. Here, as in "Brot und Wein," men in this interim of divine absence exist like the dead in Hades. Yet some men have remained loyal in divine remembrance, uncoarsened by religious indifference; they will readily rise to the first movements of ultimate song summoning the gods. "There are however many timid eyes waiting to behold the light," living in pious anticipation of the reappearance of divine radiance. They fear that sudden, direct exposure to this brilliance may blind them, unlike the "strong" souls first to evoke the gods.

Yet the speaker can also see a way to mitigate their shock at the coming light. "When, however, as if from swelling eyebrows forgetful of the world, quietly luminous power falls from holy scripture, they might, enjoying the grace, practice at the quiet gaze." The cautious ones may become as oblivious to the world as if bushy "eyebrows" shaded their eyes from light, keeping them from dangerous excesses of perception. Still, even in diminished awareness, they could encounter the subdued radiance of truth, the "quietly luminous" power emanating from "holy scripture"—the Bible and all other writings animated by divine inspiration. By attending to "scripture," they might practice their unstrenuous gaze in a gentler light and thus prepare their eyes for the full intensity of vision.

The speaker now addresses the man to whom the hymn is dedicated, the Bible-reading Landgraf von Homburg:

Und wenn die Himmlischen jezt
So, wie ich glaube, mich lieben

Wie viel mehr Dich,
Denn Eines weiss ich,
Dass nemlich der Wille
Des ewigen Vaters viel
Dir gilt. . . .   [2:171]

And if the Heavenly now, as I believe, love me, how much more [do they love] you, for one thing I know, that the will of the eternal Father much concerns you.

As gathered from Hölderlin's correspondence, the Landgraf (who aided the poet after his first bout with insanity) was a religious man of conservative views. He was distressed by the changes in the world since the French Revolution and asked Hölderlin for a poem to strengthen his confidence in traditional values.[44] "Patmos," possibly written in response, might have come as something of a shock. However, we can readily discern the fundamental (if anomalous) conservatism of these concluding strophes. If, as Hölderlin believes, the gods love him as a poet, whose task is to proclaim their coming presence to men, they must love the Landgraf even more because of his piety. This is not mere hyperbolical praise of a patron, but expression of a fundamental attitude in Hölderlin's late work—the necessity of preserving religious and societal order prior to the apocalypse. Without such order, men may behave with unknowing violence and blasphemy, and thereby provoke divine wrath. The heavenly gods love the Landgraf for adhering rigorously to the will of the Lord of Time and for upholding traditional, mediating value-structures in these perilous latter days. Moreover, the Father's own "sign," the lightning bolt, remains "silent" in "thundering heaven." Lightning, a favored emblem of dangerous, unmediated intensity of divine illumination, is here the Father's special sign to men amidst the turmoil of the epochal storm. It is communicative only to those who can grasp it as does the poet in the "Feiertag" hymn. "One," however, "stands beneath it his entire life." Christ has lived at all times standing immediately beneath his Father's lightning bolt. Not only surviving its fire, he perceives its significance and interprets it throughout the storm of Christian history.[45]

But, of course, Christ is not the only son of God; as "Der Einzige" states, many heroes or demigods have also been true to their Father. All have acted: "But the heroes, his [God's] sons, have all come and

until now the deeds of the world, an incessant race, have been interpreting holy scriptures about him and [have also been interpreting]
the lightning bolt." The sons' historical "deeds" constitute a "race"
("Wettlauf") in competitive response to the Father's will, each striving to realize perfect obedience. This sequence of pious deeds involves
an effective interpretation of God's will, whether mediated in scripture or unmediated in lightning, which they seek to "explain." Yet
the pattern of deeds is not arbitrary, for "he is there present." The
Father is secretly involved in all acts of history and has unobtrusively
been guiding processes that are essentially his own "works." He has a
controlling knowledge of these works and has always known how they
shall be executed: "For his works are all known to him from perpetu-
ity." The Landgraf's concern with the Father's will is thus vindicated
and his trepidations about the world perhaps assuaged, if, as the strophe
suggests, omniscient will has indeed been the shaping force of all history, and even the present turbulence is a part of God's plan.

The final strophe then turns again to the poet's own immediate
concerns:

Zu lang, zu lang schon ist
Die Ehre der Himmlischen unsichtbar.
Denn fast die Finger müssen sie
Uns führen und schmählich
Entreisst das Herz uns eine Gewalt.
Denn Opfer will der Himmlischen jedes
Wenn aber eines versäumt ward,
Nie hat es Gutes gebracht.
Wir haben gedienet der Mutter Erd'
Und haben jüngst dem Sonnenlichte gedient,
Unwissend, der Vater aber liebt,
Der über allen waltet,
Am meisten, dass gepfleget werde
Der veste Buchstab, und bestehendes gut
Gedeutet. Dem folgt deutscher Gesang.   [2:171–172]

Too long, too long already has the honor of the Heavenly been invisible.
For they must almost guide our fingers for us and shamefully a
power is tearing away at our hearts. For each one of the Heavenly wants
sacrifices, and when one was neglected it never brought anything
good. We have served our Mother Earth and lately have served
the sunlight, unknowingly, but the Father who rules over all loves

most that the fixed letter be cultivated, and that which exists be well interpreted. Him German song obeys.

Not only are the gods occluded, but even forms of religious service (by which men honor them) are no longer apparent. Whatever attention we give the gods seems compelled. Even "song"—the appropriate honorific mode for poets—requires divine compulsion. Yet, a violent force ("Gewalt") is wresting our hearts out of control, shamefully tearing us from holy attentiveness.[46] And yet we must strive to serve the gods, however difficult it may seem. As in "Der Einzige," to neglect any particular deity would be to slight some essential aspect of divine All-Unity, falsifying its nature. Here, we must offer the "sacrifice" of proper attentiveness to each god, or anger all the gods. We have already been serving two aspects of divinity. As elsewhere, Mother Earth is both the locus of our lives as mortals and our mortal parent, mediating Life through her structures. We have attended both to her and to the "Sunlight," perhaps as an emblem of divine lucidity, the light of truth.[47]

Yet we should now concentrate on specific tasks. Prior to the return of Christ, the Lord of Time desires that we "cultivate" the "fixed letter," texts already established, presumably the "holy scripture" of the last two strophes. We must devote ourselves to the enduring letter of these texts until it blossoms in significance and clarity for all men. This means *poetic* attention—poetic vivification and elaboration of what has already been written. The other activity the Father decrees is closely related: that everything in existence ("bestehendes") be well interpreted ("gut gedeutet")—presumably including the holy texts. The poet must become interpreter literally of all things, a task that could be considered modest only in comparison with the ultimate function of song.[48] Yet this interpretive function is merely preparatory to the final achievement of poetry. All things must first be elucidated as individual entities, and all writings authentically concerned with the truth of Being must be understood. Poetry must clearly interpret each particular aspect of its projected all-unitive vision before it can achieve final visionary synthesis. When the moment willed by the Father has finally arrived, the poet will be able to enunciate ultimate song, and Christ and the other gods will be named in fully articulated vision.

This is what "German song" observes, the course it follows: "Dem folgt deutscher Gesang." Hölderlin thought it the task of poets of his own country to implement the divine will and advance the consummate poetic work the Father has ordained for all mankind.[49]

If we now examine the structure of this poem as a whole, we see that the triadic division evident in "Friedensfeier" and "Der Rhein" is less in evidence here.[50] There are a number of ways in which the structure of "Patmos" may be conceptualized; many of these approaches are not without merit.[51] But if we are to account for the poem's inner logic, how it may have developed in the poet's mind, if we are to discern the poem's generation and intellectual necessity, we must consider it in terms of the crucial problem of All-Unity.

As noted, "Patmos" is begun at a moment when the principal goal of all Hölderlin's poetic efforts appears out of reach. The opening strophe of "Patmos" presents a graphic picture of the poet's seeming inability to achieve unitive concord. Human consciousness is fragmented with broken segments (its particulars) dwelling upon various peaks of time, loving one another though separated. They will perish if they are unable to reachieve unity among themselves and thus evoke the all-unitive God, who remains "near" though perilously "difficult to grasp." The poet prays for the means to reestablish bonds of love.

The rest of the poem evolves as a consequence of this initial prayer. The poet's flight to Asia is an ironic outcome of his request. While it represents a "going-over" of sorts, it makes no provisions for "return," but leaves the poet even more radically alienated and remote from any possibility of union. Seeking something "known," he sets out among the islands of the archipelago (themselves figures of fragmentation) for Patmos. Patmos's desolation corresponds to his own. Its associations help the poet achieve identification with St. John, who likewise found comfort here.

The poet then returns through John's memory to a moment when communion was perfectly achieved at the Last Supper. Then Christ had pronounced the ultimate articulation of all-unitive vision, that "all is good." But Christ died, and the vision and community died with him. Bereft of divine presence, the disciples lived together in memory alone, until Christ sent them the Pentecostal Spirit which re-infused them with Life but also disrupted even their residual community. This scattering of the disciples is the prototypal initiating moment of the disintegrative process which culminates in the first strophe's radical fragmentation. Yet the poet asserts that this apparently destructive process is like the winnower's toss. The all-unitive vision achieved by Christ but misunderstood after his death is fragmented throughout history, hopefully to be regathered virtually intact and purified at history's end.

Reassured, the speaker turns here to the question of poetry. He now seeks to relate his function as poet to his new understanding of history. The poet rejects the alternative of constructing a poetic image of Christ. If the poet will remain patient and docile, the consummate vision will again be granted as Christ is "named" in ultimate "Song." Unlike "Friedensfeier," the poem's conclusion offers instructions for the poet to observe prior to this apocalypse. Here a number of questions are confronted: how he might best serve the Father's will, how he should prepare himself to articulate all-unitive vision, how he should prepare others for its advent, and also (in the final strophe) how he might render "sacrifice" of poetic attention to each and all the gods.

He believes he has found the answer to these questions. Song is to be an elucidation of all things, showing the meaning of each and its relation to the whole. The work must be continued until the apocalyptic vision is achieved. By cultivating the fixed letter of scripture, and by illuminating its intrinsic truth, the poet helps others respond to the preparatory light of revelation. Through interpretation he also effectively serves all the various deities who demand poetic attention. But, most essentially, his newfound task will enable him to observe and specify the interrelatedness of all things in divine All-Unity. He can thus assist in the reunion of those isolated on the peaks of time. And in founding this community of spirit he will bring the near, elusive God (himself all-unitive Life) not merely into grasp but into the living fabric of vision, which will sustain a perfect communion. The conclusion to "Patmos," by proclaiming the mission of "German song," thus returns to its initial situation, not in mere formal reference but in resolution of the poem's central problem.

The poetic achievement of "Patmos" is thus ultimately greater and more meaningful than that of the more euphoric "Friedensfeier." It not only foresees the consummation of history but provides instructions for us prior to this event. "Patmos" also accomplishes a thorough reappraisal of Hölderlin's paramount concern: having posed with painful clarity the hindrances to achieving All-Unity, the poem evolves dialectically to a conclusion which resolves not only the questions raised in the poem but most of the questions that have yet emerged in Hölderlin's work. The final sentence, "Dem folgt deutscher Gesang," sounds like the last word on the subject of German poetry and quite likely was intended as such—but it was not. The splendid resolution of "Patmos" itself becomes subject to the dialectical negations of poetic thought. Hölderlin's last completed hymn, "Mnemosyne," is the tragic result of this final negation.

14. "Mnemosyne"

The great synthesis attained in "Patmos" soon proved untenable. The poem itself was subjected to attempts at revision, but none of these were completed past the decisive eleventh strophe. The first tentative revision was unable to work out historical implications. The last two attempts falter at the moment of Pentecost. While Hölderlin was thus able to reformulate the problem, he could no longer resolve it. None of the late versions of "Patmos" could cope with the problem of fragmentation.[1]

In his final years of intermittent sanity, Hölderlin was able to complete only three more hymns: "Andenken," "Der Ister," and finally "Mnemosyne." While the first two are interesting poems dealing with important themes, the last resumes most of these themes and itself constitutes a final statement on the now hopeless status of the problem of All-Unity. It represents virtual capitulation in the face of this problem. According to Friedrich Beissner's reconstruction of the text, "Mnemosyne" exists in three versions differing principally in the first strophe.[2] The initial strophe of the third version is radically different from that of the other two versions, and there is evidence that it was written after the completion of the second and third strophes.[3] In this chapter I will discuss the hymn's third version.

The first strophe in this version has a number of statements which (characteristic of *parataxis* in Hölderlin's late work)[4] might appear to have little coherence:

Reif sind, in Feuer getaucht, gekocht
Die Frücht und auf der Erde geprüfet und ein Gesez ist
Dass alles hineingeht, Schlangen gleich,
Prophetisch, träumend auf
Den Hügeln des Himmels. Und vieles
Wie auf den Schultern eine
Last von Scheitern ist
Zu behalten. Aber bös sind
Die Pfade. Nemlich unrecht,
Wie Rosse, gehn die gefangenen
Element' und alten
Geseze der Erd. Und immer
Ins Ungebundene gehet eine Sehnsucht. Vieles aber ist
Zu behalten. Und Noth die Treue.
Vorwärts aber und rükwärts wollen wir
Nicht sehn. Uns wiegen lassen, wie
Auf schwankem Kahne der See.   [2:197]

Ripe are the fruits, dipped in fire, cooked and tested upon earth, and a law, that all things must go in like snakes, is prophetic, dreaming on the hills of heaven. And much, like a load of logs on the shoulders, is to be kept. But evil are the paths. For wrongly, like horses, go the captive elements and old laws of the earth. And always a yearning goes into the unbounded. But much is to be kept. And loyalty is needed. But we do not want to look forwards and backwards. Let ourselves be rocked, as on an unsteady boat of the sea.

One possible source of division is suggested by Hölderlin's use of "aber" to indicate frequent shifts of thought. We thus might read the first two sentences as forming a kind of unit. In his excellent and very helpful interpretation of the poem, Jochen Schmidt notes the emphasis here on "fire."[5] This, as generally, is a figure of unmediated divine Life in its greatest intensity. Here fire is viewed as the divine vital force of Nature, as in some earlier poems—in particular, a number of motifs and emphases in the present poem are reminiscent of Hölderlin's "Empedoklean" phase. The "cooking" of earth's fruits (a metaphor for ripening) is an instance of the operation of this fire and the means by which the fruits are "tested";[6] earth is a place of trial by fire to determine how much intensity each thing can bear. There is a "law" that "all things must go in like snakes," entering the realm of death and fiery immediacy which Hölderlin now terms "Heaven," the locus of transcendent divine Being.[7] Everything ultimately perishes in fire but it approaches its end by winding, serpentine paths.

This law of universal perishing is "prophetic" in its lucidity and is "dreaming" trance-like "on the hills of heaven." The latter are possibly clouds forming a natural boundary and vantage point between this world and the next.[8] Heaven's law is thus proclaimed as if in prophetic trance from atop these clouds. The cloud-imagery is perhaps implicitly continued in the following sentence: "And much, like a load of logs on the shoulders, is to be kept." This might be understood in reference to the eleventh strophe of "Der Rhein":

Die Söhne der Erde sind, wie die Mutter,
Alliebend, so empfangen sie auch
Mühlos, die Glüklichen, Alles.
Drum überraschet es auch
Und schrökt den sterblichen Mann,
Wenn er den Himmel, den
Er mit den liebenden Armen
Sich auf die Schultern gehäufft,
Und die Last der Freude bedenket;   [2:146–147]

The sons of the Earth are, like the mother, all-loving, therefore they
also, tirelessly, the happy ones, are receptive to All. Thus it also surprises
and frightens the mortal man, when he considers the heaven which
with loving arms he has heaped on his shoulders, and the burden of joy.

As remarked earlier, these lines refer to man's loving proclivity to accept on his shoulders the burden of transcendent Life and all things beyond his comprehension. Man joyously takes on himself the task of coping with All-Unity, though it may "surprise" and even "frighten" him when he suddenly becomes fully cognizant of its weight. In the present poem what is borne on the shoulders is designated as "much" ("vieles") rather than "all" ("Alles"), but it still denotes the burden of the many incomprehensible things bound together like a "load of logs." The poet's devotion to All-Unity has become a divinely imposed onus; "we" must continue to endure this burden although it is Heaven's own law that all things (including visions of transcendence) must eventually be undone. This is only the first of the hymn's bitter paradoxes.

The second thought-unit in the strophe presents another side of the problem. Following Schmidt's persuasive reading of these lines, we may say that "paths," like those in the later versions of "Patmos," are "evil" because they are now dangerously exposed to divine fire and apt to lead us astray.[9] Both Empedoklean "elements" (modes of divine Life in the natural world) and the ancient, sacred natural "laws" of earth are now held in constraint. Their captivity is not to any alien power, but is merely the condition of earthly order and finitude, the condition which Empedokles found to be so painful.[10] Here, however, the raging discontent with finitude is felt even by the elements themselves. The divine fire now seeks to break out of its mediated bondage, thereby destroying all finite entities whose lives it supports. The immolation Empedokles sought for himself now threatens universal holocaust.

Thus, the elements and old laws of earth go "wrongly," astray like unbridled horses. And as universal anarchy is loosed, we ourselves constantly experience "yearning" for the "unbounded," Empedoklean desire to be released into a fiery immediacy, simply to *become* All-Unity rather than to come to terms with it in mediation. We seek release from the burden of comprehension, from responsible life of the mind, and from mortal life itself. Yet the speaker again admonishes us: "But much is to be kept. And loyalty is needed." We must still, despite our frustration, maintain ("behalten") the burden of our responsibilities to the many things. This repeats the main clause of the earlier sentence: "Und vieles / Wie auf den Schultern eine / Last von Scheitern ist / Zu behalten"—"Vieles aber ist / Zu behalten."

Hölderlin's obsession with the problem of All-Unity demands this reiteration; he must remind himself again of his poetic duties. There is a "need" for persevering in attention to the problem and for loyally holding up the burden.

The closing lines of the strophe have often been interpreted as a reprehensible wish to escape responsibility.[11] Yet a contrary evaluation of these lines may be preferable. Though inclined to the usual interpretation, Schmidt notes a similar episode of euphoria in *Hyperion*, where the protagonist speaks of letting himself be "rocked half asleep" in a boat ("liess vom Boote mich halb in Schlummer wiegen") and of drinking from the "cup of forgetfulness" ("aus der Schaale der Vergessenheit zu trinken").[12] Yet in the novel, after this state of near-forgetfulness, Hyperion is capable of the spiritual intensities of his love for Diotima and his later political heroism. Clearly such a moment of repose does not constitute a permanent abdication of all human responsibility—as an examination of similar instances in Hölderlin might demonstrate.[13] Hölderlin does not wish to condemn this moment of repose; if we do not want to look forward or backward, it may be that we desire not oblivion but pure realization of the present moment.[14] Our desire may indicate not flight from temporal awareness but a positive refusal to yield to inauthentic escapes into the past or an imaginary future. The willingness to be "rocked" as in a boat indicates readiness to be lulled into a minimal but lucid awareness, an experience of pure presence that would preserve the "loyalty" ("Treue") of the poet's commitment while permitting him to recuperate for the arduous task ahead. The strophe's concluding lines do not show any breach of loyalty but a mode of maintaining it under threatening conditions.

The second strophe begins by asking more specifically "how" such loyalty is to be kept:

Wie aber liebes? Sonnenschein
Am Boden sehen wir und trokenen Staub
Und heimathlich die Schatten der Wälder und es blühet
An Dächern der Rauch, bei alter Krone
Der Thürme, friedsam; gut sind nemlich
Hat gegenredend die Seele
Ein Himmlisches verwundet, die Tageszeichen.
Denn Schnee, wie Majenblumen

Das Edelmüthige, wo
Es seie, bedeutend, glänzet auf
Der grüne Wiese
Der Alpen, hälftig, da, vom Kreuze redend, das
Gesezt ist unterwegs einmal
Gestorbenen, auf hoher Strass
Ein Wandersmann geht zornig,
Fern ahnend mit
Dem andern, aber was ist diss?   [2:197–198]

But how, dear one? We see sunshine on the ground and dry dust and,
natively, the shadows of the woods; and the smoke blooms on roofs,
by the old crown of towers, peacefully; for good, if a Heavenly one has
wounded the soul talking back, are the signs of day. For snow, like
mayflowers signifying the noble-spirited wherever it may be,
glistens on the green meadow of the Alps, half-way, where, speaking
of the cross that is placed for those who once died underway, on the high
road a wanderer goes in frenzy, surmising afar with the other—but
what is this?

In asking how a pure present awareness may be loyally attained, the
poet addresses an unspecified hearer as "liebes" ("Dear"), a tone appropriate to the strophe's idyllic beginning. He then describes details
of a peaceful everyday scene. The view begins at the "ground" where
we see sunlight, a figure of divine presence, but also "dry dust," emblematical of death and fragmentation. More positive signs are stressed,
however, as the view moves upwards to the shady woods in the middle
distance. Such forest shade promises a beneficent repose like that at
the end of the first strophe. While it might also remind us that we need
protection from overly intense sunlight, the shade is itself benevolent,
associated frequently with the poet's "homeland" as a place for quiet,
hopeful waiting. Higher in the distance the viewer then sees familiar
rooftops, where chimney smoke seems peacefully blooming on roofs
next to the crests or crowns of towers.[15]

The predominantly positive character of the scene reassures the
poet, who seeks peace and contentment in the landscape to relieve an
inner "wound." An injury to the soul is mentioned in an earlier letter,
where Hölderlin declares, "wie man Helden nachspricht, kann ich
wohl sagen, dass mich Apollo geschlagen" ("to repeat the words of
heroes, I can indeed say that Apollo has struck me").[16] Hölderlin,

then living in Bordeaux, believed that he had opened his soul too un-
reservedly to the fiery intensity of life and nature there, and that Apollo
(god of light as well as of poetry) had "struck" him with a nearly lethal
dose of heavenly fire—presumably, the poet's first attack of madness.
The present lines construe this attack as a wound inflicted by a god:
"Hat gegenredend die Seele / Ein Himmlisches verwundet" ("if
a Heavenly one has wounded the soul talking back"). The passage is
extremely ambiguous. It may suggest that the god, angered by the
poet's impertinence, responded violently by plunging his soul into a
dark night of anguished confusion.[17] A more positive interpretation
might conjecture that the god in all innocence had merely "answered"
the inquisitive poet, but that this "answer," because of its divine source,
was too intense for the poet to endure. Yet however his "wounded"
condition came about, the poet finds the "signs of day" comforting in
their familiarity and simplicity. They suggest a life of calm mediation
and offer a stability which the poet needs to retain his hold on ordinary existence and residual sanity.

But the "higher" aspects of nature may themselves lead to hopelessness. The structure of the following lines consists of a complex sentence with main clause ("Schnee . . . glänzet") modified by subordi-
nate clause ("da . . . ein Wandersmann geht"), followed by another
clause asking a question ("aber was ist diss?"). The first clause describes
an Alpine landscape in spring, with half-melted snow that resembles
"mayflowers." Both snow and flowers signify the "noble-spirited":
height on the mountains may represent elevation of soul, and white-
ness might signify noble purity—the snow's "glistening" could be especially indicative of moral radiance. Yet (while these interpretations
should not be excluded) the most convincing reading might refer to
the classical *topos* of the early death of the hero, often present in Hölderlin's work.[18] Both snow and flowers share with the noble-spirited-
ness of heroes a beauty which is transient; in particular we might think
of Achilles, the greatest prototype of such tragic beauty.

Through this landscape of high meadows and snow goes a "wanderer" with an unspecified companion ("dem andern").[19] As noted
earlier in "Der Wanderer," the traveller is one of Hölderlin's figures
of the poet—he gathers diverse experiences in the hope of synthesizing
them into a type of comprehensive vision. Here, he is on an Alpine

pass; he is possibly coming from the German homeland (the restful everyday scene) to cross the Alps or to attain their summit. The wanderer walks in a frenzy ("zornig") designating a furious intensity of divine inspiration;[20] and he is "surmising afar" ("fern ahnend"), possibly with the Greek heroic world beyond the Alps, or with the unitive vision he might still achieve if a total historical view is ever attained. Yet, even as the wanderer journeys, he is also "speaking of the cross that is placed for those who once died underway." This is presumably a roadside shrine,[21] but the wanderer seems to speak of it as having special significance for himself. It commemorates those who previously died while attempting the journey he has now undertaken. The cross is therefore, even more than snow or flowers, a drastic emblem of the transiency of noble-minded endeavor.[22] And the vision of Greece which the wanderer (like the poet himself) can finally achieve now can only further inflame a psychic wound.

But we still must ask, "what is this?"—what is the end of the pilgrimage?[23] The hymn's concluding strophe will provide the answer:

Am Feigenbaum ist mein
Achilles mir gestorben,
Und Ajax liegt
An den Grotten der See,
An Bächen, banachbart dem Skamandros.
An Schläfen Sausen einst, nach
Der unbewegten Salamis steter
Gewohnheit, in der Fremd', ist gross
Ajax gestorben
Patroklos aber in des Königes Harnisch. Und es starben
Noch andere viel. Am Kithäron aber lag
Elevtherä, der Mnemosyne Stadt. Der auch als
Ablegte den Mantel Gott, das abendliche nachher löste
Die Loken. Himmlische nemlich sind
Unwillig, wenn einer nicht die Seele schonend sich
Zusammengenommen, aber er muss doch; dem
Gleich fehlet die Trauer.   [2:198]

At the fig tree my Achilles died to me, and Ajax lies by the grottoes of the sea, by brooks near to the Scamander. Once, with a roaring at the temples, after the constant habitude of unmoved Salamis, in a foreign land, great Ajax died, Patroklos however in the armor of the king. And many others died too. But on Cithaeron lay Eleutherae,

> Mnemosyne's city. For her also, when God put off his cloak, the evening
> one afterward severed the locks of hair. For the Heavenly ones are
> displeased if someone does not pull himself together, sparing
> his soul, but yet he *must*; likewise, mourning is at fault.

The goal of such a quest must be a vision of tragically necessitated
death. The first ten lines of the strophe mention the deaths of three
heroes of the *Iliad*: Achilles, Ajax, and Patroklos. Achilles is lamented
most poignantly: "At the fig tree my Achilles died to me. . . ." Critics
have noted that Hölderlin felt an intensely personal attachment to
Achilles and his fate.[24] In this regard, Schmidt quotes from Hölderlin's
earlier essay, "Über Achill": "Er ist mein Leibling unter den Helden,
so stark und zart, die gelungenste, und vergänglichste Blüte der He-
roenwelt, 'so für kurze Zeit geboren' nach Homer, eben weil er so
schön ist" ("He is my favorite among the heroes, so strong and so
tender, the most excellent and the most perishable blossom of the heroic world, 'thus born for a short time' according to Homer, precisely
because he is so beautiful"; 4:224).[25] Achilles' strength and beauty, his
nobility of spirit and particularly the brevity of his life make him the
quintessential type of the Greek hero for Hölderlin.

We might briefly digress here to recall Hölderlin's view of the
proper relationship of poet to hero. As early as the ode "Empedokles,"
the poet, while proclaiming admiration for Empedokles' noble sacrifice, insists that he himself should not "follow," since that would mean
the wasteful destruction of poetic gifts and abandonment of the "love"
that holds him to this world.[26] The appropriate poet-hero relationship
is also shown in two later odes, "An Eduard" and "Stimme des Volks."
The former is addressed to an "Eduard" who is actually Isaak von Sinclair, the political activist. It tells of the poet's determination to "follow" Sinclair not in action, but in interpretive celebration of his
heroism in song.[27] (It is interesting to note that in this ode the poet
addresses Sinclair as "mein Achill.") "Stimme des Volks" relates an
extreme example of Greek heroic self-destruction, resulting from a
simplistic and literal interpretation (in action) of a legendary mass-
martyrdom on the part of their forefathers. This devastation could
have been averted had they someone to interpret poetically this ances-
tral lore as a remembrance of Deity:

So hatten es die Kinder gehört, und wohl
  Sind gut die Sagen, denn ein Gedächtniss sind
    Dem Höchsten sie, doch auch bedarf es
      Eines, die Heiligen auszulegen.   [2:53]

Thus the children had heard it, and indeed legends are good, for they are
a remembrance of the Highest, yet there is also a need for someone
to interpret these holy things.

The final strophe of "Mnemosyne" concerns the divinely fated destruction of the Greeks in the specific instances of three legendary heroes. And here again, we might expect the poet to give a lucid interpretive account of heroic action. For we recall that interpretation of existing things and cultivation of the letter was the specific function of poetry designated at the end of "Patmos." The poet who declares "my Achilles has died to me" might thus also be assumed to maintain a proper interpretive distance. And yet, the poet's intensely personal tone here indicates that such poetic detachment might now be impossible.

While Achilles is said to have died at the "fig tree,"[28] Ajax, the second hero of the *Iliad*, "lies by the grottoes of the sea, by the brooks, in the vicinity of the Scamander." Beissner accounts for these details by reference to Sophocles' *Ajax*, which Hölderlin translated in part.[29] He also observes how they echo a passage in an early version of *Hyperion*. Afflicted by a devastating sense of loss, Hyperion "accidentally . . . hits upon" the passage in Sophocles where Ajax makes his suicide speech, bidding farewell to the beautiful forms of nature about him, the streams, grottoes, and groves by the sea—respectively emblems of destiny, dark seclusion, and idyllic rest. To these, Ajax declares: "ihr habt mich lange behalten . . . nun aber, nun atm' ich nimmer Lebensothem unter euch!" ("You have held me long . . . but now, now I will nevermore breathe the breath of life among you.") And turning to the Trojan river he declares: "Ihr nachbarlichen Wasser des Skamanders, die ihr so freundlich die Argiver empfiengt, ihr werdet nimmer mich sehen!—Hier lieg' ich ruhmlos!" ("You neighboring waters of the Scamander, you who received the Argives in such a friendly manner, you will never see me more—here I will lie without renown!"; 3:240–241.) Hyperion nearly weeps at this, for Ajax's attitude here is essentially typical of his own. Like the Greek hero, Hyperion now feels excluded from the community of human endeavor. Thus the troubled poet of "Mnemosyne" can also recall the fate of Ajax, who here lies dead by these same grottoes and brooks.

The strophe continues: "With a roaring at the temples, after the constant habitude of unmoved Salamis, in a foreign land, great Ajax died. . . ." The roaring of temples perhaps indicates compulsion by a daemonic spirit or "Genius" which (rather like the Holy Spirit at Pentecost) is experienced as a sound of roaring wind.[30] The strophe's earlier version may be cited:

> Von Genius kühn ist   bei Windessausen, nach
> Der heimathlichen Salamis süsser
> Gewohnheit, in der Fremd'
> Ajax gestorben   [2:194]

The lines speak of the "sweet" or "steady" habitude of Ajax's native island, which had reared many heroes and is constantly subject to a raging sea-wind.[31] Whatever the structure of allusion here, the poet is emphasizing two aspects of Ajax's fate—that he died in a rage of supernatural compulsion, and that he died in exile. The frenzied, daemonic character of his suicide may be contrasted with Patroklos' mode of death: ". . . Patroklos however [died] in the King's [Achilles'] armor." Aside from the obvious irony of this juxtaposition (Ajax killed himself because he was not awarded Achilles' armor), the contrast here is between two radically dissimilar ways of death. Fundamentally, the poet contrasts a death of anguished self-liberation from the confines of earthly existence to a death of stoic commitment to the destiny ordained by the gods. This opposition is more explicit in the earlier version:

> Und es starben
> Noch andere viel. Mit eigener Hand
> Viel traurige, wilden Muths, doch göttlich
> Gezwungen, zulezt, die anderen aber
> Im Geschike stehend, im Feld.   [2:194]

And many others died too. Many mournful ones [died] by their own hand, with wild courage, yet divinely compelled at last; but the others [died] standing in destiny, in the field.

The first sentence is unelaborated in the third version. Here, details are provided. Like Ajax, men were driven by grief into self-destruction, yet were divinely (or daemonically) compelled. But the others, like Patroklos, died "standing in destiny, in the field." They, too, died as the gods ordained, though in dutiful commitment to their own fates; ironically, the divine will is accomplished in either event.

While the poem's concluding lines are a meditation on this paradox, the final version interposes another passage which also has bearing on the conclusion: "But on Cithaeron lay Eleutherae, Mnemosyne's city. For her, also, when God put off his cloak, the evening one afterward severed the locks of hair." This Mnemosyne of the poem's title is the goddess of memory and mother of the nine muses; in Greek her name signifies the active power of holding things in memory.[32] She thus personifies the task the poet decrees in the first strophe: "Vieles aber ist / Zu behalten." To Hölderlin Mnemosyne is the divine patroness of the poet's endeavor to retain all things in mind for synthesis in all-unitive vision; as the principle of active Memory, she is even the divine essence of poetry itself. And yet it is observed that Eleutherae, her sacred city, "lay" on the slopes of Mount Cythera, already in ruins in later Hellenic times. And like her city Mnemosyne died long ago.[33] Her death occurred at the end of the ancient day of divine presence, when God laid aside his "cloak," the very fabric of mediation and the clothing of visible forms (in nature, art and civilization) which, as in Carlyle's *Sartor Resartus*, manifest divine presence to the world. But, as Schmidt indicates, the cloak also conceals the unmediated intensity of divine Life, protecting man from fiery destruction.[34] Thus, the image has two meanings: that the divine presence would no longer be manifest in mediated form, and that any future direct contact between man and Deity could only be destructive.

Mnemosyne's death occurs upon the removal of this mediating cloak. If the function of poetry is to express articulated response to Deity, poetry becomes impossible in the Deity's absence. This is the final, tragic answer that now must be given to the question posed (and only provisionally answered) in "Brot und Wein": "Und wozu Dichter in dürftiger Zeit?"

To recapitulate briefly: authentic poetry is humanly articulated response to divine All-Unity, and poetry strives ultimately towards all-unitive vision. "Brot und Wein" assigned it the provisional or intermediate task of providing comfort, but the late hymns from "Wie wenn am Feiertage" have been passionately concerned with the achievement of the vision itself. "Der Rhein" and "Friedensfeier" suggest that we have only to wait, and that the vision will be realized eventually through divine ordinance. "Patmos," after great difficulties, returns to the same conviction, while specifying another intermediate task, the "interpretation" of writings and all things in preparation for vision; all must be clarified and held in active memory until the vision is achieved. But now Memory, the most essential power of poetry, is dead, having perished with the end of the Greek world. Things cannot now be put in order; the all-unitive vision itself can never be achieved. The first strophe's insistence that "many things should be held" is now shown to be futile. The requisite "loyalty" cannot be maintained. There is nothing now to restrain the "longing" ("Sehnsucht") that always goes into the "Unbounded," the realm where all things not God must be consumed in his fire.

There is no alternative to mourning now. Yet mourning, too, is divinely compelled; it, too, leads to the simplicity of fire and the world of death. Even responsibility to the gods' will becomes meaningless, for everything now seems to incite their wrath:

> Himmlische nemlich sind
> Unwillig, wenn einer nicht die Seele schonend sich
> Zusammengenommen, aber er muss doch; dem
> Gleich fehlet die Trauer.   [2:198]

> For the Heavenly Ones are displeased if someone does not pull himself together, [thereby] sparing his soul, but yet he must; likewise mourning is at fault.[35]

These lines pose a dilemma to which the only possible response is despair. The gods are angered by any loss of self-possession. They have an interest in human self-control, for only then can mortals respect the limits and demands imposed by the gods. Such restraint alone permits man to "spare his soul" and to protect himself from fiery destruction.

"But yet he *must*." As in English, the German modal usually demands or at least implies another verb. Here, however, it seems likely that "müssen" is used in its absolute sense; simply, "he must." He is under compulsion; whatever he does he is forced to do. Thus, even if a man destroys his soul, he does so under daemonic necessity. And, as earlier versions of the strophe suggest, this coercion may be ultimately from the gods themselves. It is said of Ajax and all who killed themselves in wild courage that they were "divinely compelled at last": "göttlich gezwungen zulezt." They accomplished divine will as much as those who lived through their destinies and died in armor. Any freedom is illusory—whether we destroy ourselves or live out our lives we are doing the gods' will. Thus the paradox. To lose control may be to anger the gods. But we have no choice in the matter; we are merely doing what the gods compel. The gods may force us to destroy ourselves and then be enraged when we do so. As in most religious literature, it is their prerogative to be unreasonable.[36]

"Dem / Gleich fehlet die Trauer": it is in this manner that mourning "sins," or is at fault. Here as elsewhere in Hölderlin, "mourning" is an extreme condition of sad perplexity, uncontrolled grief verging on madness. Ajax is possessed by mourning when he kills himself frenzied by a sense of dishonor; so are many other heroes: "Viel traurige, wilden Muths. . . ." Mourning sins through divine compulsion that yet angers the gods; it discourages self-mastery and does not spare the soul. It is a refusal (or inability) to recollect oneself.

But not only Ajax and other Greek heroes—the poet himself may be guilty of this sin. And this is the poem's discovery. The tone of the strophe's beginning indicates that the poet may be in mourning for Achilles, feeling his loss in intense personal grief: "Am Feigenbaum ist *mein* / Achilles *mir* gestorben. . . ." Achilles has died *for* the poet, who can now no longer sing his praises. The other heroes have also died for him; he can sing only of their deaths, not their lives—he cannot make them "live again" as is traditional in verse. Eleutherae, like all Greek cities, is in ruins; he cannot rebuild it in song. But, worst of all, Mnemosyne has died. Poetry has lost not only its object but any possibility of coherence. Thus the poet mourns. Such awareness is perhaps the final reality of the wound given the soul by the god's reply.[37]

And finally, it appears that the poet cannot now withdraw to moments of pure presence and self-awareness. Nor can he be calmed by the idyllic "signs of day." For there is a symbolic dialectic in natural objects leading to transcendent concerns; moreover, even the seemingly naive picture of an alpine wanderer would bring back to the poet the futility of his quest. The culmination of such a quest is shown in the last strophe. It is an anguished awareness of death—of heroes and cities, of divine Memory, and of poetry itself. Far from comforting the poet, this vision leaves him shattered. In attempting to escape from dissolution he has confronted it at its historical origin. We are now just as the Greeks were at the end of their day, at the first onset of world mourning—"Als der Vater gewandt sein Angesicht von den Menschen / Und das Trauern mit Recht über der Erde begann" (2:94). The consolations of "Brot und Wein" are now empty; two thousand years of Christianity have brought us nothing; every comfort since the death of Christ has been illusory.[38] We remain in mourning as our world comes apart. We can do nothing since we cannot master ourselves—and this is God's will though it provokes God's anger: "Dem / Gleich fehlet die Trauer." Poetry is dead and violence alone remains, for mourning is itself a kind of violence.

Many of the remaining fragments written after "Mnemosyne" are not quite this pessimistic in some of their implications.[39] But "Mnemosyne" is Hölderlin's last completed hymn, and it ends in death.

Conclusion

Anyone who might reduce Hölderlin's later poems, including "Mnemo-syne," to mere displays of advancing schizophrenia would rob them of their value as poetry. For those who do not follow a reductive approach but consider the poems phenomenologically, Hölderlin's later works must be unsettling because they demonstrate, by precept and example, the futility of writing any poetry which seeks an ordered comprehension of life. These poems demonstrate that the failure of such poetry is necessarily correlative with the full realization of the disappearance of God. While it has become commonplace for critics to speak of a "religion of poetry," or of poetry as a substitute for religion, and to show the origins of this tendency in writers of Hölderlin's generation, the full importance of "poetic religion" still need to be examined in greater detail. This study has attempted to explore some of these implications for Hölderlin, showing their development and where it leads him; therefore, theological terms such as "immanence" and "transcendence" have been employed in charting the dialectics of his poetic thought.

While Hölderlin always assumes that God is All-Unity, the problem remains precisely *how* God is All-Unity and how—if at all—man can approach this God. All of Hölderlin's important poems concern themselves with various aspects of this problem; but their resolutions serve only further to complicate the problem itself. Hölderlin's growth as a poet is thus essentially the development of his thought regarding this burgeoning poetic obsession.

Most generally, Hölderlin's notion of God begins in something like mere pantheism (God *is* all actuality), evolves through what may be termed "panentheism" (God is *in* all actuality), and ends in a belief in radical divine otherness (God is *beyond* all experiential actuality). In theological terms: God is first wholly immanent, then immanent in things though ultimately transcending them (as in most Christian orthodoxies), and at last utterly transcendent, or withdrawn. In the first phase God has abandoned himself to the world; in the last the world has been virtually abandoned by God. This poetic direction is not of course unilinear; there are regressions and occasional sidetracks. But the basic line is clear from the Tübingen hymns to "Mnemosyne," and beyond. A late fragment offers perhaps the most optimistic statements that can be made about God in Hölderlin's last phase:

> Was ist Gott? unbekannt, dennoch
> Voll Eigenschaften ist das Angesicht
> Des Himmels von ihm. Die Blize nemlich
> Der Zorn sind eines Gottes.   [2:210]

What is God? Unknown, yet the face of heaven is full of his characteristics. The lightning bolts, namely, are the wrath of a God.

God has disappeared into himself; he is now invisible and "unknown." His "characteristics" are manifestations of his power, but not intimations of his essential Being. Although the fragment goes on to mention more appealing symbolic properties, the most typical deific attributes in the later poetry are "die Blize," emblems of an ambivalent but always threatening divine fury. The distant God approaches us now most notably in wrath.

The development leading to this radically unhappy consciousness is revealed in and through the poems themselves—from the early hymns, rapturously celebrating divine presence, to the late fragments, lamenting a disquieting divine absence. In between are *Hyperion*, the Frankfurt poems, *Empedokles*, the elegies and the major hymns—all the complexities we have observed in regard to All-Unity, the shifting visions of the essential concept and of the role of poetry in relation to it, a dialectic of resolutions which generate new difficulties and lead to new resolutions, which in turn lead to a final impasse. The last heroic synthesis of "Patmos" is ultimately negated by "Mnemosyne." Hölderlin's obsession with the unity of life, and his concern with God and poetry, lead him to a practical hopelessness about life, poetry, and God. Hölderlin has long been an embarrassment to literary historians perhaps because he so clearly anticipates this most customary state of mind for writers in our own century.

Notes

1. Introduction

1. Percy Bysshe Shelley, *Prometheus Unbound*, 2.400; *Adonais*, l. 460.
2. William Wordsworth, *The Prelude* (1850), 2.221.
3. Samuel Taylor Coleridge, "The Eolian Harp," 11.26–27; *On the Principles of Genial Criticism*, Essay Third.
4. Alfred North Whitehead, *Process and Reality* (New York, 1929).
5. William Butler Yeats, *A Vision*, rev. ed. (New York, 1961), pp.279, 210.
6. T. S. Eliot, "Choruses from *The Rock*," I.9–18, in *The Complete Poems and Plays, 1909–1950* (New York, 1952), p.96.
7. Samuel Beckett, *Endgame: A Play in One Act* (London, 1958), p.38.
8. J. Hillis Miller, *The Disappearance of God* (Cambridge, Mass., 1963).
9. Ibid., p.3.
10. Ibid., p.8.
11. Ibid., p.13.
12. Ibid., p.15.
13. Friedrich Hölderlin, *Sämtliche Werke*, Grosse Stuttgarter Ausgabe, Friedrich Beissner, ed., 7 vols. (Stuttgart, 1943–), 2:94. Textual reference to this edition (volume and page number) will henceforth be given in the text. Hölderlin's spelling will be reproduced as in this edition, except for titles of works, where the familiar modern spelling will be used. References to Beissner's commentary to this edition will be given in the notes as "Beissner," followed by volume and page number.
14. Miller, p.6.
15. See especially the stimulating essays on the topic of Hölderlin's "modernity" in *Friedrich Hölderlin: An Early Modern*, Emery E. George, ed. (Ann Arbor, 1972).

16. Ezra Pound, *Drafts and Fragments of Cantos CX–CXVII* (New York, 1968), p.26.

2. THE TOPIC OF ALL-UNITY IN THE EARLY WORK

1. Hölderlin's early interest in the topic of All-Unity is discussed in the general contexts of Hölderlin's intellectual development in Paul Böckmann, *Hölderlin und seine Götter* (Munich, 1935), pp.37–43; in Wilhelm Michel, *Das Leben Friedrich Hölderlins*, 2nd ed. (Frankfurt, 1967), pp.54–84; and in Ernst Müller, *Hölderlin: Studien zur Geschichte seines Geistes* (Stuttgart, 1944), pp.147–73. Emil Staiger, *Der Geist der Liebe und das Schicksal* (Leipzig, 1935) was one of the first books to indicate clearly the continuity of the topic of All-Unity in Hölderlin's poetry. More recently, Klaus Wöhrmann, *Hölderlins Wille zur Tragödie* (Munich, 1967), and Uvo Hölscher, *Empedokles und Hölderlin* (Frankfurt, 1965) have each dealt briefly with the topic with special reference to the Empedokles dramas, while Detlev Lüders, *Die Welt im verringerten Maastab: Hölderlin-Studien* (Tübingen, 1968), indicates the extent of Hölderlin's concern with the problems of unity and totality in the later hymns. Peter Nickel, "Die Bedeutung von Herders Verjüngungsgedanken und Geschichtsphilosophie fur die Werke Hölderlins" (Ph.D. dissertation, Kiel, 1963), offers a good review of earlier discussion and, following the example of Clemens Heselhaus, "Hölderlins Idea Vitae," *Hölderlin-Jahrbuch* 6 (1952): 17–50, points out the probable influence of Herder in mediating Spinoza's ideas for Hölderlin. H. S. Harris, *Hegel's Development: Toward the Sunlight, 1770–1801* (Oxford, 1972), pp.96–108, discusses Hegel's and Hölderlin's joint preoccupation with the concept of "One and All" at Tübingen. Jacques Taminiaux, *La nostalgie de la Grèce à l'aube de l'idéalisme allemand: Kant et les Grecs dans l'itinéraire de Schiller, de Hölderlin, et de Hegel* (La Haye, 1967), pp.128–205, discusses Hölderlin's early treatment of the concept of All-Unity, particularly in the several versions of *Hyperion*, with reference to major issues in post-Kantian idealism.

2. Max Bäumer, "Hölderlin und das *Hen Kai Pan*," *Monatshefte für deutsche Unterricht* 59, no. 2 (Summer 1967): 131–47.

3. Ibid., p.131. Hölscher (*Empedokles*, p.50) regards Jacobi as a major influence on Hölderlin's thought.

4. Bäumer, "Hölderlin und das *Hen Kai Pan*," pp.135–36.

5. Ibid., pp.131–32.

6. Ibid., p.134.

7. Ibid., p.132.

8. Ibid., p.138.

9. Ibid., p.131. Harris, p.97n, speculates that the phrase was added by Hölderlin himself.

10. Recently, increased attention to Hölderlin's political attitudes has been stimulated by two articles in *Hölderlin-Jahrbuch* 15 (1967–1968):

Pierre Bertaux, "Hölderlin und die Französische Revolution" (1–27), and
Adolf Beck, "Hölderlin als Republikaner" (28–51). Bertaux's claim that
Hölderlin was a consistent Jacobin sympathizer is fully argued in his book,
Hölderlin und die Französische Revolution (Frankfurt, 1969). For fur-
ther discussion of the topic, see Paul Böckmann, "Die Französische Revolution und die Idee der ästhetischen Erziehung in Hölderlins Dichten," in
Der Dichter und seine Zeit (Heidelberg, 1970), pp.83–112; Lawrence
Ryan, "Hölderlin und die Französische Revolution," in *Festschrift für
Klaus Ziegler*, E. Catholy und W. Hellmann, eds. (Tübingen, 1968),
pp.159–79; and the "Diskussionsbeiträge" in *Hölderlin-Jahrbuch* 17
(1971–1972), 117–32. A number of recent studies have sought to determine the exact relationship of Hölderlin's political attitudes to his esthetic,
religious, and philosophical positions; such studies include Ernst Müller,
"Die antiauthoritäre Dichter: Hölderlin und die Religion," in *Festschrift
für Friedrich Beissner*, Ulrich Gaier and Werner Volke, eds. (Tübingen,
1974), pp.288–332; Gerhard Kurz, *Mittelbarkeit und Vereinigung: Zum
Verhältnis von Poesie, Reflexion, und Revolution bei Hölderlin* (Stuttgart, 1975); Johannes Mahr, *Mythos und Politik in Hölderlins Rheinhymne* (Munich, 1972); and Franz Nauen, *Revolution, Idealism, and
Human Freedom: Schelling, Hölderlin, and Hegel and the Crisis of Early
German Idealism* (The Hague, 1971).

11. A detailed treatment of contemporaneous poets' influence on Hölderlin may be found in Böckmann's introduction to *Hymnische Dichtung
im Umkreis Hölderlins*, Paul Böckmann, ed., Schriften der Hölderlin-
Gesellschaft, no. 4 (Tübingen, 1965), pp.1–23.

12. Wilhelm Michel, *Das Leben Friedrich Hölderlins*, pp.62–63.

13. For systematic analyses of these poems, see Emil Lehmann, *Hölderlins Lyrik* (Stuttgart, 1922), pp.23–50; and Böckmann, *Hölderlin und
seine Götter*, pp.44–61. For a recent general discussion, see Wolfgang
Binder, "Einführung in Hölderlins Tübinger Hymnen," *Hölderlin-
Jahrbuch* 18 (1973–1974): 1–19.

14. On the extent of Schiller's influence, and Hölderlin's later release
from it, see Momme Mommsen, "Hölderlins Lösung von Schiller," *Jahrbuch der deutschen Schiller-Gesellschaft* 9 (1965): 203–44.

15. Michel, *Das Leben Friedrich Hölderlins*, p.69.

16. Bäumer, "Hölderlin und das *Hen Kai Pan*," p.138.

17. "Der Vergleich zeigt, dass Hölderlin . . . vor allem Heinses Ge-
danken der kosmischen Liebeseinheit des Alls übernahm. Es ist gerade das
Bild der Weltharmonie und das Band der Liebe, das Hölderlin mit dem
'Eins und Alles' der Natur verbündet" (Ibid., pp.139–40).

18. For the best discussion of Hölderlin's debt to Pietism, see Peter
Hugh Gaskill, "Christ and the Divine Economy in the Work of Friedrich
Hölderlin" (Ph.D. dissertation, Cambridge, 1971).

19. See note 10 above.

20. M. H. Abrams, "English Romanticism: The Spirit of the Age," in *Romanticism Reconsidered*, Northrop Frye, ed. (New York, 1963), pp.26–72.

21. However, Shelley (unlike Hölderlin) speaks in his hymn of various phases of religious or superstitious belief.

22. Percy Bysshe Shelley, *Prometheus Unbound*, 3.202–204.

23. For evidence of dating, see Beissner, 3:296.

24. Cf. Bäumer, "Hölderlin und das *Hen Kai Pan*," p.145. Bäumer contends that after *Hyperion* the ἐν και παν is no longer present as a fixed cliché in Hölderlin's work. While this is true, the later chapters of this book will show that the *topos* does remain a predominant theme in the poetry.

25. Lawrence Ryan, *Hölderlins Hyperion: Exzentrische Bahn und Dichterberuf* (Stuttgart, 1965). It is Ryan's general intent throughout his book to demonstrate the structural coherence of Hölderlin's novel; he also discusses in detail the novel's shifting attitudes toward All-Unity. See also Walter Silz, *Hölderlin's Hyperion: A Critical Reading* (Philadelphia, 1969); Friedbert Aspetsberger, *Welteinheit und epische Gestaltung: Studien zur Ichform von Hölderlins Roman "Hyperion"* (Munich, 1971); and Ingeborg Gerlach, *Natur und Geschichte: Studien zur Geschichtsauffassung in Hölderlins "Hyperion" und "Empedokles"* (Frankfurt, 1973).

26. The novel's conclusion has been the subject of some controversy. Böckmann (*Hölderlin und seine Götter*, p.152) sees it primarily as a final affirmation of the tensions and polarities that dominate the novel, and as admitting the continuance of mutability and "destiny." Beissner (3:488–89) reads the conclusion as a confirmation of the novel's dialectical tension between open and closed form. Ryan, however (*Hölderlins Hyperion*, pp.226–67), would insist that the novel's concluding line proclaims virtual disavowal of the attitudes expressed in the previous sentences: "Zu berücksichtigen ist noch das Schlusswort des Romans, nämlich die auf die Wiedergabe der Verherrlichung des 'einigen, ewigen, glühenden Lebens' sich unmittelbar anschliessende Bemerkung des Erzählers, in die der Roman ausklingt: 'So dacht' ich. Nächstens mehr.' Der erste dieser beiden Sätze bekündet deutlich den Abstand zwischen dem damaligen und dem jetzigen Hyperion: der Erzähler macht darauf aufmerksam, dass er soeben seine ehemaligen Gedanken wiedergegeben hat, zu denen er sich nicht mehr bekennt—an anderer Stelle hat er ja noch Reiferes, Gültigeres gesagt. . . . Aber der allerletzte Satz—'Nächstens mehr'—gibt einige Probleme auf . . . in einem anderen Sinne will Hölderlin eher den Eindruck vermeiden, dass die abschliessende, auf die Versöhnung der Dissonanzen hinweisende Stellungnahme des Erzählers das Ende seiner Entwicklung bedeutet: er will . . . die Zukunft offen halten." While I would agree with the latter statements, Ryan's insistence that use of the past tense implies negation here seems questionable. One is perhaps more readily persuaded by Gaskill's reasoned valorization of Hyperion's celebrating "einiges, ewiges, glühendes

Leben": "Admittedly these lines are placed in inverted commas, and the 'So dacht' ich' which follows suggests that the statement should be seen as relative to a particular stage in Hyperion's development, and not necessarily as reflecting the philosophy of the mature Hyperion who is writing the letter. Nevertheless, by its very position in the context of the novel it is given prominence, and it is these lines which are left ringing in our ears when we put the book down" ("Christ and the Divine Economy," pp.110–111). Gaskill would read the conclusion to *Hyperion* as confirming Heselhaus and Nickel in their insistence on the importance of the "Idea of Life" for Hölderlin at this time.

27. The question of the "exzentrische Bahn" is discussed at considerable length by Ryan, *Hölderlins Hyperion* (passim), as a major topic in the interpretation of the entire novel. See also Wolfgang Schadewaldt, "Das Bild der exzentrischen Bahn bei Hölderlin," *Hölderlin-Jahrbuch* 6 (1952): 1–16; and Ernst Müller, "Der antiauthoritäre Dichter," pp.311–17.

28. The phrase had previously appeared in a set of notes Hölderlin had written, "Zu Jakobis Briefen über die Lehre des Spinoza" (4:207).

29. On general philosophical background for the "Vorrede," see Michel, *Das Leben Friedrich Hölderlins*, pp.166–73.

3. THE FRANKFURT POEMS

1. Cf. Walter Hof, "Zur Frage einer späten 'Wendung' oder 'Umkehr' Hölderlins," *Hölderlin-Jahrbuch* 11 (1958–60):120–59. For a rather extreme theory of "Vaterländische Umkehr" in Hölderlin, see Beda Allemann, *Hölderlin und Heidegger* (Zurich, 1954), pp.11–66.

2. Following the suggestion of Michel, *Das Leben Friedrich Hölderlins*, pp.221–22.

3. For a presentation of the biographical details of this relationship, see Michel, pp.143–60. A chronology of their relationship is included in *Hölderlin: Eine Chronik in Text und Bild*, Adolf Beck and Paul Raabe, eds. (Frankfurt, 1970), pp.43–57.

4. As designated by Beissner, 1:212–22.

5. For general discussion of this poem and others of the Frankfurt period, see Karl Viëtor, *Die Lyrik Hölderlins* (Frankfurt, 1921), pp. 71–128. For another viewpoint, see Ulrich Gaier, *Der gesetzliche Kalkül: Hölderlins Dichtungslehre* (Tübingen, 1962), pp.242–48.

6. Erotic metaphors for spirituality occur frequently in some of the writings of German Pietism. See August Langen, *Der Wortschatz des deutschen Pietismus* (Tübingen, 1954), passim.

7. Cf. my discussion of the last Diotima poem, "Menons Klagen um Diotima," in a later chapter.

8. See Adolf Beck, "Hölderlin und Friedrich Leopold Graf zu Stolberg," *Iduna: Jahrbuch der Hölderlin-Gesellschaft* 1 (1944):88–114.

9. Ibid., p.113.

10. Ibid. To avoid ambiguity, however, I would prefer not to designate the present group of poems as "hymns," but to reserve that title for the later poems written in imitation of Pindar, and for the Tübingen poems.

11. William Wordsworth, "Tintern Abbey," 47–49.

12. On the "Idea of Life" in Hölderlin's poetry, see Heselhaus, "Hölderlins Idea Vitae"; Nickel, "Die Bedeutung von Herders Verjüngungsgedanken und Geschichtsphilosophie für die Werke Hölderlins"; and Gaskill, "Christ and the Divine Economy in the Work of Friedrich Hölderlin."

13. See Momme Mommsen, "Hölderlins Lösung von Schiller." For other readings of the poem, see Lehmann, *Hölderlins Lyrik*, pp.98–100; Michel, *Das Leben Friedrich Hölderlins*, pp.180–82; and Rudolf D. Schier, "Trees and Transcendence: Hölderlin's 'Die Eichbäume' and Rilke's 'Herbst,'" *German Life and Letters* 20 (1966–67): 331–41. For a general discussion of the poems of this group, see Böckmann, *Hölderlin und seine Götter*, pp.153–70. See also note 1, above.

14. For interpretations, see Böckmann, pp.153–70; Michel, pp.180–85; Lehmann, pp.100–109; and Rudolf Malter, "Hölderlins Gedicht 'An den Äther': Versuch einer Deutung," in *Saarbrücker Beiträge zur Ästhetik*, Rudolf Malter and Alois Brandstetter, eds. (Saarbrücken, 1966), pp.31–42.

15. See Jochen Schmidt, *Hölderlins Elegie "Brod und Wein,"* p.215.

16. Heselhaus, "Hölderlins Idea Vitae," pp.29–33, likewise notes how the force of Life may be figured both by plant-life and by fire.

17. On the idea of fulfillment in Hölderlin, see Karl Kerenyi, "Hölderlins Vollendung," *Hölderlin-Jahrbuch* 8 (1954):25–45.

18. One aspect of this problem is delicately expressed in a later hymn, "Die Wanderung," which muses on possible visitation by Graces or joy-bringing emissaries of Heaven:

Die Dienerinnen des Himmels
Sind aber wunderbar,
Wie alles Göttlichgeborne.
Zum Traume wirds ihm, will es Einer
Beschleichen und straft den, der
Ihm gleichen will mit Gewalt;
Oft überraschet es einen,
Der eben kaum es gedacht hat.   [2:141]

19. Mommsen remarks: "Während Hölderlin früher keinen Zweifel liess, welcher Welt er zugehört: der der heroischen, titanenhaften Existenz, erscheint jetzt neu die Aussage: dem *'geselligen Leben'* sich *'anzuschmiegen,'* daran hindert den Dichter sein Freiheitsbedürfnis; in der Welt der freien Eichbäume zu *'wohnen,'* verbietet ihm in ähnlicher Weise ein anderes Gefühl: das der Liebe. So steht er jetzt sehnend zwischen beiden Welten" ("Hölderlins Lösung von Schiller," p.231). The balance ex-

pressed in this poem is thus one of vacillation rather than contentment as in "Der Wanderer" and "An den Aether."

20. See Karl Viëtor, *Geschichte der deutschen Ode* (Hildesheim, 1961), p.163.

21. Because of their intimate subject matter, Hölderlin's odes are frequently called "personal" in tone; I would be inclined to agree only if "persona" is understood in its root meaning of "mask," and I would have to disagree, for example, with Viëtor's designation of the poems as "Oden aus dramatischem Urgefühl, Oden mit tragischem Gang" (*Geschichte der deutschen Ode*, p.152).

22. See Beissner, 1:556.

23. For an excellent, detailed interpretation of the odes, see Lawrence Ryan, *Hölderlins Lehre vom Wechsel der Töne* (Stuttgart, 1960), pp.158–229. (Hölderlin's theory of tonal changes is perhaps more clearly applicable to the odes than to other genres of his poetry.) For briefer and more general discussions, see Viëtor, *Geschichte der deutschen Ode*, pp.147–64, and Wolfgang Binder, "Hölderlins Odenstrophe," in *Hölderlin-Aufsätze* (Frankfurt, 1970), pp.47–75.

4. EMPEDOKLES

1. On fire as a symbol of Life, see note 16 of the previous chapter.

2. Because the Empedokles fragments and associated prose writings constitute an important part of Hölderlin's work and a transition into the thematic world of his later poetry, they have received much critical attention. Among the more important studies are Walter Kranz, *Empedokles: Antike Gestalt und romantische Neuschöpfung* (Zurich, 1949); Johannes Hoffmeister, *Hölderlins Empedokles* (Bonn, 1963); Uvo Hölscher, *Empedokles und Hölderlin* (Frankfurt, 1965); and Klaus Wöhrmann, *Hölderlins Wille zur Tragödie* (Munich, 1967). Ingeborg Gerlach, *Natur und Geschichte: Studien zur Geschichtsauffassung in Hölderlins "Hyperion" und "Empedokles"* (Frankfurt, 1973), provides helpful summaries of previous interpretations of the drama. Major articles on *Empedokles* are: Friedrich Beissner, "Hölderlins Trauerspiel *Der Tod des Empedokles* in seiner drei Fassungen," in *Hölderlin: Reden und Aufsätze* (Weimar, 1961), pp.67–91; Emil Staiger, "Der Opfertod von Hölderlins Empedokles," *Hölderlin-Jahrbuch* 13 (1963–1964):1–20; Wolfgang Schadewaldt, "Die Empedokles-Tragödie Hölderlins," *Hölderlin-Jahrbuch* 11 (1958–1960):40–54; Max Kommerell, "Hölderlins Empedokles-Dichtungen," in *Über Hölderlin*, Jochen Schmidt, ed. (Frankfurt, 1970), pp.213–36; and Wolfgang Binder, "Hölderlins Namensymbolik," in *Hölderlin-Aufsätze* (Frankfurt, 1970), pp.232–60. The present chapter will not attempt to duplicate these efforts, but will indicate how the topic of All-Unity is treated in the first two versions of the drama.

3. As Hillis Miller observes, there is a point of basic difference between

Hölderlin and Matthew Arnold in their views on All-Unity, represented in the difference between the protagonists of their respective Empedokles dramas: "The German poet was able in his poetry to express much more directly than Arnold the time of immediacy. He had experienced the intimacy of all things with one another, as well as the horror of their splitting apart, whereas for Arnold the age of harmony was from the beginning something he knew about only through hearsay and a kind of intuitive memory of a time he had never really known himself. . . . Arnold's Empedokles speaks with the English poet's own lucid awareness of loss." (*The Disappearance of God*, p.219.) Also, Arnold has his Empedokles speak of the unitive vision in more rationalistic terms, as philosophic truth, whereas for Hölderlin's Empedokles the philosophical ideas appear merely derivative from an immediate, extra-rational *feeling* for All-Unity as manifest in nature.

4. This designation of All-Unity occurs again in an important passage in the later hymn, "Friedensfeier" (3:535).

5. This passage may partially clarify some lines in the concluding strophe of "Patmos" (2:172) which speak of the poet's service to "Mutter Erde" and "Sonnenlicht."

6. "Earth" here resembles both Blake's "Tirzah" and the maternal Earth in Shelley's *Prometheus Unbound*. See especially I.151–152 ("Thou art immortal, and this tongue is known / Only to those who die") and III.iii.111–112, where the statement is repeated. Shelley's Earth, however, is more susceptible to transformation than Hölderlin's.

7. On this comparison, see Allemann, *Hölderlin und Heidegger*, pp.50–59; Kommerell, "Hölderlins Empedokles-Dichtungen," pp.231–33; and Romano Guardini, *Hölderlin: Weltbild und Frömmigkeit* (Munich, 1955), pp.503–507.

8. See Michel, *Das Leben Friedrich Hölderlins*, pp.242–49.

9. "In Empedokles fand Hölderlin sodann jene Liebe als grosse kosmische Gewalt, die sich ihm selbst als All-Liebe, Sympathie und Harmonie, als höchster Inbegriff der göttlichen Natur, als Inbegriff des *Eins und Alles* (ἐν καὶ πᾶν) in seiner grossen Tübinger Hymnenzyklus offenbart hat" (Schadewaldt, "Die Empedokles-Tragödie Hölderlins," p.44).

10. It might be noted that Goethe's Faust makes his pact with Mephistopheles after he had already attempted through magic to attain his own vision of the All-Unity: "was die Welt / Im innersten zusammenhält" (*Faust*, 283–383). He has been repulsed by the "Erdgeist," the spirit of the all-unitive force in earthly life, and his prospective suicide is contemplated in terms resembling Hölderlin's anticipations of joyous mergence with All-Unity in the Tübingen Hymns: "Ich fühle mich bereit, / Auf neuer Bahn den Äther zu durchdringen, / Zu neuen Sphären reiner Tätigkeit. — / Dies hohe Leben, diese Götterwonne!" (703–706). The immediate interposition of ironic consciousness, however, already an-

ticipates the very un-Hölderlinian presence of Mephistopheles: "Du, erst noch Wurm, und die verdienest du?" (707).

11. For another discussion of Empedokles' motivation here, see Kommerell, "Hölderlins Empedokles-Dichtungen," pp.225–33.

5. The Elegies; "Menons Klagen um Diotima"

1. For discussion of Hölderlin's elegies with respect to form, see Friedrich Beissner, "Hölderlins Elegien," in *Über Hölderlin*, pp.68–86. For analyses of various formal and thematic aspects see also Viëtor, *Die Lyrik Hölderlins*, pp.129–88. On the two versions of "Der Wanderer," see Andreas Müller, "Die beiden Fassungen von Hölderlins Elegie 'Der Wanderer,'" *Hölderlin-Jahrbuch* 3 (1948–1949): 103–31.

2. For more extensive discussion of this poem, see Karl Viëtor, "Hölderlins Liebeselegie," in *Über Hölderlin*, pp.87–112. Viëtor also discusses an earlier version, entitled simply "Elegie," where, as Beissner remarks (2:558), Diotima's name is not mentioned. Wolfgang Binder's article, "Abschied und Wiederfinden: Hölderlins dichterische Gestaltung des Abschieds von Diotima," in *Hölderlin-Aufsätze*, pp.263–93, speaks of the poem in the context of other poems referring to Hölderlin's parting with Susette Gontard. See also Böckmann, *Hölderlin und seine Götter*, pp.333–43.

3. Beissner notes a passage in *Hyperion* where the suffering protagonist is likewise compared to a wounded deer: "Wie ein blüthender Hirsch in den Strom, stürzt' ich oft mitten hinein in den Wirbel der Freude, die brennende Brust zu kühlen und die tobenden herrlichen Träume von Ruhm und Grösse wegzubaden, aber was half das?" (2:559). Here, however, the sufferer takes refuge in nature itself rather than in dionysian joy.

4. "Brot und Wein" later terms the ideal community of the Greeks "das himmlische Fest" (2:93), and "Friedensfeier" declares the "feast day" ("der Festtag") to be the optimal "sign of love" ("Liebeszeichen") (3:536).

5. The term "Seelengesang" also occurs in a late fragment, "Deutscher Gesang," where it apparently means the voice of the poet's own soul as distinguished from the ultimate song which might name all-unitive Life, specifically in the form of "guter Geist des Vaterlands" (2:202).

6. Beissner remarks: "Die *Liebende*, die Geliebte ist das Organ, das Medium, durch das dem Liebenden die ganze Umwelt einst erschien" (2:559).

7. On this apparition of Diotima, Viëtor declares: "in der Nacht-Zeit lebt sie als Mittlerin des Lichtes, das den versunkenen Tag-Aeon der Antiken Welt erfüllt, wie es den kommenden Tag erfüllen wird" ("Hölderlins Liebeselegie," p.97).

8. Beissner comments: "Die elegische Erinnerung vermag den Ein-

samen, der v. 55 nicht wusste, wofür er danken sollte, nun doch, 'aus leichter Brust' (v. 98) das Dankgebet zu singen" (2:560).

9. Cf. the elegy "Stuttgart," where rejuvenation in external nature is likewise accompanied by new flights of song:

> Offen steht jezt wieder ein Saal, und gesund ist der Garten,
> Und von Reegen erfrischt rauschet das glänzende Thal,
> Hoch von Gewächsen, es schwellen die Bäch' und alle gebundnen
> Fittige wagen sich wieder ins Reich des Gesangs.   [2:86]

10. Viëtor remarks:"Diesen 'gemeinsamen Boden' auf dem die Seligen sich vereinen, ihn bevölkern Gestalten des griechischen Glaubens. Erlösung aus dem Leid der Vereinzelung, ideale Gemeinschaft mit den verwandten, den göttlichen Menschen und mit den Göttern selbst—dies ist die Seligkeit, die Hölderlins Himmel verspricht" ("Hölderlins Liebeselegie," p.101).

11. The first version of the elegy has "auf seeligen Inseln" (2:74), islands of the blessed. Beissner (2:560) notes the passage in the second version of "Der Einzige" where such islands are explicitly places of asylum: "Auch einige sind; gerettet, als / Auf schönen Inseln" (2:160). In the fifth strophe of "Patmos," the island of Patmos is itself implicitly such a place of asylum for the poet and St. John (2:167).

6. "Brot und Wein"

1. Jochen Schmidt, *Hölderlins Elegie, 'Brod und Wein'* (Berlin, 1968). Another excellent, full-scale interpretation of the elegy is Emil Petzold, *Hölderlins Brot und Wein: Ein exegetischer Versuch*, reprint (Darmstadt, 1967). Paul Böckmann offers an interpretation of the poem's central image in "Das Bild der Nacht in Hölderlins 'Brod und Wein,' " in *Formensprache: Studien zur Literarästhetik und Dichtungsinterpretation* (Munich, 1966), pp.330–44. For further discussion, see Michel, *Das Leben Friedrich Hölderlins*, pp.351–54; Gaier, *Der gesetzliche Kalkül*, pp.259–64; Beissner, "Hölderlins Elegien," pp.83–86; and Max Bäumer, "Dionysos und das Dionysische bei Hölderlin," *Hölderlin-Jahrbuch* 18 (1973–1974): 105–11.

2. Schmidt, *Elegie*, pp.8–10.

3. In "Hölderlins 'Friedensfeier,' " *Hölderlin-Aufsätze*, pp.324–25, Binder notes a similar centering of structure in the hymn "Friedensfeier."

4. Cf. M. H. Abrams, "The Correspondent Breeze: A Romantic Metaphor," in *English Romantic Poets: Modern Essays in Criticism*, M. H. Abrams, ed. (New York, 1960), pp.37–54.

5. For a thorough discussion of the image of night in the poem, see Böckmann, "Das Bild der Nacht."

6. "Das Aorgische" would be Hölderlin's own term for what is amor-

phous, beyond all structures. For detailed interpretation of these lines, especially the significance of "den Irrenden" and "den Todten" here, see Schmidt, *Elegie*, pp.47–48.

7. Ibid., pp.49–50.

8. The concept of "Maas" is also important in the fourteenth strophe of "Der Rhein": "Nur hat ein jeder sein Maas" (2:148). See our discussion of the passage in the later chapter. Schmidt notes: "Das 'Maas' ist Schicksal im Sinne von Moira, als das 'Zugemessene,' uns 'Beschiedene' " (*Elegie*, p.59). Petzold, however, regards "Maas" here as only the *universal* determination of mankind: "das allgemeingültige Gesetz der Vernunft" (*Brot und Wein*, p.91).

9. From "Proverbs of Hell" in *The Marriage of Heaven and Hell*, by William Blake.

10. Cf. especially the opening strophe of "Friedensfeier," discussed in a later chapter.

11. See the previous discussion of "Vater Aether" in the chapter on the Frankfurt poems. Petzold (*Brot und Wein*, pp.100–104) and Schmidt (*Elegie*, pp.73–77) offer extensive comment on the significance of the term in the contexts of this poem. See also Schmidt's more general discussion of this designation of divinity in *Elegie*, pp.209–18.

12. On the significance of "Life" ("das Leben") here, see Heselhaus, "Hölderlins Idea Vitae," and my earlier discussion of the concept in *Hyperion* and the Frankfurt poems. Petzold (*Brot und Wein*, pp.104–107) comments at length on the term's meaning in context.

13. Schmidt comments: "Der Mensch empfindet sehr wohl die Weise, in der die Götter kommen, das Übermass, ein ungekanntes, überwältigendes Glück. Aber gerade, weil das Glück zu hell, zu blendend kommt, wird sein eigentlicher Inhalt nicht wahrgenommen, er bleibt ungewusst und unempfunden" (*Elegie*, p.89).

14. Following Beissner's syntactical reading of these lines (2:615–616).

15. The difficulties of "bearing" intense happiness are stressed in the fourteenth strophe of "Der Rhein": "Denn schwer ist zu tragen / Das Unglük, aber schwerer das Glük" (2:148).

16. For an analysis of the implications of these lines, see Paul de Man, "The Intentional Structure of the Romantic Image," in *Romanticism and Consciousness*, ed. Harold Bloom (New York, 1970), pp.65–77.

17. John Keats, letter to John Taylor (February 27, 1818).

18. Subjected to rhetorical analysis by Schmidt, *Elegie*, p.99. For the importance of Hölderlin's concept of "naming," see Schmidt, pp.95–98.

19. Schmidt analyzes the "organic" character of Greek civilization for Hölderlin (*Elegie*, pp.103–106).

20. Cf. Hegel's analysis of Greece in both the *Aesthetik* and the *Phänomenologie des Geistes*. On Hölderlin's rejection of classicistic attitudes

toward Greece, see Peter Szondi, "Überwindung des Klassizismus: Hölderlins Brief an Bohlendorff vom 4. Dezember 1801," in *Hölderlin-Studien* (Frankfurt, 1967), pp.85–104.

21. For a full account of Heinse's influence on Hölderlin see Max Bäumer, *Heinse-Studien* (Stuttgart, 1966).

22. Its significance is expressed most eloquently perhaps by Martin Heidegger: "Das ist die *dürftige* Zeit, weil sie in einem gedoppelten Mangel und Nicht steht: im Nichtmehr der entflohenen Götter und im Nochnicht des Kommenden." ("Hölderlin und das Wesen der Dichtung," in *Erläuterungen zu Hölderlins Dichtung*, rev. ed. [Frankfurt, 1951], p.44.)

23. See Beissner, 2:617–18.

24. Schmidt, *Elegie*, pp.121–25. See also Momme Mommsen, "Die Problematik des Priestertums bei Hölderlin," *Hölderlin-Jahrbuch* 15 (1967–1968):53–74.

25. The problem of the relationship of Christ to Dionysus in Hölderlin's poetry is complex; while there is no clear antithesis as in Nietzsche, it is often difficult to determine the exact degree of likeness or difference in character or function of the two. See my interpretation of "Der Einzige" in a later chapter. For further discussions of the Dionysus-Christ problem, see Schmidt, *Elegie*, pp.160–67; Guardini, *Hölderlin: Weltbild und Frömmigkeit*, pp.564–74; and Allemann, *Hölderlin und Heidegger*, pp.59–69. For the image of Dionysus in Hölderlin, see Momme Mommsen, "Dionysos in der Dichtung Hölderlins," *Germanisch-Romanische Monatsschrift* 13 (Oct. 1963):345–79, and, especially, Max Bäumer, "Dionysos und Dionysische bei Hölderlin," 97–118. For Hölderlin's image of Christ, see especially Robert Thomas Stoll, *Hölderlins Christushymnen: Grundlegung und Darstellung* (Basel, 1952); Horst Rumpf, "Die Deutung der Christusgestalt bei dem späten Hölderlin" (Ph.D. diss. Frankfurt, 1957); Gaskill, "Christ and the Divine Economy."

26. Schmidt, *Elegie*, p.142. See my discussion of "Wie wenn am Feiertage" in a later chapter.

27. It might be noted, however, that Hölderlin here utilizes the Zwinglian (rather than the Lutheran) concept of the Eucharist.

28. See Schmidt, *Elegie*, pp.150–53.

29. On the question of imminent fulfillment, cf. the concluding strophes of "Friedensfeier" and my discussion of them in a later chapter. On the general topic of "fulfillment" in Hölderlin, see Kerenyi, "Hölderlins Vollendung."

30. Cf. Beissner, 2:620.

31. Petzold (*Brot und Wein*, p.93) maintains that "der Syrier" can be seen as another epiphany of Dionysus, as well as Christ.

32. Schmidt interprets the somnolence of Cerberus here as the muting of the forces of evil in the world with the prospect of peace in Europe in 1800: "Ein sich nur noch mühsam dahinschleppender, langsam einschlaf-

ender Krieg, Vereinbarungen über Waffenruhe und Friedensverhandlungen kennzeichnen also die politische Situation während der Zeit, in der Hölderlin seine grosse Elegie schreibt" (*Elegie*, p.170).

7. "HEIMKUNFT"

1. Beissner's "Hölderlins Elegien" discusses Hölderlin's elegies as a genre form. See also Ryan, *Hölderlins Lehre vom Wechsel der Töne*, pp.229–42.

2. For more general interpretations of "Heimkunft," see Martin Heidegger, "Heimkunft: An die Verwandten," in *Erläuterungen zu Hölderlins Dichtung*, pp.9–30; Albrecht Weber, "Heimkunft," in *Wege zum Gedicht*, R. Hirschenauer and A. Weber, eds. (Munich, 1956), pp.166–81; Cyrus Hamlin, "Hölderlin's Elegy 'Homecoming': Comments," in *Friedrich Hölderlin: An Early Modern*, Emery E. George, ed. (Ann Arbor, 1972), pp.232–45; Paul Böckmann, *Hölderlin und seine Götter*, pp.369–76.

3. Beissner comments: "Das Oxymoron bezeichnet recht den Zwischenzustand, da die Tiefe des 'gähnenden Thals' vom vollen Licht des Morgens noch nicht erreicht ist" (2:625–26).

4. Cf. Earl R. Wasserman's interpretation of "Mont Blanc" in *The Subtler Language* (Baltimore, 1959), pp.195–240.

5. This reading is stressed by Heidegger: "Das Freudige ist das Gedichtete. Das Freudige wird aus der Freude in diese gestimmt. Dadurch ist es das Erfreute und also das Sichfreuende. Dieses kann selbst wieder anderes erfreuen. So ist das Freudige zugleich das Erfreuende. . . . Die Wolke dichtet" (*Erläuterungen*, p.15).

6. Beissner comments: "In den Morgennebeln ist heftig eilende, tosende und stürzende (v. 3) Bewegung, und doch weichen sie als Ganzes nicht auf einmal, sondern allmählich, eben 'langsam' " (2:626).

7. "The reader [participating in the poet's creativity] should be carried forward . . . by the pleasurable activity of mind excited by the attractions of the journey itself" (*Biographia Literaria*, J. Shawcross, ed. [Oxford, 1907], 2:11).

8. Here as elsewhere in Hölderlin the eagle is the chosen emissary of Zeus, Lord of Time.

9. The new peace in Europe may have stimulated Hölderlin's millennial optimism. Cyrus Hamlin refers to the Treaty of Lunéville, which Hölderlin thought would bring a great era of peace. He cites as evidence a letter written "just before Hölderlin left for Switzerland at the end of 1800 (6:407; No. 222): '. . . dass unsere Zeit nahe ist, dass uns der Friede, der jezt im Werden ist, gerade das bringen wird, was er und nur er bringen könnte; denn er wird vieles bringen, was viele hoffen, aber er wird auch bringen, was wenige ahnden . . . dass der Egoismus in allen seinen Gestalten sich beugen wird unter die heilige Herrschaft der Liebe und Güte, dass Gemeingeist über alles in allem gehen und dass das deutsche Herz in solchem

Klima, unter dem Segen dieses neuen Friedens erst recht aufgehn, und gerauschlos, wie die wachsende Natur, seine geheimen weitreichenden Kräfte entfalten wird, dies mein ich, dies seh und glaub ich, . . .' " ("Hölderlin's Elegy," pp.234–35). Hamlin further notes that the letter's reference to the springlike "opening" of the "German heart" is also useful in understanding the sense of mission expressed in the poem's later strophes.

10. Wasserman, *The Subtler Language*, pp.53–57.

11. Paul de Man, "The Intentional Structure of the Romantic Image," p.75, has noted the necessity for this movement. Comparing the opening of "Heimkunft" to similar passages in Wordsworth and Rousseau, he observes:

> The violence of this turmoil is finally appeased by the ascending movement recorded in each of the texts, the movement by means of which the poetic imagination tears itself away, as it were, from a terrestrial nature and moves towards this "other nature" mentioned by Rousseau, associated with the diaphanous, limpid and immaterial quality of a light that dwells near to the skies.

The movement of transcendence here is not only to serene, ethereal light as an emblem of more rarified consciousness, but to the presence of a Deity living "above" this light.

12. See note 9, above.

13. This of course does not contradict the poetic resolution achieved in "Brot und Wein"; it formulates the principal or permanent concern of poetry, while the other elegy designates priesthood of Dionysus as a temporary (if necessary) expedient.

14. On the general possibility of this, see the letter cited in note 9, above.

15. Hamlin notes the repetition here of the verb "scheinen," and remarks that "the poet acknowledges that his assessment of the situation depends upon his own surmise" ("Hölderlin's Elegy," p.240). This of course contributes to the problematical quality of the euphoria and poetic hopes in the poem.

16. Cf. the "Vorrede" to *Hyperion*, discussed in an earlier chapter. As Beissner (2:630) notes, "des heiligen Friedens Bogen" is the rainbow.

17. On Hölderlin's Pietism, see Gaskill, "Christ and the Divine Economy."

18. A striking example of this may be noted in *Prometheus Unbound* I. 603–4, where Shelley's protagonist, confronted with a crucifix, exclaims, "O horrible! Thy name I will not speak / It hath become a curse." For a thoroughgoing analysis of the problem of religious "naming" in Hölderlin, see Wolfgang Binder, "Hölderlins Namensymbolik," pp.134–260.

19. Heidegger cautions, however, that the "others" still have a duty to be attentive listeners: "Das jähe 'nicht' entbindet 'die anderen' zwar von

der Sorge des dichtenden Sagens, aber keineswegs von der Sorge des Hörens auf das, was hier in der 'Heimkunft' 'Dichtende sinnen oder singen' " (*Erläuterungen*, p.28).

8. TOWARD THE MAJOR HYMNS: THE "MANES SCENE"

1. In his excellent study, *Hölderlin and Pindar* (The Hague, 1962), M. B. Benn examines the generic form of the hymns and shows how they formally evolve from Hölderlin's preoccupation with the odes of Pindar and his attempt to parallel their achievements in German verse. The formal aspect of the hymns is also discussed by Lawrence Ryan, "Hölderlins prophetische Dichtung," *Jahrbuch der deutschen Schiller-Gesellschaft* 6 (1962): 194–228; Max Kommerell, "Hölderlins Hymnen in freien Strophen," in *Gedanken über Gedichte* (Frankfurt, 1943), pp.456–81; and Theodor Adorno, "Parataxis: Zur späten Lyrik Hölderlins," in *Über Hölderlin*, pp.339–78. An original approach to determining structures of meaning in several of the late hymns is presented in Emery E. George, *Hölderlin's "Ars Poetica": A Part-Rigorous Analysis of Information Structure in the Late Hymns* (The Hague, 1973).

2. Szondi insists that the circumstance that Hölderlin wrote some elegies and odes in the years of his first major hymns "darf nicht darüber hinwegtäuschen, dass in der inneren Chronologie seiner Dichtung die Hymnen einer späteren Epoche angehören als die beiden anderen lyrischen Gattungen." To support this claim, he notes that the hymns alone represent a new form in these years: "Abzulesen ist dies zunächst daran, dass die erste der von Pindar inspirierten Hymnen. . . , dass die Hymne 'Wie wenn am Feiertage' um die Jahrhundertwende im Werk durchaus als ein Novum erscheint. Hölderlins Oden- und Elegiendichtung hingegen reicht bruchlos in seine dichterischen Anfänge zurück" (*Hölderlin-Studien*, p.33).

3. See the earlier chapter for discussion of the first two versions of the play, and for a brief list of other critiques. For the third version and the Manes scene, however, two studies are especially relevant: Meta Cornelissen, "Die Manes-Szene in Hölderlins Trauerspiel 'Der Tod des Empedokles,' " *Hölderlin-Jahrbuch* 14 (1965–1966):97–109; and Klaus Wöhrmann, *Hölderlins Wille zur Tragödie*, esp. pp.131–39. Wöhrmann's discussion of the relationship of the Manes scene to the later hymns is also interesting. For a formal interpretation of the third version, see Jurgen Simon, "Der Wechsel der Töne im Drama: Beobachtungen zu Hölderlins Trauerspiel 'Der Tod des Empedokles' (III)" (Ph.D. diss., Tübingen, 1967).

4. Cornelissen comments on the appropriateness of Manes' coming from "Egypt": "Die Ägypter kennen die grossen Bewegungen des Schicksals. Das Individuelle nehmen sie wahr als Bild und Zeichen eines Überpersönlichen, Gesetzlichen." Manes thus confronts Empedokles as a spokesman for universal law: "Manes bringt das abstrakte Gesetz, seine

formale Seite zur Darstellung. Hieraus leitet er sein Recht zu urteilen ab
. . ." ("Manes-Szene," pp.102–103).

5. "So ist Empedokles, wie gesagt, das Resultat seiner Periode, und sein
Karakter weist auf diese zurük, so wie er aus dieser hervorgieng. Sein
Schiksaal stellt sich in ihm dar, als in einer augenbliklichen Vereinigung,
die aber sich auflösen muss, um mehr zu werden" (4:155).

6. The "Grund zum Empedokles" stresses the problematical character
of his achievement: "So sollte also Empedokles ein Opfer seiner Zeit
werden. Die Probleme des Schiksaals in dem er erwuchs, sollten in ihm
sich scheinbar lösen, und diese Lösung sollte sich als eine scheinbare tem-
poräre zeigen, wie mehr oder weniger bei allen tragischen Personen, die
alle in ihren Karakteren und Äusserungen mehr oder weniger Versuche sind,
die Probleme des Schiksaals zu lösen, und alle sich insofern und in dem
Grade aufheben, in welchem sie nicht allgemein gültig sind, wenn nicht
anders ihre Rolle, ihr Karakter und seine Äusserungen sich von selbst als
etwas vorübergehendes und augenblikliches darstellen, so dass also der-
jenige, der scheinbar das Schiksaal am vollständigsten löst, auch sich am
meisten in seiner Vergänglichkeit und im Fortschritte seiner Versuche am
auffallendsten als Opfer darstellt" (4:157).

9. "Wie wenn am Feiertage"

1. Hof, *Hölderlins Stil als Ausdruck seiner geistigen Welt* (Meisen-
heim on Glan, 1954), p.407, discusses the formal significance of this simile
in conjunction with others in Hölderlin's work. For complete interpretations of the poem, see Heidegger, "Wie wenn am Feiertage," in *Erläuterungen zu Hölderlins Dichtung*, pp.47–74, and, especially, Szondi, "Der
andere Pfeil: Zur Entstehungsgeschichte des hymnischen Spätstils," in
Hölderlin-Studien (Frankfurt, 1967), pp.33–54. For briefer discussions,
see Böckmann, *Hölderlin und seine Götter*, pp.385–87; Guardini, *Hölderlin: Weltbild und Frömmigkeit*, pp.221–28; and Jakob Lehmann, "Wie
wenn am Feiertage," in *Wege zum Gedicht*, R. Hirschenauer and A.
Weber, eds. (Munich, 1956), pp.184–90. Wöhrmann, *Hölderlins Wille
zur Tragödie*, pp.139–57, also discusses some aspects of the relationship between this poem and the "Manes Scene."

2. Heidegger remarks: "Das Wesen der Macht bestimmt sich aus der
Allgegenwart der Natur, die Hölderlin 'die mächtige, die göttlichschöne'
nennt. Mächtig ist die Natur, weil sie göttlichschön ist. . . . Diese heisst
die 'schöne,' weil sie 'wunderbar allgegenwärtig' ist" (*Erläuterungen*,
p.52). On the idea of Nature as "Life," see Heselhaus, "Hölderlins Idea
Vitae."

3. While Heidegger (p.51) assumes that the poets are said here to stand
"wie ein Landmann auf seinem Gang," Szondi would insist that the poets
are explicitly compared to the trees (and the vine): "Denn die Dichter
stehen unter günstiger Witterung, sie stehen—nach einem späteren, viel

zitierten Vers—unter Gottes Gewittern mit entblösstem Haupte, wie der Weinstock und die Bäume des Haines in der Nacht gestanden haben, aus der die kühlenden Blitze fielen" (*Hölderlin-Studien*, p.37).

4. Heidegger, *Erläuterungen*, p.50.

5. The sacred importance Hölderlin attaches to the problem of "naming" essential Nature is even more clearly shown in the incomplete hymn, "Am Quelle der Donau":

> Aber wenn ihr
> Und diss ist zu sagen,
> Ihr Alten all, nicht saget, woher?
> Wir nennen dich, heiliggenöthiget, nennen,
> Natur! dich wir, und neu, wie dem Bad entsteigt
> Dir alles Göttlichgeborne.   [2:128]

For a discussion of the problem of divine "naming" in Hölderlin, see Wolfgang Binder, "Hölderlins Namensymbolik," pp.134–260; and, also, Renate Böschenstein-Schäfer, "La théologie du signe dans les fragments hymniques de Hölderlin," *Revue de Théologie et de Philosophie*, series 3, 21 (1971):221–39.

6. We must recall, however, that the problematical elegy "Heimkunft" was written *after* this initial (and formally unsuccessful) hymn. See the remarks on chronology in "Toward the Major Hymns," above.

7. Both aspects, for example, are clearly evident in the various *Empedokles* monologues.

8. Identical with "Thaten der Welt," below. Cf. Beissner, 2:679.

9. Heidegger remarks: "Also gleicht die Natur einem Gott oder einer Göttin? Wäre dies, dann würde aber 'die Natur,' die doch in allem, auch in den Göttern, gegenwärtig ist, wieder und noch am 'Göttlichen' gemessen und wäre nicht mehr 'die Natur' " (*Erläuterungen*, p.52).

10. It is true that the phrase "hoch vom Aether bis zum Abgrund nieder" suggests the course of a lightning bolt; such a suggestion is perhaps inevitable, just as "Waffenklang" may recall the first strophe's thunderstorm. And yet, the suggestion exists merely as a shadow in the verbal structure of the strophe, which remains purely nonfigurative.

11. Ryan ("Hölderlins prophetische Dichtung," p.202) remarks: "In der Allgegenwart eines solchen Augenblicks wird diese Ganzheit [of Nature] sich dem Dichter erkennbar, die Götterkräfte sind ihm nun offenbar."

12. The original manuscript has "entwacht." Beissner emends this to "entwächst" and ascribes the original form to a recurring spelling error by Hölderlin (2:674). Most critics follow this reading, although Heidegger (*Erläuterungen*, pp.57–59) insists on "entwacht" for hermeneutical reasons of his own.

13. Szondi remarks: "Im Gewitter spricht der Gott zu den Menschen. Die Wetter sind, nach einem Wort der Hymne, das wegen der falschen

Interpunktion sämtlicher Editionen meist missverstanden wird, 'des gemeinsamen,' nach dem Prosaentwurf: 'des göttlichen, Geistes Gedanken,'
Gedanken jenes Gemeingeistes, . . . den eine andere Stelle mit dem Namen
des Weingotts Bacchus verbindet" (*Hölderlin-Studien*, p.38). In a foot-
note, Szondi then argues against Beissner's editing of the text's punctu-
ation: "Der Punkt am Ende von v. 42, der aus den Versen 43 ff. 'Des
gemeinsamen Geistes Gedanken sind, / Still endend in der Seele des
Dichters' einen neuen Satz macht, steht nicht in der Handschrift. . . . Die
Konjektur des ersten Herausgebers haben die späteren übernommen. Dass
diese Verse noch zu dem vorausgehenden Satz gehören, dass also 'des
gemeinsamen Geistes Gedanken' Prädikat und nicht Subjekt ist, zeigt aber
sowohl das Komma nach v. 43 als auch der Prosaentwurf . . ." (Ibid.). I
have followed this reading in quoting the poem itself.

14. Cf. Jochen Schmidt, "Der Begriff des Zorns in Hölderlins Spätwerk," *Hölderlin-Jahrbuch* 15 (1967–1968):128–57.

15. Szondi observes that in this poem Hölderlin still tended to believe
he could escape unscathed from contact with divine fire: "Dafür spricht
schon, dass er in der Wiedergabe des Semele-Mythos, wie sie eben zitiert
wurde, jeden Ausdruck meidet, der auf den Tod der Semele hinwiese"
(*Hölderlin-Studien*, p.39).

16. Beissner notes an interesting parallel here: "Michel . . . weist hin
auf Psalm 24, 3 F.: 'Wer wird auf des Herrn Berg gehen? Und wer wird
stehen an seiner heiligen Stätte? Der unschuldige Hände hat, und reines
Herzens ist' " (2:679).

17. Szondi, *Hölderlin-Studien*, pp.43–49.

18. "In der Hymne treibt die Unruh und der Mangel den an selbstgeschlagener Wunde leidenden Dichter zum Überfluss des Göttertisches und
macht ihn zum falschen Priester. Das Gedicht 'Hälfte des Lebens' verrät,
dass die Verschuldung nicht bloss eine Gefahr ist, wie es der Prosaentwurf
wahrhaben will, sondern die reale Verfassung, aus der Hölderlin dichtet"
(Szondi, p.50). It might be objected that the presence of part of another
poem on the manuscript would not be sufficient grounds for such a conclusion, since in the hymn itself the danger of approaching the gods as a false
priest appears to be presented as a possibility, not as a reality.

19. See Hegel, *Phänomenologie des Geistes*, Johannes Hoffmeister, ed.
(Hamburg, 1952), pp.517–19.

20. Wöhrmann, *Hölderlins Wille zur Tragödie*, p. 155, also notes that
the "false priest" of the hymn is practitioner of the false sacrifice that
Manes (mistakenly) ascribes to Empedokles. But Wöhrmann, like Szondi,
tends to read the hymn's conclusion as a kind of personal confession. For
a more general discussion of the concept of poetic priesthood here and
elsewhere in Hölderlin, see Momme Mommsen, "Die Problematik des
Priestertums bei Hölderlin," *Hölderlin-Jahrbuch* 15 (1967–1968):53–74.

10. "Der Rhein"

1. Bernhard Böschenstein, *Hölderlins Rheinhymne* (Zurich and Freiburg im Breisgau, 1968), pp.135–38. For briefer discussions of the poem, see Böckmann, *Hölderlin und seine Götter*, pp.391–400; Ryan, *Hölderlins Lehre vom Wechsel der Töne*, pp.249–77; and Guardini, *Hölderlin: Weltbild und Frömmigkeit*, pp.61–77. A recent analysis of the poem, Johannes Mahr, *Mythos und Politik in Hölderlins Rheinhymne* (Munich, 1972), seeks to demonstrate the relationships between the poem's mythical aspect and actualities such as historical events.

2. See Böschenstein, pp.135–38.

3. Hof, *Hölderlins Stil*, pp.200–202. Böschenstein argues that Hof is formalistic in interpreting the tonalities, and prefers to understand them in terms of poetic *content* (*Hölderlins Rheinhymne*, p.152; pp. 137–38). The note's relation to the poem is also discussed at length in Friedrich Beissner, "Vom Baugesetz der vaterländischen Gesängen," *Hölderlin: Reden und Aufsätze*, pp.152–61; Gaier, *Der gesetzliche Kalkül*, pp.264–75; and in Ryan's interpretation (see note 1).

4. Böschenstein carefully explicates the symbolic details in the poem by comparative interpretations of other passages where the same words or images occur. Böschenstein does an especially fine job of specifying the symbolic values of "Epheu" and "Wald" in the opening lines. (See *Hölderlins Rheinhymne*, pp.21–25.)

5. The idea of destiny as essentially *opposed*, clearly implied in this poem and elsewhere in Hölderlin, is perhaps best stated by Rilke in his eighth "Duino Elegy": "Dieses heisst Schicksal: gegenüber sein / und nichts als das und immer gegenüber."

6. Cf. Böschenstein, *Hölderlins Rheinhymne*, p.28. A naturalistic parallel might be the melting of glaciers by sunlight. The stream's parentage is confirmed in the second strophe.

7. A parallel may be found in Rilke's "Ninth Elegy": "warum dann / Menschliches müssen — und, Schicksal vermeidend, / sich sehnen nach Schicksal?"

8. Beissner notes the stream's direction, which is later changed: "Der junge Rhein fliesst zuerst in östlicher Richtung. . . . In der Wanderung v. 94–96 ist die dann eingeschlagene Nordrichtung mythisch bedeutsam" (2:732).

9. As possible sources for this implicit analogy between the Rhine and the demigod Hercules, Böschenstein (*Hölderlins Rheinhymne*, p.60) refers to Pindar's first hymn, Theocritus's twenty-fourth Idyll, and Ovid's *Heroides*.

10. Böschenstein comments: "Die väterliche Anlage im Rhein droht zerstörerisch überhandzunehmen, wenn er sich die Rolle seines Vaters . . .

anmasst und zeugend ins Innerste der Erde fahren möchte, um der Mittelbarkeit des Geborenseins zu entrinnen" (Ibid., p.61). The Rhine's divine
will here may be compared to Empedokles' mortal urge to be consumed in
the fiery immediacy of Earth by leaping into the volcano.

11. As Beissner notes (2:733), the ode "Stimme des Volks" elaborates
on the concept of streams as (generally) self-destructive destinies seeking
immediacy of dissolution in the sea (2:51).

12. Guardini (*Hölderlin*, p.70) comments: "Der Rhein nimmt das
Gesetz an; so wird seine Kraft zu reiner Fruchtbarkeit."

13. Cf. Böschenstein, *Hölderlins Rheinhymne*, pp.136–37.

14. This is a major point in Hegel's early study, *Der Geist des Christen-
tums und sein Schicksal*. Hölderlin's essay, "Das Werden im Vergehen,"
considers in detail the atrophy of structures that makes general revolution
inevitable.

15. Reading "des eigenen Rechts" as dependent on "gespottet" rather
than "gewiss." Beissner (2:734) prefers the latter reading.

16. Yet, as Ryan observes, the men were compelled to such blasphemous
violence by the intolerable fetters of their repression: "Denn nur weil er
mit Gewalt gegen eine solche Fesselung kämpfen muss, vergisst der Heros
den Abstand zwischen sich und dem Göttlichen und will in seiner trotzigen
Selbstbehauptung nicht mehr 'Ungleiches dulden' " (*Hölderlins Lehre*,
p.256).

17. Böschenstein (*Hölderlins Rheinhymne*, p.77) indicates similar
declarations in "Der Archipelagus": "es ruhn die Himmlischen gern am
fühlenden Herzen" (2:110); "Immer bedürfen ja, wie Heroen den Kranz,
die geweihten / Elemente zum Ruhme das Herz der fühlenden Menschen" (2:104).

18. Cf. Böschenstein, *Hölderlins Rheinhymne*, p.81.

19. Cf. Hof, *Hölderlins Stil*, p.201.

20. Beissner (2:731) understands the material opposition here as that
between the general discussion of typical "Vorkämpfer" in the third part
and the particular instance of Rousseau in the fourth. This, however, dis-
regards the drastic *opposition* of types in the third part itself. Böschenstein
(*Hölderlins Rheinhymne*, p.89) sees Rousseau as a mediating figure between the extremes represented by the youthful Rhein and the "wise man,"
Socrates.

21. On the Dionysian quality of Rousseau's utterances, Böschenstein
(*Hölderlins Rheinhymne*, pp.92–93) refers to "Brot und Wein," especially the "strömendes Wort" of the elegy's second strophe.

22. Cf. Empedokles' monologue in *Der Tod des Empedokles*, discussed above.

23. In this strophe the reference to Rousseau's *Rêveries* is quite clear.
Böschenstein (p.196) observes: "Die Beschreibung der Idylle auf der
Peterinsel im Bielersee hält sich wieder an die 'Cinquième Promenade.' Das

'Vergessen' gibt den Wunsch wieder, '(qu') on m'eût interdit toute espèce de communication avec la terre ferme, de sorte qu'ignorant tout ce qui se faisait dans le monde j'en eusse oublié l'existence et qu'on y eût oublié la mienne aussi.' . . . 'Sorglosarm' begreift die Wunschlosigkeit und Genügsamkeit dessen, der nun arm an Welt geworden ist. In diesem Wort durchdringt sich das Bekenntnis des Glücklichen — 'le temps le plus heureaux da ma vie et tellement heureux qu'il m'eût suffi durant toute mon existence, sans laisser naître un seul instant dans mon âme le désir d'un autre état'. . . ." (*Hölderlins Rheinhymne*, p.106).

24. "De quoi jouit-on dans une pareille situation? De rien d'extérieur à soi, de rien sinon de soi-même et de sa propre existence, tant que cet état dure on se suffit a soi-même comme Dieu" (Rousseau, *Oeuvres complétes*, 1, Bernard Gagnebin and Marcel Raymond, eds. [Paris, 1959] ,p.1047).

25. Cf. especially Schiller's *Über naive und sentimentalische Dichtung*.

26. For a detailed discussion of Rousseau's significance for Hölderlin, see Paul de Man, "Hölderlins Rousseaubild," *Hölderlin-Jahrbuch* 15 (1967–1968): 180–208. I would generally agree here with de Man's interpretation of Rousseau's presence in "Der Rhein," rather than Böschenstein's negative evaluation of Rousseau's alleged "Verzicht auf Aktivität" (*Hölderlins Rheinhymne*, p.91). As I attempt to show, Hölderlin regards the "Bielersee" episode here not as a renunciation of activity in general, but as a necessary moment of recuperation, a gathering of forces for the greater task whose final accomplishment is presented as the "Brautfest."

27. Cf. de Man, "Hölderlins Rousseaubild," pp.190–92. In the ode "An die Deutschen" (2:9–11), which in passages is virtually identical with "Rousseau," the "du" addressed to Rousseau in the latter poem is applied to the poetic speaker himself.

28. De Man comments on the universal significance of the moment of Rousseau's awakening: "Auf der Ebene der Allgemeinheit wird dieser Augenblick seine Entsprechung finden, sich auf den Gemeingeist gewordenen Willen aller erstrecken: in dem Fest, mit dem der dritte Teil des 'Rheins' einsetzt und welches das nach rousseausche Denken des Abendlandes vorzubereiten hat" ("Hölderlins Rousseaubild," pp.206–207). The "Brautfest" is clearly introduced by Rousseau.

29. See Beissner, 2:736–37.

30. Böschenstein observes: "Die Liebenden sind, wie die Götter, in unausgesetztem, ausgeglichenem Zusammenhang mit dem lebendigen Geist, sie sind sogar nicht anderes als dieser Zusammenhang selbst" (*Hölderlins Rheinhymne*, p.117).

31. Beissner (2:737) notes an interesting biblical parallel: "Zürnet and sündiget nicht; lasset die Sonne nicht über eurem Zorne untergehen" (Ephesians 4:26).

32. The question remains *why* Hölderlin should here adopt a figurative pattern contrary to "Brot und Wein." Possibly he wishes to emphasize a

different aspect of the time when divine mediation is absent. In the elegy, night is a suitable figure of privation; here, the poet stresses the dangers of unmediated transcendence signified by intense sunlight. The return of divine mediacy can accordingly be depicted either as sunrise (as in the "Feiertag" hymn and implicitly in "Brot und Wein") or as a sunset that harmonizes the world, as here. The image of sunset is clearly more appropriate when the poet wishes (as here) to present men's reconciliation with the gods as a transient state.

33. Cf. Böschenstein, *Hölderlins Rheinhymne*, pp.121–27.

34. Cf. our later discussion of the seventh strophe of "Friedensfeier."

35. Beissner (2:737–38) recounts how the appropriate details are reported at the end of the dialogue. As previously noted, Böschenstein (*Hölderlins Rheinhymne*, pp.88–90; p.125) insists on the opposition of Socrates to Rousseau in the poem. Such an opposition appears questionable, as the two occur at separate moments in the temporal myth: Rousseau before, and Socrates in the general aftermath of the Feast.

36. The poem originally had an entirely different concluding strophe, addressed to Wilhelm Heinse. See Beissner (2:729). Pierre Bertaux, *Hölderlin und die Französische Revolution* (Frankfurt, 1969), pp.135–38, sees a distinct political message in the version addressed to Sinclair.

37. See Böschenstein, *Hölderlins Rheinhymne*, p.138.

11. "FRIEDENSFEIER"

1. As might be expected of so crucial a poem, the meaning of "Friedensfeier" has been widely (and vigorously) disputed. Although the final manuscript of the hymn was not discovered until 1954 (extant earlier versions were previously considered an incomplete poem, "Versöhnender, der du nimmer geglaubt . . ."), in the past two decades more has been written about "Friedensfeier" than about any other Hölderlin poem. Its fascination for critics may be attributed to its poetic excellence, the sensationalism of its late discovery, and its obvious importance in the Hölderlin canon. The text of this poem, difficult to the point of abstruseness and almost perversely enigmatic, at once became a battleground for opposing critical views. The irony of such contention over a poem celebrating peace was immediately obvious; one of the collections of polemical essays on the hymn was aptly titled *Der Streit um den Frieden* (Eduard Lachmann, ed., Nürnberg, 1957). That title could also have been given to the *Hölderlin-Jahrbuch* 9 (1955–1956), likewise devoted to articles on "Friedensfeier." Even after the first wave of polemics had passed, new interpretations of the hymn continued to appear. A detailed discussion of criticisms of the poem and analytical summaries of the most important articles to 1960 may be found in Alessandro Pellegrini, *Friedrich Hölderlin: Sein Bild in der Forschung* (Berlin, 1965). A selected list of studies to 1965 is given by Lawrence Ryan, *Friedrich Hölderlin*, second edition (Tübingen, 1967), p.90.

Without attempting to duplicate any of these listings here (such a list would be too arbitrary or too long), I will refer to other studies of the poem chiefly to indicate points of similarity or divergence with my own reading. However, it should be stressed that my interpretation will not be concerned with the controversy, but with the poem itself. I am attempting only to explain the hymn in its relation to other poems, not to establish a position against other critics.

2. "Ich bitte dieses Blatt nur gutmüthig zu lesen. So wird es sicher nicht unfasslich, noch weniger anstössig seyn. Sollten aber dennoch einige eine solche Sprache zu wenig konventionell finden, so muss ich ihnen gestehen: ich kann nicht anders. An einem schönen Tage lässt sich ja fast jede Sangart hören, und die Natur, wovon es her ist, nimmts auch wieder. Der Verfasser gedenkt dem Publikum eine ganze Sammlung von dergleichen Blättern vorzulegen, und dieses soll irgendeine Probe seyn davon" (3:532). For analysis of the possible implications of this statement, see Binder, "Hölderlins 'Friedensfeier,' " *Hölderlin-Aufsätze*, pp.297–99.

3. Beissner insists that, though other critics see the festive hall as a "metaphor" of landscape, no such metaphor is intended here. Schmidt disagrees: "Die Grosseinteilung der Landschaft in der ersten Strophe ist durch die Vorstellung der grünen Wiesen und der seitlichen Erhebung der Berge gegeben, die in umgreifenden metaphorischen Rahmen des 'Saales' als 'Teppiche' und als 'Tische' geschaut werden" ("Die innere Einheit von Hölderlins 'Friedensfeier,' " *Hölderlin-Jahrbuch* 14 [1965–1966]:128). Binder interprets the scene as a pure symbolic construct: "Man braucht diese Züge darum jedoch nicht direkt zu deuten, weder im Sinne einer Allegorie der heimischen Landschaft . . . noch im Sinne eines realen Bauwerkes. Die immanente Symbolik des Bildes genügt; sie wäre gestört, wenn sie sich nur durch etwas erklärte, dass ausserhalb ihrer liegt" (*Hölderlin-Aufsätze*, p.300).

4. Schmidt, "Einheit," p.128, attempts detailed explication of correspondences.

5. As the identity of the Prince is the chief point of controversy in the poem, persons giving accounts of the controversy generally list the disagreements over this question. Thus, G. Schneider-Herrman, in *Hölderlins "Friedensfeier" und der griechische Genius* (Zurich, 1959), pp.83–85, lists three major categories of opinion: the Prince may be interpreted as personified Peace, as Christ, or as Napoleon Bonaparte. For example: declaring for Peace are Binder, Böckmann ("Hölderlins 'Friedensfeier,' " *Hölderlin-Jahrbuch* 9 [1955–1956]:1 ff.), and Kempter ("Das Leitbild in Hölderlins 'Friedensfeier,' " *Hölderlin-Jahrbuch* 9 [1955–1956]:88); choosing Christ are Corssen ("Hölderlins 'Friedensfeier,' " *Hölderlin-Jahrbuch* 9 [1955–1956]:32), and Hof ("Zu Hölderlins 'Friedensfeier,' " in *Der Streit um den Frieden*, p.49); opting for Napoleon are Kerenyi (*Geistiger Weg Europas* [Zurich-Stuttgart, 1955], Allemann (*Hölderlins*

Friedensfeier [Pfülligen, 1955]), and Michael Hamburger (*Reason and Energy* [New York, 1957]). Beissner, in a class by himself, understands the Prince as the "Genius of the German People" (*Hölderlin: "Friedensfeier"* [Stuttgart, 1954]). The more recent study by Peter Szondi ("Er selbst, der Fürst des Fests: 'Friedensfeier,'" *Hölderlin-Studien*, pp.74–76) lists other variants: the Prince has also been interpreted as Helios (Ruth-Eva Schulz, *Der Fürst des Fests: Bemerkungen zu Hölderlins Friedensfeier*, in *Sinn und Form*, 14 [1962] 2:187 ff.) and as Dionysus (Momme Mommsen, "Dionysos in der Dichtung Hölderlins," *Germanisch-Romanische Monatsschrift* 13 [Oct., 1963]).

6. Some adherents of the Napoleonic theory would understand "Ausland" quite literally as Corsica.

7. An earlier version of this line reads "allerneuende Klarheit" (2:130), the "all-renewing clarity" of all-unitive vision.

8. Schmidt also emphasizes the all-unitive function of the Prince: "Hölderlin empfindet deutlich den etymologischen Sinn des Wortes 'Fürst.' Er ist der 'Erste,' der oberste Gottheit. Das Wesen dieser obersten Gottheit — 'der Götter Gott' nennt sie einer der Entwürfe — ist das der Allheit. Allheit bedeutet, dass der Fürst als übergreifendes Prinzip des ἐν καὶ πᾶν zu allen Einzelnen Bezug hat und also in einem Verhältnis der Allbezogenheit steht. So kann er der 'Allbekannte' heissen" ("Einheit," pp.133–44).

9. I am assuming that these lines refer to the Prince, and not to Napoleon, as argued by Martin Trenks, "Zur Auslegung der Verse 26–28 der 'Friedensfeier,'" *Hölderlin-Jahrbuch* 16 (1969–1970):222–27.

10. Beissner comments: "Der Dichter hat — wie es scheint, in dieser Reinschrift zum einzigen Mal — die Triadengliederung durch grösseren Abstand nach jeder dritten Strophe sichtbar gemacht" (3:549). The triadic structure is thus evident.

11. See note 5, above.

12. See John 4:4–42. Schmidt comments: "Das 'geweihete Gebirg' ist der heilige Berg Garizim bei Sichar, wo die Einwohner Samarias ihre Kultstätte hatten" ("Einheit," p.146).

13. There may also be an historical reference here to the Crusaders, barbarians who came to the Holy Sepulchre, encountered it crudely, and thereby inaugurated the "destiny" of decomposing Christendom.

14. Cf. the later version of "Patmos":

> Begreiffen müssen
> Diss wir zuvor. Wie Morgenluft sind nemlich die Nahmen
> Seit Christus. Werden Träume. Fallen, wie Irrtum
> Auf das Herz und tödtend, wenn nicht einer
> Erwäget, was sie sind und begreift.   [2:181–182]

15. Schneider-Herrmann remarks a consensus on this point: "Was den

Sohn des 'Allebendigen' betrifft, so wird einstimmig Christus bezeichnet" ("Friedensfeier," p.85).

16. Szondi observes that the designation "Geist der Welt" is to be interpreted according to "einem Sprachgebrauch des späten Hölderlin . . . der gerne 'Geist' statt 'Gott' setzt, und zwar vornehmlich dann, wenn der Gott in seiner Beziehung zu den Menschen gesehen wird" (*Hölderlin-Studien*, pp.71–72).

17. Schmidt remarks: "Da Hölderlin die Allerfahrung unter dem Aspekt der Ausbildung universaler Einheit sieht, bedeutet ihre Vollendung zugleich das Ende allen Ablaufs und aller Bewegung, das heisst auch: aller Geschichte und damit das Aufhören der Zeit, Still-Stand, die Einkehr der 'Stille' " ("Einheit," p.159).

18. See Hegel, *Phänomenologie des Geistes*, Hoffmeister, ed., pp.549–64.

19. Binder comments: "Ebenso ist im 'Brautfest' der Menschen und Götter das Schicksal 'ausgeglichen.' . . . Der Zusatz 'schön' — bedeutet: in der Weise der Schönheit ausgeglichen, die immer unter der Struktur der Synthesis gedacht ist" (*Hölderlin-Aufsätze*, p.318).

20. As indicated by the brackets, there are two disputed readings in the text of these lines. The "wir" is omitted in Hölderlin's final manuscript, but most critics tacitly agree with Beissner's emendation (3:562–63), assuming the omission to be mere oversight. As Beissner observes, however, there is a lively dispute over the second reading — whether the "das" should be emended to "dass." Beissner thinks it should, and defends his choice (as any critic must) by his general interpretation of the lines. Any reading of the text is determined by one's understanding of the lines' syntax, which in turn is decided by one's interpretation of the strophe and the poem as a whole; this is the hermeneutical process. A critic must choose whether he wants a relative pronoun ("das," as in the manuscript) or a conjunction ("dass," as in Beissner's emendation); if he chooses the emended reading, it may be justified by his total interpretation. I have chosen the original reading, not simply because it is the original, but because it seems to make more sense in the context of the strophe as I understand it.

21. Cf. Schmidt (p.163): "Das 'Viel' der Teile im Gespräch — 'Viel hat . . . erfahren der Mensch' — steht im Gegensatz zu der All-Einheit des Gesangs. . . ."

22. Reading "das," a relative pronoun. (See note 20, above.) If one prefers Beissner's "dass," the lines could be translated somewhat as follows: "And the Time-Image which the great Spirit unfolds, it lies before us as a sign *that* between him and others *there is* a pact between him and other powers." As a number of critics have observed, this makes the repetition of "zwischen ihm und andern" merely rhetorical.

23. Here, again, I would follow Schmidt's interpretation: "Das Zeitbild

ist Zeichen der All-Verbindung der göttlichen Mächte. Das Liebeszeichen des Festtags dagegen ist ein Zeugnis, 'dass ihrs noch seiet.' . . . Das Wesentliche liegt in der Wendung '. . . dass ihrs noch seiet.' Sie macht klar, dass die erreichte Allharmonie der heiligen Mächte die neue Grundwirklichkeit darstellt, dass sie aber nicht als eine Auflösung der in die Allheit versammelten Einzelgestalten zu denken ist" ("Einheit," p.166).

24. Cf. Binder, *Hölderlin-Aufsätze*, pp.320–21; and Schmidt, "Einheit," p.168. Beissner (3:564–65), however, would insist that the "Jüngling" here is not Christ, but the Prince.

25. The second reading is of course preferred by those critics (such as Corssen, Lachmann and Hof) who consider the Prince to be Christ. It is also preferred by Beissner, who reads the "Jüngling" as the Prince himself, but not as Christ (3:564–65).

26. For example, the Prince is described as "Vom ernsten Tagwerk lächelnd" (3:533), while Christ is termed "freundlichernst" (3:534); the term "leichtbeschattet" (3:533) is applied to the Prince, much as the fourth strophe speaks of a metaphorical "shadowing" of Christ (3:534); both of course are "friendly" to man despite their evident divinity.

27. This is a major point in Schmidt's interpretation of the poem: "Nun ist die Gottheit zu Anfang der siebten Strophe Gott Vater, da die Verse an den Schluss der sechsten Strophe anknüpfen: 'Nun, da wir kennen den Vater / Und Feiertage zu halten / Der hohe, der Geist / Der Welt sich zu Menschen geneigt hat. / / (7. Str.:) Denn längst war der zum Herrn der Zeit zu gross. . . .' 'Der' ist der 'Vater,' und da 'der,' der das 'Tagwerk' vollbracht hat, zugleich der Fürst des Festes ist, ist der Vater Fürst des Festes" ("Einheit," p.157). It may be noted that this syllogism assumes (without proving) the syntactical identity of "Vater" and "Geist." Although the two must necessarily be *essentially* identical (as manifestations of All-Unity) for Hölderlin, the poet appears inclined to observe a *phenomenal* distinction between them: the Father as transcendent, the Spirit as immanent. Schmidt's apparent insistence on their phenomenal identity constitutes the only major instance where I would disagree with his reading of "Friedensfeier"; I am of course in total agreement with his emphasis on the centrality of the topic of All-Unity in the hymn. Szondi, who seems to be in basic accord with Schmidt on the identity of the Prince, observes a distinction here: "in der Skala der göttlichen Antonomasien, welche die Hymne gebraucht, sind die beiden einzigen, die wiederkehren, zugleich die beiden Pole: *Gott*, der ganz andere, und *Geist*, der dem Menschen verbundene" (*Hölderlin-Studien*, p.72).

28. Cf. Szondi, *Hölderlin-Studien*, p.78.

29. Cf. Schmidt, "Einheit," p.156; Szondi, *Hölderlin-Studien*, p.74.

30. See note 26, above.

31. "Der 'Feind' aber, welcher der Natur die Götter gestohlen hat, ist kein anderer als der Mensch, der sich selbstherrlich an die Stelle der Götter

setzt, wobei er dann freilich zum Zerrbild des Göttlichen, zum 'Satyr' wird" (Binder, *Hölderlin-Aufsätze,* p.323). For opposing interpretations see Beissner (3:567–68) and Ryan (*Hölderlins Lehre,* pp.298–99).

32. Cf. Hegel, *Phänomenologie des Geistes,* pp.517–19.

33. Ryan, who reads the "enemy" as "Geist der Unruh," disagrees: "Aber der heraufziehende Friede lässt alle Unruhe seltsam irreal erscheinen, so dass die Natur sie jetzt 'kennt' und 'lässt,' da ihr Feind jegliche Potenz verloren hat, ja sogar er, der Unversöhnte, in Erwartung der Zeit der Reife 'gerne fühllos ruht' " (*Hölderlins Lehre,* p.299). While some see here a reference to malevolent "titans," the late fragmentary hymn, "Die Titanen" (2:217–19), for example, is radically different in tone from the present poem.

34. Cf. the discussion of the eighth strophe of "Der Rhein" in the previous chapter.

35. Schmidt has treated this aspect of the poem most comprehensively; see "Einheit," pp.133–34.

12. "DER EINZIGE"

1. Beissner (2:753) remarks that each version provides clear indication of triadic division. For other interpretations of the poem, see Böckmann, *Hölderlin und seine Götter,* pp.428–33; Robert Thomas Stoll, *Hölderlins Christushymnen: Grundlagen und Deutung* (Basel, 1952), pp.151–84; Guardini, *Hölderlin: Weltbild und Frömmigkeit,* pp.520–30; and Detlev Lüders, *Die Welt im verringerten Maasstab: Hölderlin-Studien,* pp.19–54.

2. Beissner (2:754) notes classical precedents for Apollo's appearance as king.

3. Stoll comments: "Im Ausdruck 'Gedanken' sind Götter und Werke, die der Vater geschaffen hat, innig vermischt. Die Götter sind als 'hohe Gedanken' seinem Haupte entsprungen; der Mythos von Pallas Athene, die dem Haupte des Zeus entstiegen ist, hat dieses Bild geprägt" (*Christushymnen,* p.152). It is probably unnecessary, however, to interpret the "thoughts" specifically as "gods."

4. Beissner (2:754) notes that the sites in western Greece are all historically associated with holy athletic events: Elis, Olympia, Parnassus, and Corinth. These events were celebrated by the divinely-inspired Pindar. Smyrna and Ephesos in Ionia are connected with Homer. They are also the setting for the "heroic" episodes of *Hyperion.*

5. Böckmann observes: "In der Liebe zu Griechenland spricht sich nur das Dichteramt aus, das das Bild Gottes im Gesang feiern will, im Hinblick auf die Art, wie es unter den Menschen lebte und leben wird" (*Hölderlin und seine Götter,* p.430).

6. See the discussion of the second strophe of the "Feiertag" hymn.

7. Beissner (2:754–55) cites John 13:13 and Matthew 23:10.

8. See the discussion of the sixth strophe of "Friedensfeier." While

"Vom Allebendigen aber . . . / . . . / Ist einer ein Sohn" refers explicitly to Christ, Hölderlin elsewhere maintains, "Noch aber hat andre / Bei sich der Vater" ("Wenn aber die Himmlischen. . . ," 2:223).

9. For a detailed discussion of Herakles in Hölderlin's poetry, see Ulrich Hötzer, *Die Gestalt des Herakles in Hölderlins Dichtung* (Stuttgart, 1956). Pp.89–105 refer to "Der Einzige."

10. Cf. Schmidt, *Hölderlins Elegie "Brod und Wein,"* pp.121–22. See also Bäumer, "Dionysos und das Dionysische bei Hölderlin," 113–16.

11. Beissner (2:755) would insist that the other demigods are *more* "worldly" than Christ.

12. "Immer bestehet ein Maas, / Allen gemein, doch jeglichem auch ist eignes beschieden" (2:91); "Nur hat ein jeder sein Maas" (2:148).

13. Cf. the discussions of the eighth strophe of "Der Rhein" and the concluding strophes of the "Feiertag" hymn.

14. For instances of terrified reactions to Christ, Beissner (2:757) cites Luke 4:36; Luke 5:26; and Luke 7:16.

15. Stoll notes that "geistig" and "weltlich" are not antithetical here. Poets "must" perforce be in the world, and authentic poets are always sacral, "insofern ihre Dichtung Dienst am Göttlichen ist" (*Christushymnen*, p.164).

13. "Patmos"

1. For discussion of this hymn, see Binder, "Hölderlins Patmos-Hymne," in *Hölderlin-Aufsätze*, pp. 262–403; Böckmann, *Hölderlin und seine Götter*, pp.434–51; Guardini, *Hölderlin: Weltbild und Frömmigkeit*, pp.531–54; Emery George, "Hölderlin's Hymn 'Patmos': Comments," in *Friedrich Hölder.'.i: An Early Modern*, pp.258–76; Ryan, *Hölderlins Lehre vom Wechsel der Töne*, pp.303–309; Stoll, *Hölderlins Christushymnen*, pp.184–239; Conrad Wandrey, "Hölderlins Patmos-Hymne," *Deutsche Rundschau* 51 (November, 1924):149–64; Gaskill, "Christ and the Divine Economy in the Work of Friedrich Hölderlin," pp.39–84. Horst Rumpf, "Die Deutung der Christusgestalt bei dem spaten Hölderlin" makes frequent and very helpful references to "Patmos"; Richard Unger, "Hölderlin's 'Patmos': Song as Interpretation" (Ph.D. diss., Cornell, 1967) attempts an exhaustive, line-by-line reading of the poem.

2. E.g., Böschenstein, *Hölderlins Rheinhymne*, pp.7–11; Binder, *Hölderlin-Aufsätze*, p.731; Stoll, p.185.

3. E.g., Schmidt, *Hölderlins Elegie "Brod und Wein,"* pp.2–3; Guardini, *Hölderlin*, p.532.

4. Cf. the discussion of the central strophes of the "Feiertag" hymn, where the nearness and the problematical difficulty of all-unitive Life are explicit themes.

5. See especially the discussion of that poem's fifth strophe.

6. For a thoroughgoing discussion of eagles as *Christian* symbols, see Gaskill, "Christ and the Divine Economy," pp.74–80.

7. Cf. Stoll, *Christushymnen*, p.187.

8. Stoll seems close to such a reading: "Die einzelnen erfüllten und abgeschlossenen Epochen der sich immer weiter hinziehenden Zeit sind 'Gipfel,' auf denen die Götter und Heroen, die diese Zeit gestaltet haben, wohnen" (*Christushymnen*, p.186). For a similar but more differentiated reading, see Binder, *Hölderlin-Aufsätze*, pp.372–73.

9. Closely related to the question of the peaks is the problem of their inhabitants. Although most critics — Guardini (*Hölderlin*, pp.532–33) is an exception — seem to insist that the "Liebenden" on peaks must be historic (i.e., deceased) personages, there is nothing in these lines to indicate they cannot be actually living, as they appear, simultaneously. The operative phrase here is "Gipfel der *Zeit*" — not, as in the usually cited parallel-text, "die *Zeiten* . . . / Wie Gebirg" (2:125).

10. As Beissner (2:789) notes, the hymn "Germanien" speaks of such smoke as a "golden haze [of] legend": "Ein goldner Rauch, die Sage" (2:149).

11. Cf. Beissner, 2:789; Stoll, *Christushymnen*, pp. 190–91.

12. Cf. "Brot und Wein": "der Kranz, den er von Epheu gewählt, / Weil er bleibet" (2:94).

13. "Menons Klagen" foresees the speaker's rendezvous with Diotima "auf thauender Insel . . . / . . . / Wo die Gesänge wahr, und länger die Frühlinge schön sind" (2:79); "Der Einzige" proclaims how some men are "saved, as on beautiful islands": "gerettet, als / Auf schönen Inseln" (2:106).

14. Binder, however, notes that the speaker's westward course from Ionia already signifies some progress: "denn in Hölderlins mythischer Geographie ist die Ost-West Richtung das Korrelat des Geschichtsganges" (*Hölderlin-Aufsätze*, p.376).

15. "Alle leben sie noch, die Heroenmütter, die Inseln, / Blühend von Jahr zu Jahr. . ." (2:103).

16. Lothar Kempter (*Hölderlin und die Mythologie*, p.18) was probably the first critic to note the parallel here to Klopstock's *Der Messias*: "Unbemerkter, nicht eine der Königinnen des Weltmeers, / Ruhte zwischen Wogengebirgen die einsame Patmos" (*Messias*, XX.725–26).

17. Beissner (2:789–90) speculates on how Hölderlin may have come to the opinion that Cyprus is "rich in springs"; Ariosto's *Orlando Furioso* may be considered a possible influence.

18. Beissner (2:790) notes the biblical references for John's situation on Patmos (Rev. 1:9) and for his nearness to Christ (John 19:26). The poem's sixth strophe is clearly based on a verse from John's Gospel account of the Last Supper (John 13:23): "Now there was leaning on Jesus's bosom one of his disciples, whom Jesus loved."

19. Cf. Gaskill's reading of the poem in "Christ and the Divine Economy," especially pp.45–69.

20. In the concluding strophe of the ode "Dichterberuf," ingenuousness is also a protection against the possible dangers of divine intensity: "Furchtlos bleibt aber, so er es muss, der Mann / Einsam vor Gott, es schüzet die Einfalt ihn . . ." (2:48).

21. Binder (*Hölderlin-Aufsätze*, p.378) suggests that the phrase "die lezte Liebe" refers explicitly to Christ's new commandment of love pronounced at this time: "A new commandment I give unto you, That ye love one another; as I have loved you, that ye also love one another. By this shall all men know that ye are my disciples, if ye have love one to another" (John 13:34–35). The juxtaposition of ultimate love with "death" may be clearly noted in John 15:12–13: "This is my commandment, That ye love one another, as I have loved you. Greater love hath no man than this, that a man lay down his life for his friends."

22. The phrase "Geheimnisse des Weinstoks" thus assumes a specifically Christian meaning by implicit reference to John 15:5: "I am the vine, ye are the branches: He that abideth in me, and I in him, the same bringeth forth much fruit: for without me ye can do nothing."

23. Binder (*Hölderlin-Aufsätze*, p.378) notes that the equivalent to Hölderlin's "Zürnen der Welt" may also be found in this Gospel chapter (15:18–19): "If the world hate you, ye know that it hated me before it hated you. . . . I have chosen you out of the world, therefore the world hateth you." The "cheering" may refer to Christ's promise to send the Holy Spirit as "Comforter" (John 15:26): "But when the Comforter is come, whom I will send to you from the Father, even the Spirit of truth, which proceedeth from the Father, he shall testify of me." We must of course recall that Hölderlin interpreted the biblical passages according to his own view of the historical moment.

24. Manes predicts of the Savior's ministry: "Und milde wird in ihm der Streit der Welt" (4:136).

25. Hölderlin's insistence on the essentiality of divine "goodness" can clearly be seen in the later versions' revision of the poem's beginning: "Voll Güt' ist. Keiner aber fasset / Allein Gott" (2:173). This also reaffirms that any grasp of all-unitive Deity must be in and through community. On the axiom of divine goodness, Binder comments: "Hölderlin sieht einen . . . Zusammenhang zwischen den Wörten 'gut' und 'Gott,' den er öfters, auch in 'Patmos' mehrmals, anklingen lässt. Er stammt aus der Erläuterung des ersten Gebotes in Luthers Grossem Katechismus. 'Alles ist gut' lässt sich also geradezu mit: alles ist Gott, d.h., Gottes Wille und Tat, wiedergeben. . ." (*Hölderlin-Aufsätze*, p.378). Beissner notes that the assertion "Alles ist gut" occurs not only in *Fragment von Hyperion*, 196, but also in a letter Hölderlin wrote to his sister (March 19, 1800):

"Und so ists mein gewisser Glaube, das am Ende alles gut ist, und alle Trauer nur der Weg zu wahrer heiliger Freude ist" (2:790). For further analysis of the significance of the assertion in "Patmos," see Rumpf, "Deutung," pp.66–67.

26. Cf. the discussion of the fourth and fifth strophes of "Friedensfeier."

27. Beissner (2:790–91) observes that Hölderlin's emphasis on Christ's victory over death is paralleled in Klopstock's *Messias*, but not in contemporaneous Lutheran theology. Guardini (*Hölderlin*, p.541) speculates that there may be a reference here to Christ's final word on the cross (John 19:30). The German "Es ist vollbracht" sounds somewhat more positive than the King James' "It is finished."

28. See Beissner, 2:791.

29. This noxiousness is most fully emphasized in the last version of the strophe: "Und schadend das Angesicht des Gottes wirklich   /   Wie eine Seuche gieng zur Seite der Schatte des Lieben" (2:187).

30. Cf. the discussion of strophes three and six of "Friedensfeier."

31. Beissner (2:791) notes a variant to this line: "Den Zepter, womit   /   Er hatte geherrscht, von Asia her,   /   Seit unerforschlichen Zeiten." The image of the sun's ruling with a "scepter" may also be found in Novalis' *Die Lehrlinge zu Sais:* "dann legt die Sonne ihren strengen Zepter nieder und wird wieder Stern unter Sternen. . ." (Novalis, *Werke*, Uwe Lassen, ed. [Hamburg, 1959], p.108).

32. Reading "zu rechter Zeit" with "wiederkommen"; Beissner (2:791) reads it with "erlosch." For a detailed analysis of the concept of the "right time," and its possible sources in Pietist literature, see Gaskill, "Christ and the Divine Economy," pp.59–62.

33. These "images" may specifically be ivy plants; cf. the third strophe: "Und Zeug unsterblichen Lebens   /   An unzurgängbaren Wänden   /   Uralt der Epheu wächst. . ." (2:166). See also our earlier discussions of the emblematical ivy in "Brot und Wein" and "Der Rhein."

34. E.g., Ezekiel 8:3.

35. The disciples' state here may be analogous to the situation of the dozing men in the ode "Blödigkeit"; there the paternal God is said to keep people upright at crucial moments by similar golden strings: "Der, zur Wende der Zeit, uns die Entschlafenden   /   Aufgerichtet an goldnen   /   Gängelbanden, wie Kinder, hält" (2.66).

36. Stoll (*Christushymnen*, pp.207–209) offers a lucid analytical paraphrase of this strophe, showing clearly its relationship to the preceding strophes of the poem.

37. "Vg. Psalm 45, 3 die auf Christus gedeutete Weissagung: 'Du bist der Schönste unter den Menschenkindern' " (Beissner, 2:792).

38. Ibid.

39. A later version of this passage, though unclear even in syntax, suggests the *Logos* or One Mind: "Es ist der Wurf das eines Sinns, der mit / Der Schaufel fasset den Waizen . . ." (2:177).

40. Reading "einer" as identical with "ein Knecht," denoting a person other than the speaker.

41. Jochen Schmidt, "Der Begriff des Zorns in Hölderlins Spätwerk," *Hölderlin-Jahrbuch* 15 (1967–1968):128–57, points out that the "wrath" ("Zorn") of Deity is often the *generally* dangerous intensity of divine frenzy, not specific anger.

42. Cf. the sixth strophe of "Friedensfeier": "Und es lehret Gestirn dich, das / Vor Augen dir ist, doch nimmer kannst du ihm gleichen" (3:535).

43. As Beissner observes, an earlier version of this passage states explicitly that *all* the gods will then appear to be named: "die Götter 'ruhig in ihren Thaten erkannt, wieder die Himmlischen beim rechten Nahmen genannt sind' " (2:793).

44. For a detailed discussion of the biographical circumstances of the hymn and Hölderlin's relationship to the Landgraf, see Werner Kirchner, *Hölderlin: Aufsätze zu seiner Homburger Zeit* (Göttingen, 1967), pp.57–68.

45. It may be noted that Christ is here assigned the task which the poet sought for himself in the "Feiertag" hymn.

46. Binder (*Hölderlin-Aufsätze*, p.395) identifies "Gewalt" here as "Ichsucht." Cf. my discussion of "der Feind" in the concluding strophe of "Friedensfeier."

47. Cf. the earlier discussion of Empedokles' youthful devotion to both Earth and Sunlight (4:106). Cf. also their mythic functions in the opening strophes of "Der Rhein."

48. Stoll thus seems to misinterpret the poem's concluding statement when he declares: "Diese Schlussworte der Hymne 'Patmos' bedeuten eine gewaltige Resignation" (*Christushymnen*, p.224). Binder also appears to give undue emphasis to the statement's supposed humility: "Wer aber den festen Buchstaben pflegt und Bestehendes gut deutet, tritt als Subjekt zurück, um die Herrlichkeit Gottes zu preisen, wie sie in Bibel und Welt erscheint" (*Hölderlin-Aufsätze*, p.396).

49. As the hymn "Germanien" indicates, this attitude does not bespeak cultural chauvinism, but a modest willingness for his countrymen to be of spiritual service to the rest of humanity.

50. Beissner (2:788–89) observes a triadic structure despite the enjambment of the sixth and seventh strophes. One might, indeed, assign a dominant topic to each triad: the first (1–3) tells of the general situation and the poet's particular bewilderment and apparent helplessness; the second (4–6) achieves the poet's identification with St. John and his appro-

priation of John's memory of Christ; the third (7–9), more general in reference, implicitly continues John's memories of the fate of the disciples after Christ's death; the fourth (10–12) attains the highest degree of generality, posing and answering the question of history since the death of Christ; and the fifth (13–15), though maintaining the level of generality, provides information on the particular duties of poets. The concluding declaration returns to the poet's special situation and implicitly proposes the remedy to the general problem of the opening strophe. By cultivating the fixed letter and interpreting whatever exists, we may perhaps be delivered from our present state of "danger" in the "difficulty" of grasping the near (and approaching) God.

51. For example, the poem could be analyzed in terms of its temporal structure (how the speaker moves from the actual to an hallucinatory present, then back in memory to the time of John and Christ, and ultimately returns to the present) or in terms of its imaginary space (from Europe to Ionia, then westward to Patmos, and eventually back to German actuality in the final line). As in the case of "Friedensfeier," Binder (*Hölderlin-Aufsätze*, pp.401–402) sees a symmetrical arrangement around a central moment, much like that noted in the structure of "Brot und Wein."

14. "MNEMOSYNE"

1. For discussions of the later versions of "Patmos," see Rumpf, "Die Deutung der Christusgestalt bei dem späten Hölderlin"; Stoll, *Hölderlins Christushymnen: Grundlegung und Darstellung*; and Unger, "Hölderlin's 'Patmos': Song as Interpretation."

2. See Beissner, "Holderlins letzte Hymne," in *Über Hölderlin*, pp.113–52. Other readings of the poem are offered by Jochen Schmidt, *Hölderlins letzte Hymnen* (Tübingen, 1970), pp.50–80; Raymond Furness, "The Death of Memory: An Analysis of Hölderlin's Hymn 'Mnemosyne,' " *Publications of the English Goethe Society*, new series 40 (1970):38–68; and Karl Kerenyi, "Hölderlins Vollendung," *Hölderlin-Jahrbuch* 8 (1954): 38–45. Emery George, *Hölderlin's "Ars Poetica*," pp.267–84, offers his own reconstruction of the text of the poem into four distinct "versions."

3. See Beissner, "Hölderlins letzte Hymne," pp.143–44.

4. See Theodor W. Adorno, "Parataxis: Zur späten Lyrik Hölderlins," in *Über Hölderlin*, pp.339–79.

5. Schmidt, *Hölderlins letzte Hymnen*, pp.71–73. In this as in many other points I am greatly indebted to Schmidt's perceptive explication of the poem.

6. See Beissner, 2:825–26.

7. See Schmidt, *Hölderlins letzte Hymnen*, pp.71–73.

8. Ibid.

9. *Hölderlins letzte Hymnen*, pp.74–77. Especially significant is Schmidt's reference to one passage in the later revision of "Patmos": "und

gehalten nicht mehr / Von Menschen, schattenlos, die Pfade zweifeln ..." (2:180).

10. See the earlier discussion of the "Frankfurter Plan" to *Empedokles*.

11. Beissner's interpretation is typical: "Der Dichter möchte, auf einen Augenblick nur, sich der Verantwortung entziehen. . ." (2:827).

12. Schmidt, *Hölderlins letzte Hymnen*, p.55. The full passage from *Hyperion* is as follows: "Ich gab mich hin, fragte nichts nach mir and andern, suchte nichts, sann auf nichts, liess vom Boote mich halb in Schlummer wiegen, und bildete mir ein, ich liege in Charons Nachen. O es ist süss, so aus der Schaale der Vergessenheit zu trinken" (3:49).

13. Cf. especially Hölderlin's favorable treatment of Rousseau's slumber in "Der Rhein."

14. See Paul de Man, "Hölderlins Rousseaubild," pp.207–208. De Man points out a probable (favorable) allusion here to the "Cinquiéme Promenade" of Rousseau's *"Rêveries du Promeneur Solitaire,"* which describes a related experience of bliss and purified consciousness in a rocking boat.

15. There may be disquieting associations here, also. See "Stimme des Volks" and especially "Lebensalter," where the cities' "crowns" are themselves destroyed by fire: "Euch hat die Kronen / ... / Von Himmlischen der Rauchdampf und / Hinweg das Feuer genommen" (2:115).

16. 6, no. 240; cited by Schmidt, p.4.

17. Cf. my discussion of the concluding lines of the "Feiertag" hymn.

18. See Schmidt, *Hölderlins letzte Hymnen*, pp.57–58. Beissner's interpretation (2:827) likewise stresses the noble transiency of the snow and flowers. This reading observes a probable transition to the third strophe.

19. Paul de Man, "Wordsworth und Hölderlin," *Schweizer Monatshefte* 12 (March, 1966):1141–55, speculates that the "other" here may be the "heroic" counterpart to the poet, as typified, e.g., by Hyperion's friend Alabanda.

20. See Schmidt, *Hölderlins letzte Hymnen*, pp.58–59.

21. Cf. Beissner, 2:828.

22. See Schmidt, *Hölderlins letzte Hymnen*, p.58.

23. As Beissner (2:828) notes, the question here is identical with that posed in the tenth strophe of "Patmos"; it asks the ultimate meaning of the events just recounted.

24. See Beissner, 2:828. Beissner also observes that the opening lines of this strophe were the first that Hölderlin composed for the poem.

25. *Hölderlins letzte Hymnen*, p.58.

26. See my discussion of the ode in the chapter on *Empedokles*.

27. "Und mit Gesange folgt' ich, selbst ins / Ende der Tapfern, hinab dem Theuern" (2:41).

28. Beissner (2:828) refers to Rilke's "Sixth Elegy":

Feigenbaum, seit wie lange schon ists mir bedeutend,
wie du die Blüte beinah ganz überschlägst
und hinein in die zeitig entschlossene Frucht,
Ungerühmt, drängst dein reines Geheimnis.

While such may be its (possibly unintentional) emblematical value, Hölderlin's empirical source for the reference is perhaps a traveller's account of
fig trees by the supposed grave of Achilles; see Beissner, 2:828.

29. Beissner, 2:828–29.

30. See Schmidt, *Hölderlins letzte Hymnen*, pp.62–63.

31. Ibid.

32. Schmidt declares: " 'Mnemosyne' bedeutet im wörtlichen Sinne
'Gedächtnis' (als geistige Kraft). Die Hymne erhebt dieses Gedächtnis
zum Fundament nicht nur der Dichtung, sondern des Lebens überhaupt"
(*Hölderlins letzte Hymnen*, p.68). Beissner (2:829) also indicates this
fundamental meaning of her name.

33. Beissner (2:829–30) notes that cutting a lock of hair was an ancient
sign for death. Kerenyi ("Hölderlins Vollendung," p.45) insists that the
cutting of her hair is analogous to the tearing down of the city's walls.

34. *Hölderlins letzte Hymnen*, pp.66–67. Schmidt, like Beissner, refers
to a passage in the late fragment "Griechenland" which speaks of God's
"garment" of mediation: "Alltag aber wunderbar zu lieb den Menschen
/ Gott an hat ein Gewand" (2:257).

35. Reading "nicht" with "zusammengenommen," and "die Seele
schonend" as parenthetical. Cf. Beissner, 2:830.

36. As a parallel instance, Beissner (2:830) cites Matt. 18:7: "Woe
unto the world because of offenses! for it must needs be that offenses
come; but woe to that man by whom the offense cometh!"

37. Furness gives a relatively more cheerful reading to the poem's conclusion: while the poet "can no longer contemplate the gods and demigods of Hellas . . . it is the Christian, the medieval world, and also the
Renaissance and the Reformation which must be sung" ("The Death of
Memory," pp.67–68). We may note, however, that while Hölderlin attempts to sing about Christendom, he does not succeed—his "death of
memory" (Furness's phrase) is the demise of poetic power itself, not
merely of specific recall of the Greek heroes. Thus, as Furness concedes,
"it is perhaps inevitable that Hölderlin was unable to coordinate his
thoughts and creative faculties after this hymn" — but not merely because
of continuing emotional attachment to the Greeks.

38. This is clearly suggested in a later version of "Patmos": "Wie Mor-
genluft sind nemlich die Nahmen / Seit Christus. Werden Träume.
Fallen, wie Irrtum / Auf das Herz und tödtend, wenn nicht einer /
Erwäget, was sie sind und begreift" (2:182).

39. No hymns were completed after "Mnemosyne," though many were attempted. These attempts are difficult to understand because they are fragmentary and deficient in main verbs. For tentative discussions of some of the more important fragments, see Winfried Kudzus, *Sprachverlust und Sinnwandel* (Stuttgart, 1969); Martin Heidegger, "Hölderlins Erde und Himmel," *Hölderlin-Jahrbuch* 11 (1958–1960):17–39; and Artur Häny, *Hölderlins Titanenmythos* (Zurich, 1948). (For a good discussion of the simpler — though often impenetrable — poems of Hölderlin's madness, see Bernhard Böschenstein, "Hölderlins späteste Gedichte," in *Über Hölderlin*, pp.153–75.) Briefly, it can be said of the majority of the hymnic fragments that they are utterances of passivity and anxious resignation — sometimes hopeful of divine epiphany, more often fearful of divine fire. When the poet now speaks of All-Unity, it is of something beyond his responsibility and comprehension. His attitude is impersonal:

> Denn alles fassen muss
> Ein Halbgott oder ein Mensch, dem Leiden nach
> Indem er höret, allein, oder selber
> Verwandelt wird, fernahnend die Rosse des Herrn,   [2:227]

Though this sounds much like the end of the "Feiertag" hymn, we sense that the speaker is no longer involved — any task of all-unitive comprehension is now merely the affair of "a" demigod or "a" man. The only explicit vocation of a poet is now to insist on observance of mediation, so that God's return will not be precipitous and destructive:

> Gott rein und mit Unterscheidung
> Bewahren, das ist uns vertrauet,
> Damit nicht, weil an diesem
> Viel hängt, über der Büssung, über einem Fehler
> Des Zeichens
> Gottes Gericht entsteht.   [2:252]

Most generally, however, the speaker's attitude is one of helpless, passive anxiety. Whatever happens to the world, he will have little to say about it. His own power of active poetic memory is dead, and the broken, fragmentary state of his poetry itself attests to his inability even to approach the vision that was once his comprehensive concern.

Index

Hölderlin's works are listed in alphabetical order; works by other authors are listed under the authors' names.